*Evan,
I hope that
you live your dream!
Larry*

LIVING
YOUR
DREAM

A PRACTICAL RESOURCE TO ENHANCE
PERSONAL WEALTH CREATION AND MANAGEMENT

LARRY WILSON

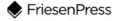 FriesenPress

Suite 300 - 990 Fort St
Victoria, BC, V8V 3K2
Canada

www.friesenpress.com

Copyright © 2019 by Larry Wilson
First Edition — 2019

All rights reserved.

No part of this publication may be reproduced in any form, or by any means, electronic or mechanical, including photocopying, recording, or any information browsing, storage, or retrieval system, without permission in writing from FriesenPress.

Care has been taken to recognize ownership of copyright material contained in this book. The author will gladly welcome any information that enables him to rectify any reference or credit for subsequent editions.

This publication has been designed to provide accurate and authoritative information related to the subject matter covered. The information presented represents the view of the author as of the date of publication. It must be recognized that the financial planning environment is dynamic which could result in the author modifying his view as conditions change. The author and publisher assume no responsibility for errors or omissions and disclaim responsibility for any liability which is incurred as a consequence of the use and application of the contents of this book.

The material contained in this book is intended for information purposes only; it is not specific professional advice. If advice or expert assistance is required, the services of a qualified, competent and independent professional should be sought in order for a customized solution to be designed.

Bulk purchase discounts are available

Author photo: Cheryl Struss Photography

ISBN
978-1-5255-5114-7 (Hardcover)
978-1-5255-5115-4 (Paperback)
978-1-5255-5116-1 (eBook)

1. BUSINESS & ECONOMICS, PERSONAL FINANCE, MONEY MANAGEMENT

Distributed to the trade by The Ingram Book Company

TABLE OF CONTENTS

INTRODUCTION 1

IN A NUTSHELL 11

PART I – PERSONAL FINANCIAL MANAGEMENT 15
- CHAPTER 1 – THE SECRET 19
- CHAPTER 2 – THE BIG THINGS 23
- CHAPTER 3 – IT'S IN THE BALANCE 31
- CHAPTER 4 – GOALS AND THE PLAN 35

PART II – EDUCATION 41
- CHAPTER 5 – INCOME EFFECT 45
- CHAPTER 6 – COST 47
- CHAPTER 7 – FUNDING (RESPs) 51

PART III – MANAGING THE BIG FINANCIAL DECISIONS 59
- CHAPTER 8 – WEDDINGS 65
- CHAPTER 9 – HOUSING 69
- CHAPTER 10 – TRANSPORTATION 81
- CHAPTER 11 – CHILDREN 85
- CHAPTER 12 – PETS 89

PART IV – DEBT 95
- CHAPTER 13 – GOOD DEBT VS. BAD DEBT 99
- CHAPTER 14 – CREDIT CARDS 105
- CHAPTER 15 – DEBT ELIMINATION 109

PART V – INVESTING 117
- CHAPTER 16 – ASSET CLASSES 121
- CHAPTER 17 – EQUITIES 123

CHAPTER 18 – FIXED INCOME 137

CHAPTER 19 – CASH 153

CHAPTER 20 – ALTERNATIVE INVESTMENTS 161

CHAPTER 21 – PORTFOLIO CONSTRUCTION AND MAINTENANCE 167

CHAPTER 22 – THE IMPACT OF INVESTMENT FEES AND COSTS 179

PART VI – WHERE TO HOLD INVESTMENTS 185

CHAPTER 23 – TAX-FREE SAVINGS ACCOUNTS (TFSAs) 191

CHAPTER 24 – REGISTERED RETIREMENT SAVINGS PLANS 201

CHAPTER 25 – RRSP CONVERSION OPTIONS 215

CHAPTER 26 – EMPLOYER PENSIONS 221

CHAPTER 27 – GOVERNMENT PENSIONS 229

CHAPTER 28 – NON-REGISTERED INVESTMENT ACCOUNTS 245

CHAPTER 29 – INVESTMENTS AND TAXES (SORRY) 249

PART VII – CALAMITY EVASION 269

CHAPTER 30 – LIFE INSURANCE 277

CHAPTER 31 – LONG-TERM DISABILITY INSURANCE 287

CHAPTER 32 – CRITICAL ILLNESS INSURANCE 293

CHAPTER 33 – LONG-TERM CARE INSURANCE 295

CHAPTER 34 – OTHER INSURANCE 297

PART VIII – ESTATE PLANNING 301

CHAPTER 35 – THE WILL 305

CHAPTER 36 – POWER OF ATTORNEY 315

CHAPTER 37 – TRUSTS 321

CHAPTER 38 – PROBATE 329

CHAPTER 39 – PERSONAL REPRESENTATIVES 339

CHAPTER 40 – TAXATION AT DEATH 345

PART IX – PROFESSIONAL ADVICE 353

NOTES 365

INTRODUCTION

Stress.

Talk with people about personal finances, and that is the emotion they exude most often. Stress. The sources of financial pressure are many, and they tend to change over time. There are a seemingly endless series of financial quandaries, all of which seem so complicated …

- I hear lots of chatter on the TV about various government programs (RRSP, TFSA, RESP). It's just a bunch of letters to me. What is their purpose and how, if at all, do they apply to my life?
- I know the kids should further their education, but should I save for them in a tax-free savings account, a registered education savings plan, or just leave it for them to figure out?
- The car is on the fritz. It's time to replace it but should I buy or lease a new one, look into the used market, or consider other alternatives?
- The mortgage is up this year. Should I continue with a variable term like Dad says or should I lock-in with a fixed term like the neighbour just did?
- My mutual fund guy just called about a leveraged investment program that he figures is just the ticket for me. He seemed to really know what he was talking about and it sounded like a "can't miss." Should I?

- George got laid off this morning. How would we survive if that happened to me?
- The man on the TV says I should check my credit score. What does that mean and what do I do if I don't like what I see?
- Should I plan to take my CPP at 60, 70, or somewhere between? What makes the most sense in my circumstances?
- Should I invest in my RRSP or my TFSA? Given my situation and where I think my finances are heading, what should I do?
- Uncle Charlie was talking up a stock at the kids' birthday party that sounded very promising. This week he is high on a managed futures fund, whatever that is. Am I missing out on something here?
- I have insurance at work and a pension plan, too. I must be good … right? How do I know?
- I haven't looked at my will in years and am not sure what happens to my finances if I have a stroke and am stuck in the hospital, unable to communicate. Where do I start?
- I don't know. I'm not sure. Is this enough …?

Not having the appropriate knowledge and tools renders decisions difficult to make and remain committed to. So in many cases decisions get deferred indefinitely. But deferred is not forgotten; the questions fester in the back of our minds, gnawing away, stealing our peace of mind, and creating stress.

Most of these seemingly impossible questions are often not overly difficult to answer once they are considered through the proper filter. For many of the this-or-that types of personal finance questions, both could be perfectly acceptable answers, with the best one perhaps decimal places better, and you might not even know which is actually better until the future unfolds. The key to moving past confusion about something and making a perfectly acceptable move is often simply gaining a little bit of knowledge and perhaps farming out certain pieces that require expert assistance to someone who is actually an expert (likely not Uncle Charlie or the mutual fund guy).

It is my hope that this book will help you figure out how to find resolution to some of the questions confronting you, and thus remove a little bit of the stress from your life. I have found peace of mind in my financial life and it is a truly wonderful feeling, one I want for you.

A Bit About Me

You probably have a bucket list or at least some idea of the things you would like to do or experience over the course of your life. One of the items on my list was to write a book on personal finance. Almost assuredly, this would be one of the least common things to show up on a bucket list, likely right alongside actually reading a book on personal finance. Nonetheless, welcome to one of the items on my bucket list, and thank you so much for participating in it. (Even if you only get this far, it still counts.)

This book is written from a personal perspective. I chose to do it this way because that presentation style is what I have found to be most engaging for me as a reader. I realize that everyone experiences slightly different circumstances that will not exactly parallel my experience, and what works for some people will not be the best solution for others. But I feel confident that the concepts discussed, and the approaches presented, will provide a solid basis to help you move your financial standing forward.

I did not come from privilege, nor was I born with physical or academic advantages that make my situation difficult to repeat. My wife and I have managed to experience a life filled with travel, entertainment, independence and, now, early retirement. Throughout this adventure, while we did not always have a bulging net worth, I can say we did have, and continue to have, financial peace of mind because of the money habits we practiced.

That being said, I think it is vital to understand the credentials of any author so that you can assess the credibility of their words. This is especially important in the world of personal financial planning because there are so many stories of scam artists and embedded conflicts of interest that cloud the reputation of the profession. So, to put what follows in context, I will introduce myself and my background.

I grew up primarily in Winnipeg, though I did live in Kingston, Ontario for six years during elementary school. In grade six, Mrs. Hefford (my teacher) asked all of us to write down on a piece of paper what we wanted to be when we grew up. This was the first time she had ever asked me to do something that I clearly understood, so I immediately wrote down *professional hockey player* and handed it in. She then accumulated the results and offered her summary to the class. She noted that she was pleasantly surprised to see that most of the class had picked respected professions ... doctors, lawyers, the periodic astronaut, all the usual jobs that will make any parent gush when asked what their kids are up to. She noted that she was especially happy to see that only one person had the ridiculous objective of being a professional athlete.

That pretty much sums up my experience in public school. My objectives didn't seem to mesh all that closely with those of my teacher. Sports and friends were my focus. Through grade 12, I'm not sure that I ever really studied for anything, much less read the full textbook provided. This keen dedication to school, not too surprisingly, found its way into my grades. I graduated grade 12 with a 64 average; my parents certainly didn't have to build a shelf for academic awards.

The one thing I did do in high school that turned out to be fortuitous was to sign up for, and complete, university entrance-level courses. Another thing that turned out to be somewhat fortunate was that my girlfriend at the time was university bound, and since I had nothing else planned, I followed her and enrolled in all of the classes she did. She had done very well in high school and wanted to be a doctor. I figured I was likely getting myself in over my head, but thought that if I actually spent some time trying to learn, something good might come of it. In any case, it beat the alternative of getting a job or continuing to stock shelves at the local Shoppers Drug Mart.

Much to my surprise, university turned out to be a great experience. I started off a little slow, but once I learned how to study, I found that I could easily achieve, even surpass, the level of most of the other students. The classes were informative and challenging, the professors (well, many of them) seemed to really enjoy what they were doing, and they presented the material in a way that provided a glimpse into how it mattered in the real world.

The most engrossing moments I can remember from a high school class were keenly focused on the foam accumulating at the side of my history teacher's mouth and hoping for it to land on someone other than me. In university, I had an information technology professor who had a gland problem which caused him to sweat continually and profusely. He would start class with a dry shirt and by the end of class the shadow from his arm pits would meet at or around the middle of his shirt. Had this been one of my high school teachers, my sole focus would have been on the time it took for the two shadows to intersect; in university, though, this was just a side benefit. The professor was very enthusiastic, extremely informative, and that is what got my attention and kept me focused on learning ... or maybe I just matured a bit over the summer.

I ended up spending six years in university and graduated with two degrees: a science degree in agricultural economics and a commerce degree (accounting). I was on the dean's honour list my last four years and graduated from commerce *with distinction*. I managed to get through high school without ever threatening to get an A. In university, over my six years, I earned 30 A's. When you find something you are passionate about and engaged in, even the average among us can excel. Five foot six, combined with an immense lack of skill, put an end to my dreams of a hockey career. Hard work and dedication formed the foundation of my professional career.

After university, I landed at job Peat, Marwick, Mitchell & Co. (now KPMG), where I articled and obtained my CA designation (recently rebranded as CPA, CA). This job was, well, brutal: tons of overtime, huge responsibility after very little practical experience, many days where you didn't see the sun (the drive to work was in the dark, the drive from work was also in the dark), combined with ongoing coursework and a final exam that promised to fail half of those who dared challenge it. I began to envy the gas station attendant who filled my car; he knew when he was going to start and end work every day, and he was getting paid substantially more than I was at the time.

The Uniform Final Exam (UFE) was a four-day, four-hour-per day ordeal that still pops up in nightmares even after all these years. Exams were something that I had come to really enjoy throughout university. (Odd, I know.) I always viewed them as an opportunity to demonstrate that the hard work I had put in was time well spent. The UFE, however, was a monster. In fact, you took a couple of months off work simply to study and practice writing past exams just to get the hang of how to manage the complexity and challenge it presented. One of my counterparts at KPMG, a member of Mensa, a lawyer, and the smartest person I have ever met, challenged it three times. (He is now a Senior VP at a huge financial institution.)

"Marks day" was one of the most stressful days of my life, as it was for all who wrote. Back in my day, after two months of waiting for the result, you had to drive downtown to get the piece of paper that told you, your employer, and the rest of the world if you had managed to achieve the magical 240 score. You would arrive at the institute office and watch someone sift through the box of envelopes to locate the one emblazoned with your name. The envelope was handed over with no more fanfare than if it was a utility bill; meanwhile, this thing in your hand felt like it held the answer to whether you were a fraud and an idiot or had the potential to have a meaningful life. It was the single biggest moment in my academic and professional career to that point and I did not feel good about it.

Most people opened the envelope in the elevator on the way back to their car. Not me. I had developed the habit of opening my university transcript in my parent's kitchen. It worked well for university, no need to change the routine for this unveiling. I drove 20 minutes home; all the while that envelope was staring at me, riding shot-gun in the passenger seat. It looked really thick. My thinking was that it clearly had an enrolment form included for my next attempt. It got thicker each time I looked at it.

When I was finally in my spot in the kitchen, I took a deep breath and opened the envelope.

The first line that caught my eye was "A final candidate who wishes to appeal his examination results ..." it blubbered on further about the appeal process; this was not good. I then looked above that and there was a line that said:

Result: Pass.

The relief was beyond immense. I briefly lost my mind and didn't know what to do. Kind of like when we told my mother we were expecting our first child. She walked around in circles, totally unaware of what was going on. It was pure unadulterated joy.

Having said all of that, the UFE aside, the KPMG work experience was life changing. I audited dozens of very successful businesses over the course of those years and saw the vision and dedication of the people who made those businesses the successes they were. I prepared tax returns for some very successful individuals and saw the financial rewards that were possible with hard work dedicated to creating value. I also had the honour of working with extremely dedicated partners, managers, and staff who brought their A games to work every day and complained remarkably little about the hours and demands placed on them.

Four years of that was enough. I saw first-hand the impact the lack of work/life balance had and in particular the toll that it took on people and families. There was certainly more to life than just work.

My next employer provided better balance for many years. I did find that once I moved into senior management roles, balance tended to disappear. In the end, I found myself working just as hard as I had during my articling years. At age 55 (my wife was a couple years younger), having achieved financial independence, we decided to retire.

My family is living proof that if you work hard, invest prudently in both yourself as well as "the markets," and have a financial plan that is implemented with appropriate discipline, you can find the freedom you desire before you are too decrepit to enjoy it.

Also of importance to establish my credibility are the other professional credentials in addition to having been designated a CPA, CA:

- I won the gold medal in the Canadian Securities Course (1999),
- I became a Certified Investment Manager (1993),
- I became a Certified Financial Planner (2001), and
- I also became a Derivatives Market Specialist (2006).

My objective in writing this book is to share my experience and help others achieve their goals through efficient financial management. I am not planning to leverage this book in any way for personal gain. (In fact, I fully expect to lose money—not a smart financial planning move.) For me, this is fun.

The Limitations of this Text

It is not possible to cover all of the ground I delve into within this book in a complete or timelessly accurate manner. At any time, with the stroke of a pen, government programs that are crucial to your financial plan can change in very substantial ways. Any of the rules I discuss related to TFSAs, RESPs, RRSPs, RRIFs, RPPs, CPP, OAS, etc. may have changed between the time I wrote about them and when you read it. There are scads of details involved with each of these programs, and their resiliency is at the whim of the federal and/or provincial government.

In those areas covered by provincial legislation and regulation, the rules can be many and varied. Quebec especially has developed unique policies, programs, and approaches in many areas that are influential within financial planning. For instance, there are several consequential differences between the Canada Pension Plan (CPP) and the Quebec Pension Plan (QPP), though they are often talked about as though the two are interchangeable. The approach taken in Quebec is also quite different in many areas relevant to estate planning, especially when it comes to the legal framework.

Come to think of it, Quebec takes a different approach to a wide variety of things. All of the best Grey Cup festivities I have attended were in Montreal. The only time I really enjoyed Cirque Du Soleil was in Quebec City, where they did a free performance using a series of overpasses as the setting. Who could forget all of those trips with the boys and family to see the Montreal Expos and Youppi in Jarry Park and later the Big O. Ahhh, the memories.

It isn't just Quebec, though; all provinces have taken different approaches to income tax policies and offer a wide variety of programs designed to encourage certain actions, discourage others, and/or offer a unique take on a variety of support programs, many of which will or may be relevant to your planning.

You should always confirm your understanding of the current rules, as they apply within your province, before executing any particular strategy. But don't let this discourage you; the Government of Canada and the provincial governments tend to do a very good job of providing up-to-date, relatively user-friendly guidance on their official web pages. It is not difficult to confirm your understanding of a program by spending a few minutes scanning the materials they provide in advance of implementing a course of action.

Having said this, the majority of the ideas presented here are generally enduring. Core ideas—like building human capital through advanced education, designing and implementing a financial plan, spending less (hopefully substantially less) than you earn to facilitate goal attainment, effectively managing big expenditures, prudently managing debt, investing with a well-designed low-cost strategy tailored to your situation, protecting your income, assets, and family in a cost-effective manner, understanding the income tax implications relevant to your situation, purchasing professional advice necessary to enhance your plan effectiveness, and thinking through your estate-planning options to direct asset flow upon death in the manner you would most prefer—are virtually timeless. The details and available applications may change from time to time but the main principles that should be embedded in your financial endeavours tend to age well.

Much of what I have included in this text is based on my opinion, which in turn is based on my education and experience. I don't know about you, but I have been known to make the odd mistake, and it could well be proven that some of what I am presenting here turns out to be suboptimal in one way, shape or form. This book covers topic areas that, if discussed in a fully comprehensive manner, would require several volumes. Clearly, this book is too succinct to offer fulsome coverage of all of the topics touched upon. I will, within these pages, point you in the right direction to obtain further information where I feel it is important to do so.

Boring Alert

All that said, any credible discussion of personal financial planning must dive into details at certain points, in order to be useful. Not all details of potential actions need be understood by everybody—some things just are not applicable. If at any point in the book we are getting into something that is not relevant to you, simply skim it or skip it if you just can't take it any more … try not to let a deep dive into a subject area discourage you or inhibit your progress.

You will notice that at certain points in the book I include the phrase "boring alert." (My kids think I should have put that on the cover.) Generally these are segments of the book where we get more deeply into program or planning details. These are some of the areas in the text that can be a challenge to stay awake through, especially if they don't really seem relevant to your situation for one reason or another. The alert is my attempt to help you keep engaged and perhaps refocus. While the material may not hold you captivated in the same way that a juicy *Survivor* Tribal Council can, when it is applicable to you, it is important to have awareness of it. If the material is not important to you at the moment, it might be later, so skimming it for general awareness is always a good idea.

IN A NUTSHELL

Personal finance is a subject matter that, like it or not, is not an optional undertaking. It is up to you if you apply your resources to efficiently achieve your goals, or if you instead stumble and bumble from one financial decision to the next without a coherent strategy. One certainty is that your financial life will happen; it is entirely your decision if it happens on purpose or by default.

There are several key principles that I outline in this text that I have found worked well for me. Everyone can do this stuff.

1. Develop Human Capital

    The ability to earn a healthy living is a core element of a sustainable financial plan. Human capital is built and enhanced through post-secondary education and continuing education. There are a number of government programs and savings vehicles that are designed to enable the development of human capital—take advantage of them. The inescapable equation behind a successful financial plan is that income must exceed expenses (hopefully by a substantial margin). If you earn *more* income, you give yourself more options, period. The path to earning more is through building and maintaining human capital.

2. Purposeful Spending

   Clearly articulated goals help direct the use of funds to where there is the greatest personal value. There are a number of areas where people tend to get tripped up and spend excessively (cars, houses, consumables, etc.). Having a plan around expenditures, supported by explicit personal goals, helps better direct money to where you will experience the greatest level of satisfaction, as defined by your value system.

3. Strategic Investing

   Effectively converting capability into cash flow, combined with a purposeful expenditure program, should provide excess income. The excess income must then be effectively invested to support the funding of well-articulated longer-term goals. The investing program should include due consideration of tax efficiency, a personalized asset allocation, effective diversification within and across asset classes, and cost minimization strategies. Investment strategies are where people make mistakes on a regular basis, which is unfortunate because it is one of the aspects of personal finance where simple, effective, and low-cost options can be readily designed and implemented.

4. Protection

   Events and outcomes with potential to be game changers should be identified and managed through an appropriate mix of behaviour management and risk transfer. Like it or not, insurance has a critical role to play in a well-designed financial plan. It is the one expenditure you make with the hope that it never pays a return other than to provide peace of mind.

5. Good Record Keeping

   Documentation of your financial plan, income, and use thereof, as well as investment program, provide feedback that is key to understanding progress and identifying behavioural modifications required on a go-forward basis. Knowing where you stand financially, how you got there, and where you want to go is essential to efficient and continual progress.

6. DIY with Sprinkles of Quality Advice

    There are a lot of moving parts associated with a comprehensive financial plan—personal financial management can be a daunting undertaking. It is up to you to be an active participant in the development of your plan and implementation of the strategies designed to get you to where you want to be vis-à-vis your goals. In order to be an active participant, you should develop a certain base understanding of all areas of personal finance and hire qualified assistance to help as appropriate. No one cares more about your finances than you; take responsibility for your plan.

7. Estate Management

    Arrangements should be made to ensure the ongoing management and/or distribution of your estate in the event of incapacity or death. Formal legal arrangements appropriate to an individual's specific circumstances need to be designed and enacted.

I have just returned from a Baltic Cruise with my family. When I sat on the balcony of our cabin, each day, without exception, I took a moment to reflect on how fortunate I was to have been given the opportunity to have the family I have been blessed with and the experiences that life has granted me. My wife and I have worked hard for what we have achieved and we have been purposeful in arranging our financial affairs to provide the support for the life that we have lived and plan to live going forward. But I know that we have also been lucky. We were lucky that we were born in a wonderful and generous country and lived every day of our lives with a supportive, loving family. To say I feel fortunate is the understatement of the year.

Having peace of mind is a wonderful state to find one's self in. Designing, implementing, and maintaining a comprehensive financial plan provided a strong foundation that helped us achieve our current situation.

I am five foot six with average abilities. If I can live my dream, you can too.

PART I – PERSONAL FINANCIAL MANAGEMENT

My parents did not spend a lot of time planning their financial future. Dad finished high school, completed a limited amount of specialized technical training, got a job that had a good benefits package (including a defined benefit pension plan), and worked for the same employer for the vast majority of his career. Mom stayed home with my brother and I until we were in school, then she got a job to help bring in a little extra cash and kept that job until Dad retired; then, a little while later, she retired. The income side of the financial picture was modest, consistent, uninterrupted, and long term. This is the way many if not most parents did it when I was growing up.

My parents didn't have an itemized budget, but they avoided any sort of lavish spending. We lived in a series of non-descript houses in family friendly neighbourhoods that met our needs. All of our houses were near large empty fields where we could shag flies, build skating rinks, and fly a kite. When we moved to a house that didn't have a community pool, my dad bought a cheap above-ground pool that occupied many a summer afternoon for my brother and I, as well as our friends. Each time we moved, the pool came with us.

My dad bought second-hand automobiles that matched our transportation requirements. It was a treat when we went out for dinner and it was always to either a family restaurant or fast food establishment, never anything fancy. We went on family vacations every summer that utilized the tent trailer and campgrounds. I don't recall any family vacations as a kid that involved air travel, all-you-can-eat-whenever-you-want buffets, or theme or water parks.

The only debt they ever took on was a mortgage. Given that all of the houses we lived in were modest, the mortgage was never an oversized burden. We never had a custom-built house; apparently we were always able to find something that matched our needs in the inventory of homes available for purchase. Everything, other than housing, Mom and Dad bought was on a strictly cash basis. (In the later years, they did use credit cards for some purchases but the balance was paid off every month.)

My parents didn't have a clue about investing. They did have some savings because they always lived well within their means. I remember them purchasing Government of Canada Savings Bonds and maximizing their contributions to RRSPs because they somehow stumbled on the idea that this might be a good thing to do. Interest rates were higher in those days so there was a decent return to be earned without taking much risk. The core of their financial plan was living within their means and the core of their retirement plan was my dad's defined benefit pension plan, supplemented with government programs and whatever savings they happened to accumulate along the way.

I remember an annual visit from the insurance salesman, where my parents sat around the kitchen table nodding a lot. My dad developed heart problems rather early in life, so he became uninsurable at a relatively young age. But they did keep up the small permanent life insurance policies they had taken out on him for years and years. It never occurred to them to purchase any insurance on my mother; an opportunity missed by the salesman because I am sure he would have been able to convince them of the merits. The policies on my dad would have been woefully inadequate to help in any meaningful way, but luckily they were not needed when he passed away. I suspect he had additional coverage through work that would have filled-in some of the gap during his working years, but the personal policies he purchased had no strategic value whatsoever.

I think this was pretty typical of the approach to finances that was taken by my parents' generation. If you didn't have it, you didn't spend it and you counted on the work pension and government programs to look after you in retirement. In your retirement you looked forward to relaxing, golfing, and getting together with friends to play cards. My parents had some additional savings, which were untouched and amounted to a modest portfolio in the end, but they certainly were never subject to a formal investment plan during most of the asset accumulation phase of their lives.

While this approach worked for my parents, it is unlikely to work as well today. The spending limits that my parents took for granted (their pay cheque) are not as strict now as they were back then. Cash is now used very infrequently, if ever. Credit is readily available for virtually every type of purchase and it is pushed as hard now as the box set of encyclopedias was by door to door salesmen back in the day. Jobs are no longer as secure and the benefits packages are far less generous, on average, than were made available to my parents' generation. The investment options available now are almost boundless compared to the options that were known to my parents. The tax system is more extensive, complicated, and impactful than it was in the formative years of my parents' lives together. The world has undergone dramatic change; along with that change, personal finance has become more complex.

Managing the finances of the household today takes more time and effort than it did for my parents' generation. The responsibility for planning has shifted more to the individual, but the tools available now are far superior and more cost effective than the options Mom and Dad had.

If you invest the time to develop a comprehensive financial plan (or have one developed for you by a qualified professional) and do a good job of sticking to it, you can live a far more interesting and fulfilling life than at any time in history. But, the onus is on you to make prudent informed decisions that will allow this to happen for you and your family.

Takeaways from Part I

- ✓ You will make mistakes along the way as you manage your personal finances. Learn from them, adjust as necessary, and move on. There is nothing to be gained by beating yourself up over being human.
- ✓ Rather than focusing on all financial decisions with the same level of analysis and zeal, focus your efforts on getting the big decisions approximately right; this is where your time and effort is best spent.
- ✓ Some of the big financial decision areas you need to focus on, in my opinion, include:

- education and continuing education
- marriage/cohabitation
- borrowing (or not)
- managing large and/or recurring purchases
- investment planning
- tax planning
- insurance planning
- estate planning

✓ Effective financial management requires a certain amount of ongoing rigour and effort. Planning, tracking, and documenting are essential habits to develop and maintain.

✓ Living below one's means is a vital concept to embrace. If you find you are not moving toward your goals with the appropriate consistency and speed, then you need to consider increasing your means, decreasing your expenditures, or deferring goal achievement. Enhancing human capital is probably the most foolproof way of manipulating this formula in your favour. If you have the capacity to generate more means, then you have more options.

✓ Living below one's means does not mean becoming a Scrooge. It simply requires that an appropriate balance between current consumption and future consumption be planned for and managed.

✓ Setting and maintaining written goals, which are clearly articulated and valued, form the foundation of an effective financial plan.

✓ If you don't have the ability to create and maintain a comprehensive financial plan, hire qualified assistance to design one, then either implement it or have it implemented on your behalf. Regardless of the process you select, be an active participant ... no one cares more about your finances than you.

CHAPTER 1 – THE SECRET

When it comes to achieving financial independence there is no secret. Sorry.

Success in personal finance is not about doing any one thing right, and it certainly is not about doing everything exactly right; it is about doing the big things approximately right. There is a lot of room for imperfection in your approach and the sum total of your small mistakes shouldn't have a significantly detrimental impact on your end result. Indeed, you can't have the perfect approach because there are too many variables that you would need to anticipate correctly.

- Do you know what inflation is going to do for the next twenty or thirty years?
- Do you know which asset class is going to be the best performer next year or over the next five years?
- Do you know when the stock market is going to correct/crash next and when it will subsequently recover, allowing you to perfectly time your exit and re-entry?
- Do you know how long you and your family members are going to live?
- Do you know if your income will increase faster than inflation over the next decade, or if it will increase at all?
- Do you know if your wife/partner will come to her/his senses and figure out that there are better partners available than you? (So far, I've

successfully managed to distract my wife from thinking about this with any clarity.)
- Do you know if your kids are going to become independent when you would like them to be?
- Do you know if your parents are going to need some financial help, or alternatively, if they are going to leave you an inheritance that will solve any financial issues you may have?

As I am writing this, Donald Trump is President of the United States and Las Vegas, in their first year in the NHL, is playing for the Stanley Cup! Wow! Having watched the debates leading up to the election and knowing what the polls were saying, Trump's victory was almost an unfathomable result. Las Vegas in the Stanley Cup Finals? Get real! But there you have it. The world is full of surprises that just can't possibly be envisioned in advance, and it is this environment within which you must design and implement your financial plan.

The really cool thing is you can turn on any business news station at any time of the day and there is someone willing to tell you exactly how the future is going to unfold. They do so with detailed, articulate reasoning and unbridled confidence. The trouble is, they don't know what is going to happen with any more precision than you do. (Often, at the end of their dissertation, they will flash up a quick disclaimer that says as much.)

I especially love the highly qualified stock analysts that present their best stock picks on the business news. They blast out a clear cut and insightful argument that demonstrates the obvious value in the recommendations they are making, presented with the *you're stupid if you don't* undertone. Often when the prior stock picks are reviewed, which were also ushered in with the same flair and fanfare, they show the fallibility of the analyst. On the day I was reviewing this particular piece of the book, there was a well-respected and very successful money manager presenting his best stock picks, all of which sounded to be no-brainers. The net performance he demonstrated on his prior stock picks over the course of the following year was -10.33% during a time when the index returned a modest positive return. Hmmm, maybe I shouldn't run out and fill my portfolio with his newest picks after all.

Personally, I view much of the business news as entertainment at best, but for people who give it too much credence, it can be very dangerous. If you are prone to acting on the basis of the business news, perhaps the best investment you could make would be to reduce the cost of your cable package in favour of watching a few reruns of *Gilligan's Island* rather than giving the financial guru of the day edge-of-seat attention.

For your financial future to work out nicely for you, you don't need to know everything with precision and you don't need to do everything robotically following the set of golden rules as you have come to understand them. If you get the big stuff mostly right, you'll likely be fine. If you get some of the little stuff right on top of that, you'll likely be even finer. (I should have paid more attention in language arts.)

One of the key pitfalls to avoid in managing your personal finances is becoming bogged down in details to the point where it impacts your ability to act in a manner such that you get to the point of doing things mostly right. There is time as you move forward to refine what you are doing and how you are doing it. Through practice and patience you will have an opportunity to improve on your plan as time unfolds; you don't need the perfect solution before you start.

The best time to design and implement your long-term plan was back in the day, but the second best time is right now. Second best is often pretty good. If you ascribe to the contention that Wayne Gretzky was the best hockey player of all time, it isn't too bad if you just turn out to be Gordie Howe, or Bobby Orr, or whoever your version of number two is.

My friend Bernie and I had the distinct pleasure of picking up and driving Gordie Howe to an event once. He was a very nice man, and it was a short drive I will never forget.

CHAPTER 2 – THE BIG THINGS

So you are probably wondering what this guy thinks the "big things" are that you need to get approximately right in order to earn financial independence. The list will change somewhat depending upon where you live and your individual circumstances, but for most people I believe the big things include the following (not necessarily in order of importance):

1. Education and Continuing Education

    For most of your life your biggest asset is, well, you. Knowledge and talent convert into cash flow. The more knowledge and talent you possess, the more potential you have to achieve a substantial, consistent, and durable income. Some people are born with a talent they can readily convert into financial success once they identify it and hone their skills. (Connor McDavid, Josh Donaldson, Greg Bridges come to mind … Greg is someone I went to high school with; he got A's in his sleep, and is now a tenured university professor.) Most of us need to define and develop our human capital through ongoing training, study, practice, and hard work (not to say that Connor, Josh, and Greg don't work hard, but I do believe they had an advantage that allowed them to flourish in a way that not everyone can.)

Successful completion of well-targeted education, combined with maintaining marketability through sufficient and appropriate continuing education, provide the path to enhanced human capital. When human capital is ultimately converted into cash flow, one key ingredient to ultimately realizing financial independence is in place ... but as all the high income earners who are broke continue to prove, this alone is not enough.

2. If you Partner, Partner Well

I'm not talking about finding a sugar daddy or mommy. I'm talking about finding someone with whom you can achieve long-term compatibility if you so choose a partnered lifestyle. Apart from the emotional toll splitting up can take, it is also extremely expensive, to the point where it can be financially devastating.

I did a quick internet search to see what the divorce rate was in Canada and found a wide array of statistics that were somewhat challenging to understand and authenticate. Without getting into too much detail it looks like the odds of getting a divorce are somewhere in the high thirty to low forty percent range, depending on many variables, including where you live, how old you are when you get married, if you have been married before, etc. Apparently, we are not great at achieving long-term compatibility.

In his book *Straight Talk on Your Money*,[1] Doug Hoyes notes, "One in seven insolvencies in Canada is caused, at least in part, by a relationship breakdown. More than a quarter of people filing bankruptcy are divorced or separated at the time they file." Add to that the post-split time period when you walk around like a zombie due to the emotional toll splitting up entails and it seems to me that marriage is a decision that deserves cold-shower scrutiny at the outset.

Divorce is costly in every imaginable way, but it may well be the only reasonable option once nuptials have been executed and reality has presented a previously unforeseen truth. Sufficient up front due diligence to ensure a high probability of marital success is advisable, as is a prenup when unequal financial wealth is contributed by the participants. What a sophisticated process of due diligence entails in this realm is just a wee bit outside of my area of expertise (as in Dustin Johnson hits his drive just a wee bit farther and straighter than I do). Kevin O'Leary, in his book *Cold Hard Truth on Family, Kids & Money*,[2] ventures into this area if you want some advice from the Shark, Dragon, and once Conservative Party leadership candidate.

3. Planning, Tracking, and Documenting

Knowledge is power. Having a financial plan and tracking progress related to your plan, while tedious and boring for some (exhilarating and entertaining for others—well, me) is absolutely essential in order to maximize the likelihood of achieving your goals. If you don't have documented goals and strategies, and you don't track your progress, you really don't know if you are on course or not. Knowledge is essential to help you correct when you stray and reward when you achieve.

4. Living Well but Comfortably BELOW One's Means

I do not believe in depriving one's current self to overly enrich one's future self. You don't know what life has in store, so it is my philosophy that you try to use your financial resources to live well over the whole of your life. The trick is defining what living well means, and making sure that you are following a path that reasonably levels out your expenditures to achieve a proper balance between today and the future; this is what a well-designed financial plan should help you accomplish.

My wife and I have always targeted to save well in excess of 20% of our income; this rate of saving allowed our family a buffer that provided ongoing peace of mind. There were some higher expense and lower-income years around the time we were having and raising our kids where meeting our saving target was not possible, but we planned and executed in a manner that allowed us to exceed our target most years without undue sacrifice to the lifestyle we enjoyed.

5. Avoiding/Minimizing Debt

Current consumption can be satisfied in one of two ways; paying now or paying later. Paying now is what you want to do in almost all situations.

Paying later has the attraction of allowing for immediate consumption without any immediate pain. The problem is, and it is a big problem if you fall into a pattern of taking on debt, you pay more. Compounding this problem, and this too is a big problem, is the tendency to buy more than you require. This doesn't mean you buy two Honda Civics rather than one when you need a car. (That is obviously stupid.) It means you buy that gorgeous V6 SUV with low profile tires, a sun roof, leather interior, and 46 cup holders instead of the Civic. Paying more, and too much, is a very dangerous path to follow if you want to achieve your longer-term goals in a reasonable time frame.

Paying now, on the other hand, means that you have delayed consumption while saving for the purchase. When you save first you have a clear memory of the effort involved in earning and saving the money, which has a tendency to better focus you on the need the purchase will fill and arms you to better fend off the urge to buy more than you need. For instance, my daughter has a very different view of the cost of the jeans she is looking at when she considers the number of hours she worked at Subway to earn the money required to pay for the jeans. The hard work has a way of making the evaluation of the pending purchase more thorough and grounded. Does this mean she won't buy the jeans? No. Does this mean that she makes sure she values those jeans more than dinner and a movie with her boyfriend? No. What the hard work does do is encourage her to consider if the jeans represent a fair trade for her time. If the answer is yes, she buys them. If the answer is no, maybe she takes another look at the sale rack or waits for a price reduction such that the trade-off makes sense.

When purchase decisions are disconnected from the earning process, as they can be with heavy reliance on debt, there is a much greater risk of encountering financial challenge as the future unfolds.

6. Managing Life's Large Expenditures

   Some of the most common large expenditures that people seem to have trouble controlling include the following:

   - Housing
   - Transportation
   - Weddings
   - Children
   - Pets (yes, Rover)
   - Some hobbies
   - Repetitive/habitual purchases that endure

   Lots of financial literature focuses on perfecting the use of your limited funds, often targeting expenditures made on little daily pleasures. I think that it makes sense to focus hard on the large expenditures you are likely to make as well as the habitual expenses that accumulate to substantial value. The goal is not to eliminate them or even reduce them necessarily; after all, enjoying your life is kind of the point. The objective of looking at these areas of expenditure is to force you to think about the commitment they entail in the context of the potential impact on your longer-term goals. A dollar spent is a dollar gone, regardless of what it is spent on, so your goal is to make the vast majority of your dollar expenditures count.

7. Prudent Consistent Investing

   Efficient and effective investment of savings in both registered (RRSPs, RRIFs, TFSAs, RPPs, etc.) and unregistered accounts are important. It also, believe it or not, is not overly difficult or complicated.

8. Understanding and Managing Income Taxes

   I keep a spreadsheet that shows me the running tally of the income taxes (federal and provincial) my family and I have paid from the time my wife and I married to the present. The total, my friends, is a very healthy sum.

How healthy you ask? Well, let me frame it this way … my youngest child and I took a trip from Winnipeg to Oahu, home of the famous Waikiki Beach. We were there for a week and did all of the expensive touristy things, including a submarine ride, a helicopter tour, a two-day specialized sightseeing tour, a sunset cruise with five-star dinner, a tour of Pearl Harbor, an evening luau, and eating out every day, including cheesecake dinners and breakfasts on the balcony looking out at the ocean. This was a very expensive short trip! Well, we have paid enough income taxes for us to do that trip 200 times!

You may not be inclined to become a tax expert (I certainly do not consider myself to be a tax expert), but you should make an effort to understand the basics and hire experts to help with the details where it makes sense to do so. Doing this piece of your finances right is absolutely critical. There is much more to know about income taxes than I will cover in this book, but we will cover several important concepts.

9. Protecting Income, Property, and Investments

Insurance is the perfect product to disaster-proof the financial side of your plans. Money cannot fix every potential disaster, but for a good many of them, it can help.

10. Planning for Departure

A comprehensive estate plan, tailored to your situation and your wishes, is something that Canadians do a terrible job of, according to my research. Love your family enough to put the time and effort into drafting a will and power of attorney. Put some thought into how, if at all, a trust or series of trusts will help achieve your goals and provide protection for your beneficiaries. Consider the probate and tax implications that come with death and organize your wealth transfer approach with these costs in mind.

Each and every one of these aspects needs to be fully considered, many on a recurring basis. But again, your goal is to get the major decision points approximately right and adjust moving forward. We all make mistakes and missteps; when you do, just regroup and learn from what happened.

Prudent, consistent investing is where lots of people make the most glaring mistakes. I can recount many investing mistakes that I have made. For example, I purchased units in a labour-sponsored venture capital corporation. I got a nice tax write-off, and followed that up with a not as nice capital loss as its value plummeted. To this day I have the "investment" because the fund is no longer accepting redemptions due to liquidity limitations of its holdings.

In another instance of being stupid—I mean imprudent—I purchased shares in Nortel Networks. I thought they must be worth more than the value the shares had fallen to by the time I bought them ... I wasn't stupid enough to buy the shares at $120 each, but if you buy them at $25.69 (like me) and sell them at $2.52 (like me), that is the same percentage loss as buying at $120 and selling at $11.77.

In spite of these investing mistakes and others, I did manage to get the big picture approximately right. I developed an investment policy, established a conservative asset allocation appropriate to family circumstances (reviewed and modified annually), and followed it in a manner that contained the impact of any errors I made. The vast majority of our investments are targeted at a low-cost, diversified equity and bond portfolio. Because of the structure I implemented and the care I exercise to respect the limits I have set, I can readily absorb the laughable but relatively few glaring errors I make.

When it comes to personal finance, perfection is impossible—don't expect the impossible of yourself. Set yourself up in a good circumstance, practice patience and due diligence, and you will likely not do anything that is so stupid that you can't recover. Spend the time to understand your goals, build a financial plan, and implement a framework in support of those goals. Follow the plan and you should do a fine job of moving toward your goals by doing the big stuff right and limiting your screw-ups to the edges. So long as you contain the impact of your screw-ups, while they will bother you, they won't hurt you all that much in the long run.

We will spend much time on each of these areas (except for partnering) over the course of the remaining pages.

CHAPTER 3 – IT'S IN THE BALANCE

The purpose of a personal financial plan is to help you manage your actions (and money) in a fashion that maximizes your life experiences across the whole of your life in a balanced and prudent manner. You need to bring into focus what you want to achieve/experience in your life and how money and time will be used to help realize your objectives. A financial plan provides the structure vital to keep your goals in focus and to help make tough decisions as you move forward.

Financial success inevitably requires that you spend less than you earn, but the big question you will have to answer is how to best use your surplus to experience the life that you will most enjoy. Mindlessly living below your means and saving each and every extra penny should not be the objective here. There are many examples of people who have lived their life spending the bare minimum so that they could build more security, ultimately accumulating a bigger pile of money that they never enjoyed. That, to me, is every bit the mistake that overspending is. Finding the correct balance is crucial.

My wife and I have retired early (mid/early 50s). We could have continued in our jobs and accumulated more wealth. We could have saved every penny not designated for an essential expenditure and had a greater "pile" to be saved, spent, or gifted in the future. But the "pile" was never our objective. Money was simply a means to help achieve a series of well thought-out written goals that had been considered and refined over a number of years.

For example, one of our goals was to *maintain a prudently affluent lifestyle both before and after retirement.* We then had a series of component goals that described more clearly what that meant in terms of how we were going to use our financial resources—essentially defining in operative terms what *prudent affluence* meant to us. This thought process, which we documented and updated annually, gave us the structure we needed to guide our decisions related to how and when we used our financial wherewithal, and how to balance our current versus our future use of resources.

We chose to prudently spend our surplus over time, and the focus was not on *stuff* as much as it was on having experiences that brought more value to our lives. For instance, my wife took a leave of absence in her late twenties and spent a year travelling around the world. In order to do something as extravagant as this, there were certain conditions that needed to be achieved through a well-considered plan of action that balanced our current and future spending plans. We had to be able to afford to pay for the trip without going into debt. (If you really want to do something like this, it is my position that you must pay for it first.) In order to get to this point, we needed to have developed skills that were both marketable and financially rewarded. Then we had to build a lifestyle that allowed us to save the money that was required to fund such an adventure. Unless you have an appropriately integrated plan, an adventure of this scope simply stays on the bucket list and likely becomes a member of your regrets list further down the road.

If you are going to lease and drive the latest SUV with a trade-up every couple of years, or buy too much house before you can afford it, or spend everything that is coming in (or more) on the "nice things," then the trip around the world, while you are young enough to really experience it, is out the window. For my wife, being prudent with her money was not a sacrifice as such; rather, it enabled the early achievement of an experience that she would remember forever and that would form the foundation of her outlook on life.

Some of our friends thought we were nuts (more precisely, thought I was nuts) for separating for a considerable length of time in our early married years. I knew that travel was very important to my wife and if we were going to have a long marriage this was an area where I would have to make some sacrifices. I had no interest in going to many of the areas of the world where she was intent on spending a remarkably long amount of time. So I went along for four months during the easy parts of the early trip (Fiji, New Zealand, and Australia) and went back for a several-week visit in Thailand later in the year.

The time spent in Thailand very quickly made it evident that my having avoided much of the low budget, low GDP parts of the trip may have saved our marriage. I don't need to live in the lap of luxury, but I still to this day do not view a sit-down toilet as being too fussy. For my wife, it was all about the experience, which meant spending as little as possible on the extraneous elements like meals, hot showers, individual rooms with an actual lock on the door (if there was a door at all), or proper rodent control (she woke up in India with a rat sleeping on her) … for her, it was about spending a night on the Great Wall, sailing up the Gold Coast, experiencing a camel safari in India, scaling Ayers Rock, trekking to the Annapurna base camp in Nepal, and sleeping above the biggest noisiest pig in a house made with twig construction lit with a bunch of perilously balanced kerosene lamps in the middle of the Thai jungle. (That was my memory; I doubt she noticed.)

Not a chance we would still be together if I had been there the whole year. Her eyes saw all of the beauty and splendour of the cultures and ways of life practiced around the world. She saw beauty in all of the flowers, nature, people, and geographic wonders that she got to experience first-hand. A nattering buffoon of a husband would likely have taken considerable shine off what she was experiencing. She often says if she were to die while she was travelling that would be the best way to go. Clearly she has not considered the cost of flying her body home for a proper funeral.

I too see the beauty in her pictures, but the torture endured in getting the picture I could do without. For instance, we were in Africa on a subsequent trip and my wife took a photo of the Nile River and there happened to be a dam in the picture. Not an overly interesting picture; however, when we emerged from the bush a guard with a machine gun approached us and demanded she pass him the camera. My immediate response would be to give him the camera, apologize, accidentally drop any cash I had in my pocket for whoever might want to pick it up and hop back in the bus we were travelling on and hope it all went away. My wife simply said NO. It then turned into a staring match; and somehow my wife won. She wasn't about to give up her role of film with other treasured photos on it. Travel, and those pictures were a very important piece of the documentation of her experience and she was not going to easily concede on retaining her "proof of life." Likely she barely remembers this episode, yet it is one of the many similar sorts of experiences that I hold dearly in my nightmares.

The point of this dissertation is that people are unique and what they want out of life is also, to a large extent, unique. You only have one life, so putting thought into what you want to achieve, how you are going to fund it, and documenting the whole plan is an important step to take. It is some work, sure, but isn't everything that is worthwhile?

Some people might get this right flying by the seat of their pants, but most people without a plan would simply bumble into their result and then have to live with it. A bit harsh, perhaps, but finding the proper balance between spending now and later does boil down to doing the thinking.

CHAPTER 4 – GOALS AND THE PLAN

If you spend some time and effort thinking about what you want out of life, you can then organize yourself to get much, if not all of it. If you want to accumulate two million dollars, you can organize your occupation, spending, saving, and investing program to accumulate two million dollars. I'm not sure what that does for you other than to allow you to say you have two million dollars, but hey, that was your goal, not mine … *fill your boots*. (I don't know what that means, my brother-in-law always says it.)

If you think more deeply about what you want, you can refine that *two million dollar* goal into more meaningful terms. When I hear goals expressed in dollar terms, I think what people are trying to say is that their goal is financial security, and the number they pick is what represents financial security to them. To me that goal is more appropriately expressed as something like "I want to accumulate enough capital so that I can work on my schedule and focus my time living on my own terms. Living on my own terms means …" It is when you get to the level of defining the details that support the broad objective then you are putting some meat on the bone (or tofu on the carrot, if you are vegan like my youngest). The details add purpose and meaning to the goal; they are what make the goal important and drive the willpower needed to make any concessions that may be necessary to achieve the greater, albeit delayed, result.

Goals are very important; without them life will just kind of happen. The more thought you put into your goals, the better your understanding of them will become and the more dedicated you will be to doing what is necessary to achieve them.

For a goal to be effective it needs to be SMART (specific, measurable, attainable, realistic and timely or time bound).[1] A properly structured financial plan always starts with SMART goals. Each goal should be written in terms that demonstrate the five components that meet the criteria of being SMART.

The first part of our family financial plan lays out our goals and forms the foundation of everything else included in the plan. In the first iteration of our financial plan, we started with a very basic plan and as we progressed in our lives together, my wife and I added more detail and numerical support to our plan during our annual updates. As with all things, getting started is the main hurdle to overcome. There is time to refresh your approach and add colour as you move through life and your understanding of what you want evolves. The perfect financial plan for you is not likely the one you will start with, but rather one that takes shape over time as you gain experience and come to better understand what you want and how best to achieve whatever that may be.

When my wife and I were young and just getting started as a couple, we didn't have a formal financial plan. We simply fumbled along, following a few simple money management principles that seemed to stand us in good stead. We were both pretty good savers, which helped us get off on the right foot as a couple. We established allowances and held our spending within them. We had no debt, and never bought anything we didn't have the money for. We lived in a tiny apartment, furnished with lawn furniture, until we could afford more. Our lifestyle purchases fully respected our modest means. We heard RRSPs were a good idea, so we made a point of purchasing a registered GIC each of our first couple of years together. Maxing out our contributions was something we got in the habit of doing and have done every year of our lives together. Life went on, following these few basic principles.

For my family, formal planning became important once we started to formulate a clearer idea of what we really wanted to get out of life and how the associated plans would be supported by our income. Formalizing the plan, considering all relevant elements of our financial needs and wants, was a very important step in making sure we were moving toward what we wanted our money to help us achieve. Pen to paper (fingers to keyboard) is a very empowering step to take. It adds formality and an element of responsibility that isn't there otherwise.

The practice standards[2] of the FP Canada Standards Council (the standards setter for financial planning in Canada, a division of FP Canada the licensor of the Certified Financial Planner (CFP) professional certification marks) includes a clear ten-step process that CFPs are to follow:

1. Explain the role of the financial planner and the value of the financial planning process
2. Define the terms of the engagement
3. Identify the client's goals, needs, and priorities
4. Gather the client's information
5. Assess the client's current situation
6. Identify and evaluate the appropriate financial planning strategies
7. Develop the financial planning recommendations
8. Compile and present the financial planning recommendations and supporting rationale
9. Discuss implementation action, responsibilities, and time frames
10. Implement the financial planning recommendations

Whether you go through the process of developing your own financial plan, or you employ the services of someone to help you, the rigour embedded in the above process should be followed. I believe that most financial plans are better if the owners are taken through the process by a qualified independent advisor. This step is important and needs to be done with appropriate diligence, thoroughness, and understanding; thus, the advisor needs to have appropriate credentials and not have any embedded conflicts of interest (this is discussed more thoroughly in part IX). A financial plan is not something that can be done for you without your active participation.

My family's current financial plan contains the following broad elements:

- Goals

    We have five main goals that are specific, measurable, attainable, realistic, and timely. Each of these goals has subcomponents that, when taken as a whole, effectively drive our financial choices. Our goals focus on several themes: lifestyle and the sustainability thereof, funding for our kids' education, managing the impact of death or disability, and tax management. The manner in which you express and breakdown your goals will be personal to you and will likely look different from how my family has chosen to express ours. The important characteristic to strive for is to have your goals clearly describe what you want to achieve and thereby have them help you arrange your finances to move toward their achievement in a prudent and continual manner.

- Net-Worth Summary

Net worth is a single number that is arrived at by valuing all of your assets and deducting the value of everything that you owe. Ultimately, hopefully, it will simply become the total of your assets because you have eliminated all of your debt! (Any debt you have should likely form a prominent element in the goals section of your plan … just sayin'.)

Our net worth summary includes not just the number for the current year, but also the number for each of the previous years. Obviously your first plan iteration will have no history, but each annual update of the plan adds a layer of experience. Your current year net worth demonstrates your cumulative financial achievement to date and the growth pattern the number takes on over the years shows you how the enduring effort you and your family have put into your finances has resulted in where you find yourself. It is motivating to see that your hard choices result in financial advancement as the years unfold.

- Cash Flow Summary

The way I have built this summary shows, on one line, family take-home pay for the year (gross pay minus all source deductions), family expenses for the year, and the amount saved. I also include a very concise description of any major expenditure made during the year such as the purchase of a car, expensive trips, amounts spent on kids, etc. Again, in our case, the summary shows many past years.

- Expense Summary (optional)

This summary shows us the detail, by expenditure category, of where we spent over the course of each year. I'm an accountant, I love this stuff ... so much good information!

- Income Tax Summary

This is a simple summary of major categories that show up on our annual tax return. It is nice to have a solid number that you can throw back at your parents when they suggest that our (Canadian) taxes aren't all that bad. Income taxes truly are a huge burden and you need to do everything you can to manage them within the rules. This is the reason that we have built one of our goals around income tax management.

- Target Asset Allocation

I will spend more time on asset allocation later, but in short, the asset allocation target shows the percentage of investment assets to be maintained within each of the major investment categories across the full breadth of our family investments. It is displayed in terms of the target ranges appropriate to our circumstances as well as the actual percentages at the time of the plan update. This shows us if we are sticking to the plan or if something needs to be adjusted.

- Retirement Strategy

For years, one of our lifestyle goals was focused on retirement and this piece of the financial plan was designed to more fully explore the financial aspects unique to retirement and to review our readiness over time. Now that my wife and I have reached this stage, I maintain a separate spreadsheet that is designed to forecast our income expectations and expenditure requirements across the breadth of our retirement horizon.

- Insurance Strategy

    Life, disability, property, and other forms of insurance pertinent to one's situation are a necessary evil. Having this section in our financial plan forces us to consider our risks and how we are managing them on an annual basis.

- Estate Strategy

    I am sure I will die someday; you will too. It is essential to give clear thought to how assets will be managed/disbursed in the event of disability/demise.

- Education Funding Strategy

    This section relates to a specific goal my wife and I have, which is designed to provide our kids with every opportunity to develop and maximize their human capital. In order to be clear on what we want to do, how we will do it, and how we are doing at any point in time, this section forces an annual consideration of all the relevant elements.

It sounds like a lot of work putting together a document that covers this variety of topics. In truth, it is a fair amount of work, but it relieves a lot of stress because what you are doing becomes purpose driven and very personal. It gives my wife and I great peace of mind as we go through this process to refresh our views and results on an annual basis.

Always keep in mind that this is your plan and it needs to be designed to meet your requirements … you are the focus here. Your plan can and should grow and change with your needs over the course of time. It is fine to start off simple and add colour and breadth of coverage as your financial means and needs grow/change over time. The key is to get started and to work with a plan that you find informative and helpful as you move forward.

As previously stated, if you don't feel that you have the skills to do all of this yourself, and you don't have any interest in building the necessary skills, then you should work with a qualified financial planner who can supply the tools to simplify the process.

PART II – EDUCATION

The cornerstone to a viable financial plan is enhanced earning potential, plain and simple. In almost all cases, the foundation for enhanced earning potential is advanced education and skill development.

There are some exceptional individuals who are able to build a financial empire and fulfill their life's dreams without substantial formal tutelage. I admire those who were provided with such a gift. However, those people are the exception. The rest of us need more assistance in developing a skill set that is both valued and financially rewarded.

The simple math (simple is my specialty) says it is much easier to spend less than you earn if you *earn more*. I may be wrong, but I doubt the days will soon reappear where a high school graduate (or drop out) can get a job at "the factory," work there for 35 to 40 years, and retire with a defined benefit pension plan that will provide them with a sufficient reliable income for life. That was a viable strategy in my parents' generation, and to a much more limited extent in mine, but it won't work as easily now and in the future. You may luck out, but you probably should widen your marketability such that you have a few more embers available to nurture.

There are two phases to education and skill development that are important to engage. The first phase is post-secondary education. It normally starts in one's late teens or very early twenties and ends four (plus) years later. The second phase of education is also very important—that of continuing education. The world is changing at an unprecedented pace and it is vital that skills are both maintained and enhanced across the whole of one's career. Continuing education can be the difference between an okay career and an exceptional career.

For example, while working in a prior job, I became acquainted with an engineering technologist who was well thought of and valued as an employee. He was well placed, with his set of skills, to continue along the path he was on and have a respectable career that he could enjoy and would support a reasonable lifestyle for himself and his family. However, he recognized that he had the aptitude and ambition to do more. He sought his employers' help (funding and work hour flexibility) to go back to university while working, and over time he completed an engineering degree. He very quickly, after having completed the degree, moved up the organizational structure and ultimately became a very important, and well paid, piece of the management group. He saw what he wanted and he did what was necessary to get there through improving his educational standing … oh, and he worked hard to prove his worth to the organization every day.

I have also seen the other approach, where initial education is sought and obtained but it is not nurtured through continual dedication to skill development and enhancement. In many cases these individuals have had, or are in the midst of, respectable careers but they never really seem to progress to the level of their potential. If your goals can be satisfied with the income this approach provides, and you get the value you want out of your life by simply having a little more free time to be fully conversant in what is happening in the latest season of *The Bachelorette*, then good for you. Continue on. If you want a little more from your career, then look for opportunities in continuing education and take advantage of the support that many employers provide. This can be one of the most valuable employee benefits offered and it is amazing to me how often the hand up is not taken advantage of.

Takeaways from Part II

- ✓ Advanced education, all else remaining equal, enhances earning potential and broadens career opportunities.
- ✓ Post-secondary education is expensive. In order to graduate without a substantial debt burden, it is important to develop and implement a saving strategy in support of education funding. Parents have a lot of demands for their savings at the same time that their kids' education savings becomes a priority. If grandparents are able, this is an area of

- ✓ support where they may be more than happy to lend a financial hand; give them a nudge!
- ✓ As the end of high school approaches, a thorough search for available scholarship opportunities should be undertaken. Many scholarships have clear qualification criteria and require an application be submitted. If you don't apply, you may be leaving money on the table that is there for the taking.
- ✓ The government realizes the societal benefits that flow from advanced education and offer a number of support programs. Take them up on their generosity as it applies to your situation.
- ✓ While there are a number of approaches to education funding available, my favourite by a country mile is the Registered Education Savings Plan. The key benefits of the RESP include:

  - Government support. Up to $7,200 of Canada Education Savings Grants are available for those who qualify and care to take advantage. Free money is a good deal!
  - Tax-free compounding. There is no tax to pay on the earnings and grants while they remain in the plan.
  - Tax savings. When investment earnings and grants are taken out of the plan, they are taxed in the hands of the student, who is likely to be in a low tax bracket. This can be a very effective (and legal) income splitting tactic.
  - Administrative simplicity. Depending on the plan chosen, there are usually few restrictions on accessing the funds once a qualifying education program is entered by the student. There is a limitation as to the balance that can be accessed over the first several weeks, but after that the program limitations are slight.

- ✓ Achievable financial plans require one to live within one's means. To the extent that means and marketability are enhanced through advanced skill development, the probability of achieving the personal goals specified in a well-articulated financial plan is greatly enhanced.

CHAPTER 5 – INCOME EFFECT

In *The Cumulative Earnings of Post-secondary Graduates Over 20 Years: Results by Field of Study* (who names these things?) published by Statistics Canada in 2014, it is made abundantly clear that there is real economic value in well directed, advanced education. The study, as the title suggests, looked at cumulative employment earnings over a period of 20 years ending in 2010. The overall finding was that "Bachelor's degree and college graduates earned considerably more than did high school graduates."[1] I probably could have come to that conclusion without doing the study, but the details provided are enlightening. While high school grads demonstrated median cumulative 20-year earnings of $882,300[1] (male, constant 2010 dollars), this number was improved upon by a college education and a bachelor's degree by 1.3 and 1.7 times, respectively. That is a very substantial bump; markedly greater than the cost of the education.

The study also highlighted that the post-secondary education premium was not consistent across all fields of study, and there was considerable variability within each field of study. As one example, while the median business administration degree for a male yielded 1.8 times more cumulative earnings over the 20-year period than a high school grad, those in the 90th percentile improved their earnings by a factor of five.[2] (The results were even more dramatic for women.) While the numbers were different for other fields of study, the same trend generally endured. If students distinguish themselves within their chosen field, a substantial improvement in salary can be achieved.

Prudence needs to be exercised because education in and of itself does not guarantee substantially enhanced earning potential. For instance, one can get an undergraduate degree, and follow that up with a masters and doctorate, but if that advanced education is in a narrow or unmarketable field, it may be very difficult to translate that into a reliable, substantial, and sustainable income stream.

A friend of mine has a friend (how is that for convoluted?) who devoted many years of post-secondary study to the history of one relatively small island nation. That type of focus, while it may be fascinating, does not open a multitude of doors. I believe, in this person's case, it worked out nicely and he is now an academic sharing the knowledge he gained from his many years of study with another round of students. But that, in my view, is placing all of your eggs into a rather small basket. One of the key foundational principles of financial planning is diversification. Having a wide array of employment or business opportunities to which your skills are applicable provides a solid foundation for a stable, reliable, and substantial income.

I think a lot of people get the education equation wrong. The sole focus should not be on what interests the student. It is what provides value to others that is likely to provide the student with the income level necessary to build and support a family as well as to fund a lifetime of satisfying experiences. Finding a calling of personal interest is important, don't get me wrong. Hating every moment of your work life would be rather depressing. However, you need to do something from 9 to 5 that brings in the cash that provides for your needs, some wants, and supplies extra to fund your goals and aspirations.

I'm not going to get into where one should focus their educational efforts here, but there are lots of resources that can easily be found with just a couple of clicks that may help. Statistics Canada provides extremely useful segmented information and is a good place to begin a search. Keep in mind survey information of this type tends to be based on averages (or medians) and individuals may be an exception on one side or the other. In fact students should do all they can to be the exception, get into the 90th percentile, and take advantage of the wage multiple that is there for the taking!

When planning for education, a little research can go a long way to ensure desired results can be realized. Once a course of education is started, there will be lots of opportunity to adjust along the way, but having a plan is always a good way to begin the journey.

CHAPTER 6 – COST

If well thought out, money spent on education is an investment that will pay off more than most (or all) other investments a person will make over the course of their life. If not well thought out, the cost has the potential to be a significant and long-lasting burden. According to the Government of Canada website:

> A student attending CEGEP, trade school, college or university full-time today can expect to pay between $2,500 and $6,500 per year—or more—in tuition. Books, supplies, student fees, transportation, housing and other expenses will only add to that total. In fact, full-time students in Canada paid an average of $16,600 for post-secondary schooling in 2014–2015. That is more than $66,000 for a four-year program.[1]

The cost of an education is highly dependent on the degree/diploma sought, the institution attended, and whether or not the student stays home or leaves home for their studies. However, in terms of the overall broad picture, if the average student is paying just under the $70,000 mark over the course of their post-secondary education, that represents a lot of saving or, more likely, a lot of debt. In Manitoba, that would mean working over 6,000 hours (about three years) earning minimum wage, assuming no income taxes (as if!).

From my perspective, in order to reduce cost, it makes sense to get an undergraduate degree (or the equivalent) from an educational institution located close to home. While the cost associated with living away from home is highly variable, it can easily double (or more) the cost of an education. If avoided, that represents a substantially reduced level of debt for a new graduate.

If it turns out that a graduate degree or specialist designation is in the cards, at that point consider if it is worth the extra cost of going to an out of province/country institution. While there are some employers who place great value on where an education is received, in my experience, they are the exception. Most employers are simply looking for a degree or diploma in a relevant field along with strong academic performance. The periodic employer will require a degree from *Hogwarts*, but most often, the local universities and community colleges do a good job of delivering the base skills and it is up to the student to enhance their value through experience and ongoing training.

In addition to the financial component, the adjustment to a post-secondary setting, when compared to a high school setting, is in itself significant. Learning how to live independently at the same time the student is trying to figure out how to study, balance a social agenda, and manage unsavoury roommates, is a substantial undertaking. If the moving-away-from-home elements are removed from the picture, the opportunity to flourish at a post-secondary institution may be greatly augmented.

Provincial government programs should also be investigated because they can have a financial component significant to a decision. For example, the Province of Manitoba had a nifty Tuition Fee Tax Rebate program that refunded a hefty percentage of education costs for students who chose to remain and work in Manitoba after graduation. (I believe other provinces use similar styles of incentive.) Government programs frequently change, so it is important to do research in a timely manner. A case in point is the Tuition Fee Tax Rebate program I just mentioned. The Province of Manitoba announced, almost immediately after I wrote about it, that it is to be phased out (and to think I voted for the party in power, *grumble*). Governments have a tendency to do this so making long-term plans based on their programs can be somewhat frustrating. Don't be discouraged, though; effective financial planning is about making the best decision at any given point in time and adjusting as the landscape changes.

No matter how you slice it, the cost of post-secondary education is substantial. How substantial the cost becomes can often be controlled to a degree through research and well-chosen strategies around the educational institution selected.

While I won't focus on scholarships in this text, it would be imprudent of me to not mention that there are tons of them available to deserving applicants, thereby reducing the cost of education. My daughter won a couple of scholarships as a result of her high school performance and used them to reduce the cost of her initial year in university. Our friends' son, Scott, was an accomplished amateur golfer and he was awarded several scholarships for his academic achievements and later earned a scholarship to play on the university golf team that gave him substantial monetary and non-monetary advantages (course selection privileges, registration flexibility, etc.). Given his parents' lack of golf prowess, Scott certainly deserved a full ride for overcoming seemingly insurmountable genetic odds. (Okay, full disclosure: Scott's dad is a better golfer than me … that was hard.)

The internet is your friend when it comes to researching scholarship opportunities. Most require that certain qualifying criteria be achieved (either academic or non-academic) and an application be filed. Many of these opportunities are readily available to the average among us who are able to demonstrate a distinctive element related to the eligibility criteria that stands-out from the other applicants. It's not necessary to be able to stick-handle like Connor McDavid, invest like Warren Buffet, or have the academic prowess of Alex Dunphy (I love *Modern Family*), average with a twist is good enough to win many of the scholarship opportunities out there. They are worth a look.

CHAPTER 7 – FUNDING (RESPs)

Some parents believe that a student should be responsible for funding their own education. After all the kids have been fed, clothed, housed, and entertained through the bank of Mom and Dad for the first 18 (or so) years, now it is their turn. Some also believe that the kids may be more likely to take a dedicated approach to study and achievement if in fact they have some financial skin-in-the-game and take responsibility for at least a portion of the funding.

I understand and respect both of these positions, but I feel that advanced education is just too important to leave solely in the kids' hands. I have two main concerns. The first concern is based on the present-day cost of financing an education versus when I went to school. The second concern is the lost opportunity if a young adult does not develop their human capital early in their working career.

In my day it was possible to save enough money before and during post-secondary to cover all, or the vast majority, of the cost of a good education. I know I was well able to cover the tuition, books, and entertainment costs (I lived at home for the six years I spent in university), *but* that was at a time when we still used punch cards for the computer programming course. Remember those days?

Ahhh, punch cards … You would spend hours upon hours at a device that looked like a typewriter (*keyboard* for those who don't know what a typewriter looks like), which poked holes into cards that, when read by another big machine, would produce the final product of your vision … sometimes. This was essentially a test of your keyboarding skills. To produce the outcome you were looking for, you would have in the area of a three-foot stack of paper-thin cards that the machine would have to accurately separate and read at a very high speed, then provide you with a printout of what you had programmed. Often that printout was gibberish, which invariably meant you either typed something wrong or you had an error in logic; good luck figuring out which. When presented with gibberish, you then had to sift through each and every punch card to see if there was a typing error, and after that joyful process, if you were still awake and had found nothing, you would have to review your programming logic. If you were smart, you did it the reverse order (a hard learned lesson).

The whole task was arduous and painful. But if you actually did get the banner output that clearly enunciated, "Happy Sixth Kim" (my future wife) built in little sixes (it was our six month anniversary when I was taking this course) you beamed with pride and walked with a certain swagger that everyone in that computer room was envious of. Remember that? I didn't think so.

That was university at a point in history when students could readily afford to pay for education with the time available for work. Nowadays with the cost of education, and the nature of jobs that are available for high school grads, it is very difficult to work enough to pay for a degree outright. Even if they hold down a job while attending post-secondary and over summers, it is a stretch to earn enough money to make a substantial dent in the cash requirements associated with being a student without overly compromising grades.

Gail Vaz-Oxlade, in her book *Saving for School*,[1] noted that the Canadian Federation of Students had calculated that the average debt for university graduates was almost $27,000. If a student happens to meet their significant other at university, on average, they get to start their lives together in the hole $54K. Yikes! This is also at a time when housing prices are reaching unprecedented heights and well-paying full-time employment is very challenging to find. I think, if the parents and/or grandparents can afford it, a little help with the cost of education is in order, but that is just my opinion. (My kids seem to agree.)

The other concern I have with not helping the kids through the financial challenge of advanced education is the higher probability that their potential human capital will remain untapped for longer and perhaps forever. Some students may take a gap year in order to earn money to help fund their education, but as demonstrated earlier, the cost is highly unlikely to be covered by taking a single year off. Also, once in the workforce, and away from the grind of studying, it becomes more and more difficult to go back to school. Finding the time to dedicate to education is more difficult the longer you delay largely because other financial responsibilities tend to creep in as life unfolds.

I do believe that having financial skin in the education game is a reasonable expectation of any parent. I have hired many grads over the years and found that the majority of applicants took longer to get their degree than the expected number of years. A four-year degree, accomplished in just four years, seemed to be the exception. Having some level of financial responsibility may well cause more urgency in getting the work done. I also believe that having a level of financial responsibility, for some kids, will cause them to study harder and achieve at a higher level.

I do recognize that there are situations where parents' priorities can rightfully rest with obligations other than financing their kids' education. If debt is a problem, it is likely more important to take care of that than to fund education savings. If saving for retirement is behind schedule, then it is not unreasonable to attach a higher priority to funding retirement than to investing for the kids' education. If a family is running a fiscally responsible household and there simply is no extra cash available, then it is reasonable to take a more conservative approach to funding the kids' education (though there are lots of government programs that can help with funding in these situations). There could be any number of valid reasons why it is impractical for a parent to set up an education fund for their children. I do not believe it is a parental duty to fund their kids' education at the peril of their own financial stability.

Assuming it makes financial sense to help with education funding and you are not philosophically opposed to helping your children with this type of support, then the question becomes one of how to go about doing it. There is considerable debate in the literature about the best way to save for post-secondary education. You can use trust accounts (formal or informal), personal unsheltered savings accounts, Tax-Free Savings Accounts (TFSAs), or Registered Education Savings Plans (RESPs). While each has advantages over the others, for my money, there is a clear and obvious best choice ... the RESP.

The main reasons I prefer RESPs boil down to the following:

- FREE MONEY. The government provides a grant of 20% on the first $2,500 of eligible annual contributions to the plan (government funding maxes out at a total of $7,200). There are also some additional government benefits available to lower-income Canadians. The list need go no further than this, but I will venture a little further into some of the highlights.

Other characteristics of the RESP that warm my heart include the following:

- Tax-free compounding. Earnings are tax free while they accumulate in the plan, exactly the way it works in your registered retirement savings plan and tax-free savings account. Tax-free compounding is a significant benefit over any unsheltered approach and the free money from the government grant amplifies this particular benefit within the RESP.
- Income splitting. When the earnings and government grants are extracted from the RESP to pay for eligible education costs, they are taxed, but they are taxed in the hands of the student. This should result in a much lower overall tax burden in normal circumstances. In many instances there will be no income tax to pay at all.
- Ease of use. RESPs, if you select a good plan provider, do not have a heavy administrative burden in terms of paperwork or management (the plan promoter may disagree with this because most of the additional work falls to them). My experience with our kids' RESPs has been administrative-burden-lite and our promoter has been very efficient in managing the grant and payment side of the equation. There is a process that you need to go through to set up the account initially, and certain documentation is required to be provided every time you seek payment from the plan, but the time and effort required is minimal.
- Control over fees and expenses. There is a wide array of RESP promoters; thus, you can select one with a keen eye to minimizing administration fees and management costs. For instance, you can choose a self-directed plan and take advantage of low-cost exchange-traded funds, or use a low-cost mutual fund family.

- Risks are manageable. There are risks associated with the RESP option, but in most situations, there are actions you can take to optimize the outcome. The unique and primary risk you must assess is the possibility that the named beneficiary may choose to end their educational path before taking full advantage of the RESP. If this situation were to occur, there are potential tax consequences and potential penalties that will have to be planned for. There are actions that can be taken to manage the negative impact.

I should also point out that funding an RESP is the perfect feel-good way for the grandparents to help enrich their grandkids' lives. Several sets of grandparents that I am familiar with have really loved this method of contributing to their grandkids' lives. Both my parents and in-laws saw the value.

The tricky part is that grandparents may not be familiar with this opportunity to help out, or they may think based on your two careers, fancy house, and the SUVs in your driveway, that you are flush with cash. The fancy house and SUVs are more likely to be an indicator that you are not flush with cash, but it won't look that way to them. For that matter, you may not have any better understanding of their financial situation than they do of yours; looks can be deceiving. But this is a great topic around which to engage in a family finances conversation. The focal point of the discussion is the grandkids and this is often an easy starting point to have a conversation. Grandma and Grandpa will likely be aware of news reports of the escalation in the cost of post-secondary education and if they are in a position to help with the grandkids' prospects for a comfortable life with a fully satisfying career of their choice, they are likely to be all-in.

Keep in mind though, what goes around comes around ... if you are lucky you will be a Nana or Grandad someday down the road and it will be your turn to help out. Personally, I can't wait! No, that's wrong. I can wait—my kids are too young for that stage. When they get there, though, one of the first things I will be suggesting is that they get a social insurance number for Lawrence Junior and set up an RESP (which I will gladly contribute to).

For Further Information on RESPs

Canada Revenue Agency (CRA) has issued a publication titled *Registered Education Savings Plans*[2] that walks you through how the RESP works. I would suggest you print off a copy and take it out to read over a nice breakfast. (Treat yourself to the full strength syrup rather than the low calorie stuff; it will give you the energy boost you need to get through the information.) That publication will also alert you to further Canada Revenue Agency bulletins and publications that may serve as a useful reference, given the details of your situation.

It is possible to write an entire book on RESPs if you want to get into all of the nitty gritty. In fact I have read a number of such books. If you are interested in a nice, short read, I mentioned previously a book written by Gail Vaz-Oxlade in 2013 entitled *Saving for School*. Another very good book on this subject is *The RESP Book*,[3] written by Mike Holman. This book was last updated in 2011, but Mike also has a blog that he updates regularly to highlight any changes to the disclosures made in the book and to help enhance your understanding of RESPs and related strategies. Both of these books present the details of the RESP program at a level that I don't have room to cover here.

Continuing Education

While your initial post-secondary education is of utmost importance in establishing your human capital (and hopefully elevating your paycheque) it is continuing education that serves to both keep your knowledge current and build additional skills. Don't make the mistake of thinking you are done once you finish your initial degree if you want to progress well over the course of your career.

Many employers have programs that support ongoing education. At my last employer, there was even a program where they would pay for you to earn your MBA! All they insisted on in return was that you agree to stay for five years or pay back the support if you chose to leave. I mentioned some of the additional credentials I managed to earn over my career; the majority of the cost associated with those was borne by my employer. Naturally I had to kick in all of the time associated with the study, but that was just the fun part. I believe that the educational component of my training over the course of my career was a substantial contributor to having achieved a high-profile position with a corner office on the top floor of head office.

The extra effort involved in continually developing and enhancing your skills is necessary to maximize your progress and improve your remuneration along the way.

PART III – MANAGING THE BIG FINANCIAL DECISIONS

While it is very important to understand where all of our money is going, the main focus of this section will be on a few of the more substantial expenditure areas that have a far-reaching and enduring impact on a family's financial progress. The decisions you make around housing, automobiles, children, and other similar big ticket items will be key determinants as to how likely you will be to achieve your financial goals. Purchase decisions you make related to other common areas of substantial expenditure, such as weddings and pets, are also important to understand because they too can have a surprisingly oversized financial impact.

In addition to the big expenditures, there are all kinds of smaller expenditure items that can become more or less habitual in nature. These, when considered on a cumulative basis, can also have a significant effect on finances. In the table below, we take a look at the cost of three potential habitual (daily) expenditures: a fancy coffee, fast food takeout, and a deck of smokes.

EXPENSE ITEM	COST	ANNUAL COST	50 YEAR CASH OUTLAY	ANNUAL INVESTMENT AT 5%
Fancy Coffee	$4.75/day	$1,734	$86,700	$363,000
Take Out	$10/day	$3,650	$182,500	$764,000
Smokes	$15/day	$5,475	$273,750	$1,146,000

The message to be taken from this is that our habits can cost us, and cost us dearly. The pack of butts doesn't seem so bad when you are dropping $15 per day, but over time it can produce an opportunity cost equivalent to the value of a fleet of Teslas! The "annual investment at 5%" column helps to understand the actual opportunity cost of the cash flow. For the sake of mathematical simplicity, it was assumed the whole of the annual deposit was made at the end of each year. The numbers also do not incorporate any tax on the investment income, but they are representative of what could be achieved in a tax-free saving vehicle (such as a tax-free savings account) invested in a balanced portfolio utilizing current long-term return expectations.

So does this mean that you will never be able to retire if you have coffee, eat out, and smoke? Obviously not, but expenditures that are habitual and/or individually costly will certainly make the equation more challenging. Smoking aside, I think focusing on cutting out all of these niceties is unrealistic. (If you smoke, please stop.) I love to go out after dinner, by myself, and have a coffee at Tim's with a good book. I also really enjoy going out for breakfast and either reading a book or having a nice conversation about financial planning with my wife. (She likes the breakfast, not the conversation so much.) When I was working, I ate lunch out fairly regularly. If I didn't, then I would end up staying at my desk and working through lunch, which I did far too frequently. These were/are all little breaks in my day where I feel a modest amount of money is well spent and justifiable. I feel that I get a lot of value out of these little pleasures.

Sure, I could make my coffee at home, eat a bag lunch, and never go out for breakfast, but each of these little indulgences adds value to my life and to my way of thinking, more value than they cost. But, the thing is I know what they are costing me and I have a very good appreciation for the extended value of each of them over the course of my life. I don't do them every day; they would lose their value to me if I did. But I can afford them and I choose to spend my money on them.

How you choose to spend your money is all about achieving an appropriate balance between spending and saving. My family and I make saving a priority and our spending is balanced in terms of our income, and in full view of our financial goals and objectives. The value I place on these smaller expenditures exceeds the value I put on buying a massive house using massive debt. I value my coffee and reading time more than I value driving the latest SUV and upgrading it every couple of years. I value going on vacations with my family more than I value an extravagant wedding. The choices my family and I make in spending our wealth are balanced with our short- and long-term goals. We have a very solid understanding of our means, both current and future, and our expenditure plans are expressly designed to live below them. We understand the cost of our lifestyle and how that impacts competing interests.

At one time we were more frugal when we had less of an understanding of our means and wanted to make strong progress toward our longer-term financial goals. My wife points out that being on a weekly allowance was really beneficial for her as it made daily financial choices very obvious. What she had to spend was limited by what was in her wallet. She set aside some money each week so that she was able to treat herself with something she really wanted when the occasion arose. Her stash allowed her to buy earrings or other treasures occasionally when she valued that item more than the smaller weekly consumable purchases.

Cutting back on the little luxuries should be a priority if you are in debt, cannot afford them, or they are impacting your ability to meet your longer-term financial goals. The key is to be aware of the cost of each of the elements of your lifestyle and ensure that you feel that you are gaining appropriate value for what you are spending. Knowledge is power.

I should also mention here that a separate chapter has been included later in the book that delves into the impact of excessive investment management fees and what you can do as an investor to control them.

Takeaways from Part III

- ✓ One of the keys to effective expenditure management is knowing what you are spending, where you are spending it, and the impact of that spending on your ability to achieve competing goals. The ultimate objective is to spend your money in a manner that maximizes the personal value received.
- ✓ If an expenditure is highly valued and affordable in the circumstances, go for it. Use your financial resources in the manner that provides the greatest value to you. No regrets!

✓ There are a couple of expenditure categories that generally have greater impact on a family's finances, and thus deserve a more thorough and considered approach:

   a. Those that are individually significant. This class of expenditure requires careful planning and consideration to ensure that the cost is well aligned with the value experienced. These expenditures, which will be considered in some detail following, include but are not necessarily limited to:

      - Weddings. The cost of the average wedding these days is eye-popping. The cost of the more extravagant weddings is jaw-dropping. Where you decide to fall in the range of possibilities is a choice that deserves careful consideration.
      - Housing. Everyone needs a place to live. So often when it comes to housing, though, "need" gives way to "want"; and "want" costs a lot more than "need." Every time I walk through a show home I see lots and lots of "want." Renting, often outright rejected as *throwing your money away*, is a valid alternative to consider and for many is the right financial and lifestyle choice.
      - Transportation. Getting to and from work and around town can be successfully accomplished in a number of different ways and at a number of different price points. For many, mass transit works just fine and is a very cost-effective choice. For some a BMW SUV makes sense … I guess. But a quick drive about town demonstrates that there certainly are an awful lot of people making the BMW SUV choice (or the equivalent).
      - Children. Parents have a lot of control over the couple of decades of cost decisions involved in raising a family. Ultimately the total expended will be substantial, but there is a lot of variability from one family's experience to the next; the cost need not be debilitating but it certainly can be if your choices take you down that path.

- Pets. This is one of those areas that families often fall into without ever thinking of the financial implications. Rover may become an integral part of the family, but he is far from free.

b. Those expenditures that are smaller by instance but repetitive in nature, as we have already seen, have the potential to accumulate to a formidable sum. These expenditure areas can be insidious in that you may not be aware of their impact on your ability to achieve your goals. Over time, they eat away small chunks of your disposable income, thereby undermining your saving objectives. Awareness is key.

✓ Expenditure management is not about deprivation. Rather, it is about being purposeful in using limited resources to bring the most value possible. A dollar spent is a dollar gone. Some dollars will give you immense pleasure or serve a critical need, others will be wasted. The idea is to maximize the valuable dollar spend and minimize the wasted dollar spend. Dollars directed to well thought-out and articulated goals tend to be the dollars that provide maximum value.

CHAPTER 8 – WEDDINGS

My wife and I had a lovely wedding. It took place on my in-law's front lawn, a friend was the bartender, a fellow articling CA played his Ukrainian Bandura as guests arrived, my brother played the piano to accompany the walk down the aisle, and my wife and I planted an apple tree. (It is still alive even though my nephew ripped off most of the branches a few years later.) We had just a few close friends and relatives in attendance and one bee. I never saw this alleged bee, but my wife claimed a bee stung her and that was what caused all of the tears while we were exchanging vows. I figured the tears were the result of her having come to the realization, albeit too late, that she was in the process of throwing away her life with a buffoon for a husband. Other than that little wrinkle, things went pretty much according to plan.

After the ceremony, several invited guests joined my wife and I for a fantastic prime rib meal at a restaurant called the Round Table (recently closed, such a pity). It was a great restaurant; they would give you a hunk of meat that just melted in your mouth, and you could never finish it because it was cut to be darn near the size of your head. Ahhh, good times. They also had every kind of beer you could imagine on tap before it was the fashion, nice! I couldn't really have asked for a better wedding than the one we had.

It cost us $30,717.

Not even close! But, according to *weddingbells'* Annual Reader Survey of more than 2,000 brides-to-be, that was the expected average wedding cost in Canada for 2015[1] (including the honeymoon). Our wedding cost us an itty-bitty fraction of that number. We have rings (mine is somewhere, I never did like jewellery), we have a tree, we have a wonderful set of memories, we have a piece of paper that proves it all happened, we have a couple of lettuce spinners that continue to work, and I still have my wife—the wedding seems to have served its purpose and it didn't break the bank.

Maybe a survey of 2,000 brides-to-be is not a perfectly accurate reflection of what the actual cost of the average wedding really is, but in the solid couple of hours I spent on the internet reading about this stuff (I'm clearly not much of an expert on weddings), it appeared that this number was fairly repeatable and remained relevant in 2019, with only a slight uptick. One site was nice enough to provide me with a planning spreadsheet that showed me what I should expect to spend in each cost category if I were getting married in Southern Ontario. It presented three different budgets, one each for what were termed *tight* ($17ish thousand), *average* ($38ish thousand), and finally *gala* ($101ish thousand). I wonder what the term is for the wedding my wife and I had; skin-tight, constricted, cramped, stingy, miserly ... reasonable?

I really have trouble understanding why on earth the average wedding has to be so extravagant. By all monetary accounts, my wedding should have been a miserable disaster. Yet, I don't think it was. My wife is very practical (except maybe for that taking a year off to travel around the world thing). She wanted a small intimate wedding and she even found a wedding dress that she was able to wear on several subsequent occasions that cost a couple hundred bucks. This approach seemed to work, and yet we weren't married by an Elvis impersonator (though that could be fun).

Imagine, a smart couple of university graduates complete their degree with the average level of student debt, then decide to have the average wedding. These smart kids have developed above average human capital that they are about to turn into real money, great move! Well, if their parents aren't there to foot the bill, they had better turn the potential into money because they are about to start their new life together with about $85,000 of debt. And they don't have their fancy house with an oversized mortgage yet, but if they continue to act "average," they are about to get one of those too!

I have two beautiful children and I want them to have the best life possible. But I also want them to inherit some of the practical thought process that was so evident in their grandparents' generation, and currently in their mother. A beautiful wedding, for sure, if they choose to go that route. A university education, yes please. But I sure don't want them to start off adult life with a mortgage-sized debt load without the house!

The same principle applies to weddings as applies to everything else; if you can afford it, go for average, or even gala, go to town! However, be clear on what *afford it* means. It does not mean borrowing from future you and your future family; it means paying for it upfront. Maybe your parents will pay the shot (there goes a big chunk of your potential inheritance, by the way). Maybe you wait a couple of years and save up for it. (That will give you a little more time to make sure the buffoon isn't too "off" and the whole thing has a chance to endure.) But please, do all you can to avoid starting life together with a huge bill that will just add stress and pressure.

If this is a second marriage for you because the first one ended in divorce, hopefully you have learned your lesson about going overboard on the wedding. How special does that first one feel now? If you can't pay for the second one out of pocket, well, I expect your aren't reading this book anyway so I will stop with the lecture.

When it comes to weddings, like everything else, be prudent in your spending. A big lavish affair is fine if that really adds a lot of value to your life and you can afford it. But don't lose site of the fact that money spent on one thing isn't available for something else. Thirty thousand bills can provide a lot of something else. In fact, that $30,000 would grow to become over $320,000 at retirement if invested at 7%, just sayin'.

CHAPTER 9 – HOUSING

When my wife and I got married, we spent our first couple of years in a small apartment. We later bought a small, newish home where we stayed for several years. When that became too small because we were expecting our second child, we moved up to a modestly larger newish home where we still live today.

From a financial management perspective, in my opinion, we did a number of key things right over the course of our home ownership progression, including the following.

1. At each stage, we never bought a home that offered more than our midterm foreseeable needs demanded.

   Our apartment was tiny, we couldn't afford a house, and we needed time to save an appropriately sized down payment. Our first house was just over a thousand square feet and was sufficient to accommodate my wife, myself, and one child. Our current home is about fifteen hundred square feet and adequately accommodates the whole family; we will never need more house than we have. This approach meant we did not at any time:

   a. Have an oversized mortgage and the accompanying excessive interest payments and stress.

b. Have the oversized operating expenses that accompany a super-sized house, such as higher property taxes, higher maintenance costs, higher heating and cooling expenses, etc.
  c. Have a bunch of little used space that needed to be furnished, cleaned, and maintained.
  d. Have any of the costs demanded by living in a more exclusive neighbourhood such as lavish landscaping, expensive driveway decorations, higher-end furnishings, etc.
  e. Other than in the very early years of our first house, have a disproportionate amount of our capital tied up in a single asset.

2. We made mortgage destruction a key focus of our financial lives.

We paid off the mortgage on our first house over the course of three and a half years. We made use of all the prepayment options that our mortgage provided. We had three such prepayment options available to us:

- to increase the amount of our weekly payment,
- to prepay up to 10% of the original mortgage amount once per year, and
- in the case where prevailing interest rates were at least 1% greater than the rate attached to our mortgage, to make discretionary haphazard additional payments on a regularly scheduled payment date at our discretion.

We had a guaranteed rate of return of 10.75%, our mortgage rate, on all extra money we dedicated to mortgage destruction.

3. We monitored and rewarded ourselves for meeting and exceeding our mortgage destruction objectives.

I find that the best way to progress toward the achievement of a goal, like debt elimination, is to regularly measure progress. I set up a spreadsheet that captured each and every mortgage payment, breaking the payment down into its component parts of interest and principal. This was a simple measurement mechanism to design and it was fun to update each time we made a payment. (The internet has all kinds of readily available calculators that make this even easier to do now.) It was incredibly rewarding to see the balance owing dwindle over time. It was especially invigorating to see the impact of the lump-sum payments and the effect they had on the time remaining to the end of the mortgage, as well as the new profile that the next weekly payment took on vis-à-vis the amount that went toward principal as opposed to interest.

As we met milestones we would have celebratory dinners or similar modest events—this type of reflection is important to reinforce the positive behaviour that lead to the accomplishment.

4. We paid cash for our second house.

Our total interest cost for housing across the whole of our lives together accumulated to just under $13,000.

5. We did not spend excessively on renovations.

My wife finished our first basement with some help from our fathers. I was there for most of it, but I don't know that what I did would qualify as "help." We had a friend put a bathroom in the basement of our first house (and yes we are still friends even after taking full advantage of his skills—thanks again, Jim). We are in the process of making some modest updates to our current house because it is now 20 years old and requires a refresh (twenty-year-old carpets are not so nice). All home renovations were paid for out of savings.

6. We did not move other than when we really needed to.

The cost of moving is substantial, with real estate commissions, moving company services, land transfer taxes, lawyers, labour, and stress.

I realize that not everyone is in a position, especially in the current housing market, to follow the same path we did. Probably you can't pay cash for a house in the early years of your career; the market in much of Canada will not allow for that. But the principles behind what we did are still entirely relevant. Buy what you need, not what you dream to one day own. Build up a substantial down payment before you buy. Focus on mortgage elimination. Monitor progress and reward accomplishments. Limit turnover and all of the associated cost. This is as doable today as it was in the past.

Housing is one area of life where I believe people are generally very challenged to maintain a prudent approach to financial management. Given the cost of housing, how well we are able to manage this single area of expenditure can go a long way to determining how much extra wealth is available to meet other highly valued goals and objectives.

It is amazing to me how many TV shows there are dedicated to demonstrating how skilled craftsmen and talented designers can, over the course of an hour, take a dilapidated old house add a second storey, fix the wiring and plumbing problems (which always seem to catch them by surprise), add a walk-in closet that looks like it is bigger than the original bedroom, redesign the ensuite to make it something Hugh Heffner would applaud and take out seemingly every wall to enrich the space with an "open concept." Along the way, they also cure the asbestos and mould problems they encounter; pure magic to people like me who were born with ten thumbs and no creative vision. Then they unveil the figures and show how much added equity has been created through the whole process. (BTW, take these estimates with a grain of salt.) Wow, sign me up!

Who hasn't wandered through the most recently erected show homes in their city and thought how nice it would be to have the latest design, fancy appliances, and enough space to have a game of catch with your kids in the living room, and the family room, and the great room, and the kitchen, and heck, in some places you could play catch in the closet or the library off the master. Then you go to the bank and find out that it doesn't have to be a dream; they will lend you enough to make it a reality! After all, if the bank will give you the money, they are smart people, it must make sense. Also, property values *only go up* so it is also a great investment. In fact, not only is this possible, it would be stupid not to … and you wouldn't want to be stupid.

Oh, the mind games we can play with ourselves. Don't listen to yourself. Stay true to what you need and can reasonably afford.

If you can truly afford the big and fancy, go for it, you deserve to treat yourself if that is what you really want to spend your money on. So if you can forward an offer with a cheque to cover the price, and have enough additional spare cash in the bank to cover all of the associated costs including the new furniture, cars to decorate the driveway, future maintenance, and the butler, of course (cuz your new neighbour has a butler), have at it. But if your world is more financially constrained than that, stay true to what your means allow and never lose site of the other goals you have so diligently documented in your financial plan.

By the way, even though you may not recall a period where Canadian housing has lost significant value, it has happened, and I am very confident in saying that it will happen again. The fact it hasn't happened recently may well provide you with a reason to give that very possibility due consideration.

No one in the United States was quite ready for what happened to them just a few years back. In fact, as I write this I am sitting in the den of our "cottage" in Phoenix while our daughter tells me it has begun to snow in Winnipeg. Our Phoenix property is a very modest 1570 sq. ft. bungalow on a 7200 sq. ft. lot, which we were able to purchase fully (and tastefully) furnished, beautifully landscaped, complete with an outdoor hot tub for $140,000 US. (Paid in cash, of course.)

We have some dear American friends down here who were recently trying to sell their massive and beautiful property (over 2800 sq. ft. on a 10,000 sq. ft. lot) for $379,000, which is slightly less than 75% of what they paid for it … ten years ago! I just got off the golf course and had a wonderful citrus beer on the patio of the golf club, at dusk, without a mosquito in sight. This is not exactly a tough place to fall in love with. Yet, house prices were absolutely decimated a decade ago and have yet to fully recover. Could this same thing happen in Canada? Why not?

I am certainly not an expert when it comes to real estate. But I have come to learn that close to 70% of Canadians own their homes, which is high compared to historical Canadian figures and high compared to many other countries in the G20.[1] While home ownership appears to be revered in many parts of the world, there are several very wealthy countries where a different slant is taken. For instance, home ownership is well under 50% in Switzerland; Germany and South Korea also are major economies where home ownership is much lower than is the case in Canada.

Alex Avery recently wrote an excellent book entitled *The Wealthy Renter*,[2] which makes a very compelling case for renting as opposed to home ownership. His book is well worth the read and the modest cover price. Mr. Avery looks in detail at the six largest Canadian housing markets and analyzes their characteristics in an interesting and thought-provoking manner.

When one takes a few moments to think about it, there are a number of substantial benefits that accrue to renting that really aren't given a lot of consideration, given our predisposition to home ownership. Some of these include:

- Stress advantages. If you don't own a house, there are a lot of things that just don't concern you and you don't know what those will be until you own a house and they find you. I remember feeling anxious whenever the clouds rolled in while I was at work because we had a window well, conveniently hidden under our deck in the back yard, that would sometimes fill up with water and drain through the window onto my computer.
- Few housing related expenses accrue to renters. Need a new roof? Call the landlord. Furnace breaks? Call the landlord. Hot water tank springs a leak? Call the landlord. Mould forms in the dingy corner of the basement? Call the landlord. If you own a house, all of the unexpected costs accrue to you. From experience, if your sump pump is going to stop working, it will do so at around midnight on a long weekend and that will leave you and your whole family bailing out the sump pit until you can find someone to come and address the situation ... if you were renting, call the landlord.
- Renting does not involve the same investment risk. Renters don't need to be concerned about a potential housing correction. None of the people renting in Phoenix, Las Vegas, or Florida in 2007 were particularly hurt by the crash in housing prices. If the house they were renting was subject to foreclosure, they had to move—inconvenient but not gut wrenching net worth destruction like it would have been for the owner.
- Likely there will be substantial cost advantages associated with renting. See the example of my situation below.
- Freeing up cashflow provides more options to invest in a diversified manner. If you tie up investment capital in a home, it will form a

significant, likely the most significant, asset on your net worth statement and therefore limit your ability to use other investment options.
- Renting provides substantially more freedom than the alternative of home ownership. As a renter, you can pick up and go in short order with relative ease when your needs change or opportunities present themselves.
- Moving is relatively cheap when you are a renter. When you rent and choose to move, there are no hefty commissions, lawyer fees, land transfer taxes, mortgage related fees, fix up the house for sale expenses, inspection costs, etc. Moving is expensive when you own.
- Renting is easy to understand from a cost perspective. If you are renting, you know exactly what it costs every month; there is no mystery.
- Renting, in many cases, frees up time. You may love much of what you are required to do as a home owner, or you may hate the tasks that come with a house. Many of those tasks are avoided or reduced for a renter.

I can feel the vitriol coming through my computer screen as I write this because it challenges the deeply held belief of many that home ownership is the only reasonable alternative. I absolutely believe that for many people owning a house is the right way to go. Everyone needs to live somewhere, but the decision of how to accomplish this should be done in full view of the cost of your choice and the risk exposure embedded in the decision you come to. Renting is a reasonable choice to consider; it doesn't place you in some lower class or mean you are somehow insufficient or less-than-Canadian.

Let's take a quick look at the cost side of the equation, using my family situation as an example (the numbers will differ by location). This is what our monthly cost of housing (or "rent") looks like:

CATEGORY	ANNUAL	MONTHLY
House Insurance	$ 870	
Utilities	$ 2,956	
Property Tax	$ 3,974	

CATEGORY	ANNUAL	MONTHLY
Maintenance (2%)	$ 8,000	
Opportunity Cost (or mortgage interest)	$ 19,960	
	$ 35,760	$ 2,980

The first three cost categories (house insurance, utilities, and property tax) are all self-explanatory and easily valued.

Maintenance cost is trickier to define. There are a lot of elemental costs that go into this total that occur regularly and are easy to measure, but these pieces also tend to be only a moderate portion of the overall cost of maintaining the house. The hard part to account for are those more significant things that happen only periodically, like replacement of appliances, a new roof, new flooring, house painting, sump pump replacement (I have a thing about sump pumps—I need a good therapist), fence replacement, furnace replacement, hot water tank replacement, driveway slab adjustment, foundation repairs, window replacement, etc. You may go years without having to do many or any of these things, but their time will come and you need to account for their true financial cost in your assessment of the real cost of home ownership.

I did an internet search to try to figure out a good way to approximate the cost. There are lots of guesses out there in internet land. I don't know what the best rule of thumb is, but I saw lots of estimates that were in the area of 1–4% of the property value. I decided to go with 2% of our property value for the purposes of this example.

The other cost element that needs to be explained is opportunity cost. Since we have paid for our home, we don't have a mortgage (and do not have the associated interest expense). Because we chose to put our money into home ownership, it is not available for us to use in other ways. The best way to put a cost on this is to consider the return we would be able to get if we invested that balance in a portfolio of investment assets (because that is what in fact we would do). In order to be both conservative and realistic, I have used the expected return from a balanced asset allocation in accordance with the FP Canada Standards Council Projection Assumption Guidelines 2019. This portfolio, which is invested in 50% cash and fixed income and 50% equities, is expected to produce, on average, a gross return of 4.99%.[3] That is the number I used to calculate the opportunity cost associated with our home.

All of this taken together suggests that the "rent" we are paying on our home is $2,980 per month. If we were looking to rent a comparable place in our neighbourhood in the current market, we would have a number of options available for about $2,000 per month. Lo and behold, renting would be cheaper.

When my wife read the draft of the book, she noted that I need to point out that while the cost of running the house may indeed be as I have stated, and yes we could rent a house in our neighbourhood for the number quoted, it is important recognize that the value of our property has appreciated. To this I concede, yes absolutely, the house has appreciated (and when you simply look at the purchase and current value figures it looks like it has been a great investment). But when I calculate the annual net return, and analyse it a little, it is a much less impressive result. In fact, it is quite a bit less than a balanced portfolio would have produced over the holding period, and this is at a time when the housing market has performed very well due to declining interest rates and high demand for housing.

Your housing choice will have a huge impact on your quality of life. If you have considered the plusses and minuses of both options and have decided that home ownership is really the right path for you and your family, then you need to ensure that you take that step in a prudent and thoughtful manner.

Here are some of the key considerations you should take into account as you move forward.

1. Debt, do you have any?

    If you have credit card debt, student loans, consumer loans of other sorts, then I would strongly advise that you eliminate them (or at the very least get them under control) before adding to your obligations with a mortgage.

2. How much have you amassed for a down payment?

    A conventional mortgage loan is equal to or less than 80% of the property value. As soon as you are contributing less than 80% [20%] of the property value by way of a down payment, you are venturing into a high-ratio mortgage. A high-ratio mortgage comes with additional costs, including expensive mortgage loan insurance. This is a very peculiar type of insurance where the homeowner pays for the insurance, but the sole purpose of the insurance is to protect the lender, not the homeowner. I believe that you should have a down payment sufficient to get you into the conventional mortgage area, as a bare minimum; preferably, you are able to put down much more than 20% of the value and have a spending plan to support aggressive mortgage elimination. If you don't, consider renting (and saving the difference) a little longer. Take advantage of your parents for as long as is reasonable!

3. How much house can you afford/do you need?

There is often a big difference between the housing option that a family needs and the housing option that a family wants. I strongly favour tending away from "want" in favour of "need" when it comes to this trade-off. Wants are limitless and needs are finite. CMHC has a couple of affordability rules outlined in their *Homebuying Step by Step Guide*[4]:

a. Your monthly housing costs should be no more than 32% of your average gross household monthly income; this is referred to as your gross debt service ratio. Housing costs include mortgage payments, property taxes, utilities, condo fees, etc.
b. Your monthly debt load should be no more than 40% of your average gross household monthly income; this is referred to as your total debt service ratio. Your "debt load" includes housing costs defined above, plus the cost all of your other debt obligations. These other debt obligations would include credit card debt, car payments, line of credit payments, student loans, support payments (child/spousal), and all other debt obligations you have managed to amass.

To my way of thinking, if you are considering a purchase that is getting you even close to these percentages, you are dedicating too much of your financial capacity to housing. Too many families get themselves into a situation where they are house poor. Don't ever let the bank tell you what you can afford. Their goal is to maximize the loan so that they can make more money off you.

By the way, in general, I love banks … as an investment. I love how much money they make and how generous they are paying tax-efficient dividends to investors. But it is your family who have to make a life with what is left over after the housing payments. It is up to you to do a detailed budget to ensure that the housing purchase you are considering allows you to make the necessary progress toward your other goals that also require financing in a steady and prudent fashion. Too much house, in my opinion, is one of the fastest ways to derail your financial plan.

4. What is the best kind of mortgage for you?

There are a number of things to look at under this heading; frequency of payment, rate structure, and flexibility are the only ones I will briefly comment on here. (This is a big topic. Make sure you do some research if you are in the market for a mortgage.)

When we had a mortgage, it was a weekly pay mortgage. This made sense for us because both my wife and I were working and we got paid bi-weekly on alternate weeks. Thus, we had weekly cash inflow to support our payments. What you want to do is match your payments to your cash availability. Try to target payments very close to when you receive your income so that the money attacks the mortgage as soon as possible.

We went with a fixed rate mortgage, rather than a variable rate mortgage, because it added certainty. All the studies say that going with a variable rate will save you money. It is true that this worked in the past, but that was during a largely declining interest rate market, one which is very unlikely to continue in my opinion. I like fixed rate because it provides certainty, and therefore allows you to plan effectively—there will be no surprises before your next renewal date.

As far as flexibility goes, more ability to pay down the debt without penalty is better than less. Ensure you have some options to pay down the debt early in the event that you come into some money (bonus, inheritance, raise ... it could happen). Take the time to understand the prepayment options you have and plan to take advantage whenever you can.

5. What happens if _____?

When it comes to one of your largest areas of expenditure, housing, you will want to make sure that you have a buffer. The best way to do this is to keep your payments manageable in the event something bad happens. Leave room in your plan to enable you to adjust as necessary.

Buying less house is a great start. You should also ensure that you can afford the payments if the interest rate were to substantially increase from the current level. (This is referred to as stress testing.) Either get the mortgage provider to do the calculation for you (keeping the amortization period constant—they can play games to make it look like nothing happened by making the mortgage last longer) or do it yourself using one of the calculators on the internet (www.ratehub.ca has some useful calculators; there are many other sites also). Figure out what the monthly cost would be under an alternate rate scenario and make sure your budget (including your goal funding objectives) remains viable with the elevated payment schedule.

There are "stress test" requirements that apply to federally regulated financial institutions that became effective January 1, 2018. Under this set of rules, the bank is required to ensure that you qualify for the mortgage based on the higher of a couple of different interest rates. The rate they must use depends on if the loan requires mortgage loan insurance or not, the current Bank of Canada conventional five-year mortgage rate, and the interest rate you negotiate with your lender. Stress testing is something that anyone looking to buy a home should have always been doing, regardless of a legislated requirement.

How you manage housing costs over the course of your life will have a huge impact on your financial wellbeing. Consider your approach to housing analytically rather than emotionally. There is nothing wrong with choosing to rent until you are ready/able to buy, if in fact you are ever ready to buy.

CHAPTER 10 – TRANSPORTATION

Choosing their ride is another area where many people expend beyond their needs, and I am guessing, beyond their means too. When I drive around I marvel at all of the new and very costly cars and trucks that are on the road. I live in one of the larger urban areas of our country—can anyone explain to me why there are so many huge 4X4 trucks driving around? Very few of these trucks seem to be transporting anything other than their driver. (I always thought hauling was the purpose of a truck. That's what the advertisements seem to portray. Silly me.)

The Canadian Automobile Association has a neat little feature called the *Driving Costs Calculator*[1] available for use on their website. The calculator looks at the cost of operating different classifications of automobile for the province of your choice. The calculator shows the total annual driving cost and provides insight to the components that go into making up the annual cost. Clearly your specific situation may be such that you vary from the calculated cost, but the assumptions are laid out and if you really want to, you can make modifications to better dial-in on your specific circumstances.

When using the calculator, the first thing you will note is that the cost of operating a vehicle, any vehicle, is substantial. Even if you opt to run what they classify to be a subcompact, it would cost you something north of $7,500 per year to operate. If you chose a SUV as opposed to a subcompact, the annual driving cost would be in the area of $12,000 per year depending on your province. To give you a flavour of provincial cost variation, I ran the calculator for three provinces (calculated results change regularly as inputs are updated):

Table 1: Provincial cost variation, compared by vehicle type, July 2019.

	ONTARIO	**MANITOBA**	**BRITISH COLUMBIA**
Compact	$8,959	$8,295	$9,530
SUV	$11,889	$11,219	$12,571
Luxury	$15,243	$14,629	$15,850

Having a little fun with the numbers provided by the calculator, let's imagine you are an individual from Manitoba whose first car purchase is made at age 18. Your transportation needs dictate a compact car, but you really want, and purchase, a SUV instead. Repeating that process across your driving career, what will it cost you to go with what you want rather than what you need? In that simplified series of assumptions, the additional cost is $2,924 annually (according to the calculator on the day I ran the numbers); let's assume the cost differential remains consistent. If you were able to invest that difference with an annual return of 5% (in a TFSA to take taxes out of the equation) you could have accumulated $1.034 million dollars in your investment account by the time you turn 78 … just because you selected the need vs. want ride and invested the difference consistently over 60 years.

We could even take the above example further and if you were to go for a transit pass, which would cost about $1,000 annually, instead of the SUV … now you are talking real big money! I know, the "what if" game can be silly. For instance, you could have saved even more if you had decided to go with the SUV instead of a Lamborghini Aventador. But the point of the example I chose is if you go with the mode of transportation you need as opposed to the one you want, you can save oodles of money. Sometimes that means the difference between an F150 and a Honda Civic; other times that means the difference between a Fiat 500 and a transit pass. If you live in Toronto, Montreal, Vancouver, or one of the other large cities in Canada, for many people transit is a viable option for the majority of their transportation requirements. On those occasions when you need a vehicle, rent one. When you're retired, and you can now afford that 121-day luxury cruise around the world, you will be very happy you chose your ride wisely.

Okay, let's assume you need a car because you live in the suburbs, bus service is infrequent, and even though city hall keeps talking about extending the subway out to your area, they are a little slow in getting the project going. (Sound at all familiar?) You are aware of the costs associated with vehicle ownership and you have selected the class of vehicle you need to get you from point A to point B, and you can afford it. The question will likely now become, should I lease or should I buy?

I like to keep my life simple, and leasing is anything but simple. If you are so inclined, David Trahair has created a spreadsheet that you can use to work through this question with the specifics of the vehicle you are considering. The spreadsheet can be downloaded from David's website at www.trahair.com. There are situations where leasing may be your best choice, but there are a lot of elements of each lease that you really need to keep a sharp eye on so that you do not get caught with unplanned costs.

The biggest concern I have with leasing is that it makes car ownership look like it is cheap and that may cause you to take more car than you need. It is easy to go into the car dealership and be talked-up a class or two of vehicle when they are so readily able to demonstrate that your cash flow can handle the payment. It is up to you to consider how this commitment will impact your other, likely more important, financial goals.

If you are a good shopper (I am not a very good shopper), your most cost-effective option is almost always to buy a quality used vehicle and keep it for its remaining life. A car that is about three years old will allow you to avoid much of the depreciation expense and provide many of the advanced features available in current models. If going this route, you should research the maintenance and accident history of the vehicle as well as identify any existing liens before making a purchase decision.

In our thirty years together, my wife and I have purchased a number of vehicles and have paid $0 interest to car dealers or banks in support of the purchase. I did buy our first van using dealer financing, but only because they offered a financing rate of 0% and would not give me a discount for paying cash. In general, my feeling with respect to automobiles is that if you can't pay for the purchase outright, then you can't afford it.

I like paying cash because it is a simple tool for ensuring that I have the means for the ride I have selected. After all, that is all I see a car as being: a way to get from point A to point B. A certain amount of comfort and safety is required for sure but spending as much on a depreciating asset as some people do on a house just doesn't make any sense at all to me, none.

If you are one of those people who gain substantial satisfaction from your automobile, and you can afford the vehicle of your dreams without undue harm to your other financial goals, hey, buy whatever Land Rover, Jaguar, BMW, or Tesla you want ... you have earned that freedom.

For many people, a car is necessary to function efficiently within their lifestyle. Anything beyond what you need is simply additional driveway decoration. Anyone who is in a city with good public transit, and especially those who are early on in the process of turning human capital into financial capital, should seriously consider the cost benefits of public transit. If you live fairly close to work, you could even walk, rollerblade, or cycle ... health benefits, environmental benefits, and financial benefits ... the whole trifecta!

CHAPTER 11 – CHILDREN

I got this email in 2007 from my oldest daughter …

Hi dad,

I love you Soooooooooooooooooooooooooooooooooooo
oooooooooooooooooooooooooooooooooooooooooooo
oooooooooooooooooooooooooooooooooooooooooooo
oooooooooooooooooooooooooooooooooooooooooooo
oooooooooooooooooooooooooooooooooooooooooooo
ooooooooooooooooooooooooomuch!I cant whate untill you come back! We got to by gomme this week because last month we got it the week before and because we wher at Wall Mart aniwase mom wouldn't let us take a speshile trip.I also got new pants/cuprees/shortes.

LOVE

KAYLEE

P.S.I found my baseball glove it was in the box where we put our backpacks, I cant whate to play baseball with you!

What is the value of this? It made the crap I experienced that day lose importance.

At this point in her life, gum (gomme) was very important to Kaylee, important enough that she was compelled to write me an email while I was out of town on business. Apparently gum was much more important to her than learning to spell or learning how to use spellcheck.

Whatever the total is that my wife and I have spent on our kids, it was and continues to be money spent without regret. Before we had kids, I did do the research to understand what the financial commitment was likely to be. I think it was important for my wife and I to sit down and think through both the financial as well as the life impact that having a family would have on us.

MoneySense magazine did a detailed study in 2011 that estimated the average cost per child to raise a kid to age 18 for middle-class couples with two children across the country; the total came in at $243,656 per. The magazine then updated the figure in April 2015 with the revised cost coming in at $253,947.[1] A quick search of the internet provides links to other studies, which proclaim much different cost profiles. Some arrive at annual expense figures of $3,000 to $4,500 additional cost per child. They too describe a rather rigorous research process.

Well, there you have it: two very different numbers. Helpful, isn't it? Both of these numbers are before you even consider the cost of post-secondary education, if you plan on kicking in that for your kids. In addition, do the costs actually stop at 18? They have not for us. In fact, I don't anticipate them diminishing substantially any time soon.

What I get from these numbers, both of which are different than the number we came up with at the time we did our number crunching, is that there is a substantial cost to raising a child, and how much it costs is highly dependent on the path you choose. Private school costs more than public school. Grandparent daycare is way cheaper than paying for it. Breast feeding costs less than formula (at least I think it does). Cloth diapers cost less than disposable (though I couldn't imagine using cloth diapers). Hockey costs more than chess club. Braces are expensive, but if you catch a break, you may not have this expenditure.

Parents make choices every day that impact the total cost of raising their children. Your kids need not cost you the quarter million to age 18; but they sure can if that is what you choose. On the other hand, there is a certain base level cost that is very difficult to penetrate. The main point, though, is that it is largely up to you what you spend to raise your kids.

LIVING YOUR DREAM

Hopping on a plane with my youngest child and spending a week in Hawaii was a piece of my life that I (hopefully, we) will cherish forever. Spending two days searching for locations used in the filming of *Lost* was wonderful. This was her favourite TV series at the time and the reason I chose the location for our trip. We spent time every night leading up to the trip watching the show together. The sunset cruise, taking a helicopter tour over the island, visiting Pearl Harbor, making bagels for lunch, eating leftover cheese cake for breakfast—all are memories that I will cherish because it was an opportunity for me to spend time with and get to know my beautiful child. If having a kid was purely a financial decision, I would have missed out.

My other child has different interests, so we have taken a couple of trips to engross ourselves in sports. We drove down to Minneapolis to watch the Twins play a series. On the way back, we had to hunker down in a little gas station in a tiny village to wait out a tornado that passed very near to us. I have never before, and hopefully will never again, see a sky as menacing as it was that day. We also hopped on a plane and took in a couple of Toronto Blue Jays games and even got the opportunity to go down on the field before one of the games to test the turf and take a few pics. The chocolate crepes at the little restaurant near our hotel were amazing! If having a child was purely financial, I would have missed out again.

These two little instances are a clear case in point of where we could have had virtually the same experience, but done so on a much tighter budget. I simply could have made time to sit down with my youngest to watch *Lost* once a week for the season (or for several seasons). A bucket of popcorn, a glass of juice, an hour of intrigue ... priceless. I could have taken a finance-lite approach to the ball games, too. A bowl of munchies, put on the team uniform and cap, settle in for a couple hours of ball (we would have missed the *roof report*, but the meat of the experience would have been similar). For anyone who has not been to a Blue Jays game, they play in a covered stadium with a retractable roof. The *roof report* consists of one of the players projected onto the score board looking up at the sky and saying either "it's open" or "it's closed" ... we laughed every time.

Kids will be an expense and they can be very expensive, but the quantum you experience is largely up to you and the decisions you make over the 18+ years you have to make them. Your kids will have a long list of needs and an endless list of wants. Funding their wants has to be filtered through the impact they have on your other financial priorities.

CHAPTER 12 – PETS

Not many financial planning books talk about the cost of pets. I decided to include a section on pets because so many families do the pet thing, and almost none that I have talked to have any idea what they have committed to financially by adopting Rover.

We currently have two pets: a dog named Chester and a bunny named, wait for it, Bun (that was a tough day on the naming front). Before these two cherished family members we also did the natural progression through a number of goldfish (Goldie, Reddie, Slate, and several others) and a couple of hamsters. This probably sounds familiar to many families. Also, like us, many families wouldn't hesitate to pay whatever is required to keep their pets healthy. In looking at our Chester file, the cost is certainly anything but insubstantial.

Full disclosure, I was not sold on the merits of getting a dog. The other pets I had no problem with because they do not require as much effort and money to maintain, essentially, I could ignore them if I chose to. While I was continually petitioned for a dog, I was quite resolved in my immediate and unwavering response of "no." Usually I will try to offer sound reasoning to substantiate a "no," but for a dog I felt that it was important to demonstrate a strong, firm, and unwavering stance on the issue. End the discussion without a discussion, so to speak.

Then along came a family weekend stay at a fishing lodge. We had gone there several times before and had a great time swimming, hiking, and the girls really enjoyed fishing while I took the opportunity to read. This particular weekend, though, it rained continually. We were locked in the cabin, playing cards with endless repetition; given my disdain for cards, this was an agonizing outcome. The first night the question of adopting a dog came up, and I immediately shot it down. Over the course of the weekend, it came up again and again, each time with an immediate and consistent response of "no." Then, in a moment of laziness, I did not respond with the same level of emphatic disapproval when questioned and a chink in the armour, however small, was detected by all three girls. The onslaught began.

I thought the issue through a little bit more and decided that it wasn't really my place to dictate this outcome without a little more analysis. So I passed an assignment back to the girls. It was their responsibility to figure out what a dog would cost over the course of its lifetime and how the time requirements associated with dog ownership would be managed within our busy household. No promises were made; I figured this would bring an end to the saga. But I was very wrong—very, very wrong.

The kids and their mom did some hunting around online to figure out the cost of maintaining a small dog across the breadth of its lifetime. They called a local vet to find out what kind of maintenance costs would be associated with a small mutt and the nature of the associated veterinary care that could be expected. Together we did an annual cash flow and present value for the stream of cash envisioned. I forget the final total that came out of the exercise but it was in the vicinity of $24,000; and they had a list of tasks that showed a minimal level of time requirement from me. They had done a thorough financial and task analysis; I was very impressed by the effort. After several attempts to advocate for an alternate/better usage of the money, each of which was rebuffed, I caved. Chester (a Yorkie Poodle cross) is now a valued member of our family.

Chester is the most wonderful little guy. He loves to keep you company and gives great feedback when things are going the way he likes, which is almost always. He hates being left alone, but he dutifully goes to his bed under the kitchen table when instructed to do so. As soon as someone turns on the TV, he is right there to curl up beside or on them. He tries to please everyone because he knows he is loved.

Chester has exceeded our expectations in terms of his affection and dedication to the family. He has also met or exceeded our financial projections.

Chesterfield, as my friend refers to him, developed a talent for growing funny little bumps on his body. This led to a research project for my wife. The research suggested that a dog chiropractor might be able to come up with a solution, but alas we had difficulty finding one who thought he could help. (Imagine, a shortage of dog chiropractors). Ultimately we hired a dog nutritionist to help design a better diet for him in an attempt to avoid surgery. Now Chester is on a raw meat diet with so many supplements it is a real project to feed him.

When my wife and I recently returned from a short golf retreat, Chester came bounding up the stairs to greet us but then immediately started to fall over as his back legs lost their strength. This led to an overnight at the vet, which cost more than the honeymoon suite at any downtown hotel in Winnipeg. Boarding costs are also substantial when we leave town as a family. The regular and surprise costs that have accompanied our little guy have been, and thankfully continue to be, constant.

Pet ownership is a decision that needs to be taken in full view of the costs associated with the animal you are intending to adopt. It is very easy to overlook the financial commitment involved if all you do is look at the adoption cost and the price of a bag of food that looks like it will last for a year (it doesn't). Chester cost us a mere $350 to purchase from Manitoba Small Dog Rescue Inc. The cost of purchase was immaterial; the maintenance cost is anything but.

The Ontario Veterinary Medical Association (OVMA) put the overall cost of owning a dog at $3,051[1] per year (just under $45,000 assuming a 13-year life and 2% inflation); and a cat at $1,842[1] per year (just under $32,000 assuming a 15-year life and 2% inflation). The Winnipeg Humane Society places a lower annual ownership cost than OVMA on a dog and cat (still substantial) and provides an annual budget for rabbit ownership of $674[2] (a rabbit!).

None of these costs consider the damage that can and likely will be done to your house. Bun chewed up a spot of carpet in my daughter's bedroom. Chester, like a little baby, has the odd accident. Sometimes his raw meat diet doesn't agree with his pace of gobble and running around too soon after eating. This rather unattractive pile can be difficult to get entirely out of a light-coloured carpet. (He will do his best to eat it again, but he doesn't get it all; just thinking about that almost led to a pile on my keyboard.) Also, he has not found his way out of the house each and every time nature has called … sometimes his fault, but more often ours. Again, on the light-coloured carpet. As you can imagine, the grass in the back yard is a continual project.

As I sit here we have three very nice and hardworking gentlemen replacing all of the flooring on our main level. We had to go with a "luxury vinyl" product due to moisture and scratching concerns ... the week-long project is going to come in somewhere around $20K. This is not all due to the pets, but they certainly hurried along the need for action.

Chester and Bun are a part of our family that we wouldn't be without. They are worth the cost of admission. My wife would postulate Chester easily brings $24,000 worth of love to compensate for all of the cost and inadvertent damage that he has caused. It was a great decision to bring Chester into our house as it turns out, money well spent. I suspect a large portion of the supply of animals to shelters comes from people who are not prepared for the ultimate cost of owning one.

Pet ownership is one of life's great responsibilities and pleasures. The cost needs to be fully understood before entering into the contract. Over and above that, the cost needs to be within your means and considered within your financial plan. Pets are not an immaterial financial decision once you are beyond the goldfish and hamster stage.

Dogs formed a very important part of my parents' lives as well. When Cori, one of their precious little mutts, was diagnosed with a life-ending ailment, my parents were distraught. He delivered the following poem tucked under his collar to my mom the night before he was euthanized:

> Thank you for everything ...
> Thanks for the walks in the sun, rain and snow they were the highlight of my day.
> Thanks for all of my toys, the things we made toys and the Christmas presents. Thanks for playing with me.
> Thank you for my special cookies, the periodic scraps from the table and making sure I ate what was good for me.
> Thanks for letting me on the couch, putting up with my barking, and letting me hide my treats in all the right spots.

Thanks for taking me with you when you could and staying home with me when there was going to be thunder ... I always felt safe when you were around.

Thank you for cleaning up my poop, the stuff I would sometimes cough up, and the messes I would make when I wasn't feeling well.

Thanks for considering me and my feelings. Thanks for caring.

Thank you for brushing me, patting me and talking to me ... it always felt nice to be near you.

Thank you for letting me off my leash and giving me room to explore and learn and make mistakes. I never really wanted to catch a squirrel, but it was always fun to try.

Thanks for giving me a bath when I needed it, trimming my nails, cleaning my teeth and taking me to the vet when it was time to go.

Thank you for finding me and making me a part of your home and family when I didn't have one and needed one.

My life has been blessed. I loved every minute you spent with me.

I have always trusted you to make the decisions that were in my best interest and you have represented me well ... I couldn't have asked for more.

If I could have selected my life, it would have been the one that I lived.

If I could have selected my family, I would have chosen you.

I thank you from the bottom of my heart, I have cherished our time together, I will always be with you ... I love you!

Cori

Obviously having a pet is much more than just the cost side of the equation, but it is important to understand the costs and what that means you may have to give up. If you can't afford a pet, but really want the animal experience, consider volunteering with your local pet shelter as an alternative to direct ownership.

PART IV – DEBT

I'm sure you have noticed by now that my views on debt are very much old school. In general, I like the way my grandparent's generation did it; if you didn't have the cash you didn't buy it. Period. End of story. In many cases, they did it that way because there was no other option; credit was not readily available as it is today. So their approach to debt was not so much a choice as it was a function of the financial environment of the time. I don't think they were necessarily smarter when it comes to debt management; they just weren't given the opportunity to make the mistakes that are available (and availed of) today.

As I am writing this in 2018, the national ratio of household debt to disposable income is about 170% demonstrating strong growth in both mortgage credit and consumer credit. Canadians have the highest household debt relative to income in the G7. Much of this debt load is due to Canadians' propensity for home ownership and the growth in housing prices. But Canadians' infatuation with debt is not solely related to the house they are living in. In the second quarter of 2018, TransUnion reported that the average Canadian consumer owed a balance approaching $30,000[1] in non-mortgage debt and within that total the average credit card debt was north of $4,000.[1]

Generally, I am not a big fan of talking in terms of averages. After all if you, I and Warren Buffet were all together in a car, *on average* we would be billionaires. Maybe you are a billionaire, but I'm not, so the average of us doesn't mean a thing to me. The problem I have with using averages as a benchmark is that extremes can drastically influence the result. However, with population-based averages I think the number is meaningful.

On average, Canadians are not leaving much of a buffer between themselves and financial hardship. Being average in many areas is fine. Be an average golfer, average cook, have average handyman skills, average bone density (I must be getting old if that is popping to mind) … but, please, don't be of average indebtedness!

Takeaways from Part IV

- ✓ Canadians rely heavily on borrowing to finance their lifestyle.
- ✓ Not all debt is equally concerning. Debt that is used to smooth consumption in a measured and prudent manner is a reasonable approach to take in modern society. Debt used to acquire an appreciating asset, where the risks are manageable and fully understood, can also be a reasonable use of borrowed capital.
- ✓ Borrowing to finance an otherwise unsustainable lifestyle is a recipe for financial disaster.
- ✓ Not all "good debt" is in fact good debt. Borrowing to invest in excessive housing consumption, or to finance an overly aggressive investment program, can be fraught with peril. Huge mortgages, and disproportionate investment loans, are often justified under the banner of good debt … it is not.
- ✓ It is very difficult to function in modern society without some use of temporary borrowing. All transactions that utilize other people's money should be carefully considered, and subject to a repayment plan such that interest expense is well managed.
- ✓ Credit cards, when paid on time and in full (with the help of automated payments to take human error out of the equation), offer many advantages. When not paid on time and in full, they have the potential to quickly erode financial peace of mind. If you don't know how to dismantle a bomb, don't dismantle a bomb … if you can't properly manage your credit card spending, don't use one.
- ✓ In instances where borrowing levels have become a problem, a dedicated debt elimination plan should be designed, implemented, and maintained. This plan should include:

- Remittance of all minimum payments on time.
- Focused effort on eliminating high-interest non-deductible debt on an ASAP basis.
- A dedicated though pragmatic approach to the elimination of lower interest rate and deductible debt.
- Debt counselling services where professional assistance would be of benefit to promote a higher probability of success.

✓ Everyone should make it a habit to review their credit report periodically to ensure the information is accurate.
✓ Adopting quality debt management strategies and practices is essential to establish and maintain a good credit score.

CHAPTER 13 – GOOD DEBT VS. BAD DEBT

Not all debt is created equal.

Most people at one time or another will use debt to finance the purchase of a home, car, investment, or quasi-investment that would not otherwise be possible. Most people will also use a credit card for certain aspects of their day-to-day purchases for reasons of safety, convenience, or cash flow management. Debt, in one form or another, is a feature that permeates the financial profile of most consumers in modern society.

When debt is taken on as a means of smoothing consumption in a measured and calculated manner, it can be used to enhance current lifestyle without unduly hampering future lifestyle. After all, it is over time that a person converts their human capital into financial capital and not all purchases are best delayed to the point where cash is on hand. (It pains me to say that just a little.) For debt to make sense, though, the interest and repayment terms must be such that the individual is well able to absorb the commitment without unduly hampering their ability to save toward their other goals and objectives. Current consumption should not be over-emphasized, nor should it be underemphasized; an appropriate balance needs to be struck. The only way to make sure the balance struck is reasonable in the circumstances is to have a plan that guides your spending and saving decisions. Don't manage your debt by default; be purposeful in its use, management, and destruction.

My belief is that almost all purchases should be delayed until cash is available to settle the transaction in full. For example, under no reasonable circumstance should anyone consider a payday loan. Period. End of story. (I would have said under no circumstance whatsoever, but my wife says I need to be careful in making blanket statements because there could be, and likely is, a situation I have not considered.) Under no reasonable circumstance should a person run a balance on their high-rate credit card for a non-life sustaining purchase. Yet, payday loan companies and credit card purveyors are flourishing, based almost entirely on the poor credit management practices of what are mostly hardworking (though likely disorganized) people.

I loved the way Robert R. Brown describes payday loans in his book *Wealthing Like Rabbits*:

> Payday loans are like chomping down on a big wad of moldy chewing tobacco until it morphs into a thick, slimy gob of carcinogenic goo in your mouth and horking it into a dirty, butt-filled ashtray before you use a filthy, discarded needle to mainline the viscous shit-brown gunk directly into your lungs.[1]

I believe, based on the above quote, that Mr. Brown is not a big fan of payday loans either. (BTW, his is an excellent book. I suggest giving it a read.)

Whether it is appropriate to take on debt is dependent on the nature of the expenditure and the ability to retire the obligation within a reasonable period of time. The nature of the expenditure is important because when you take on debt you are not only taking on the burden associated with paying back the amount borrowed but also the additional kick in the financial gonads associated with interest expense. If you are living within your means your need for debt should be very limited.

The financial institution that is the source of a loan is not a good barometer for deciding if you can afford the loan or if the use of the funds makes financial sense. In fact, their goals related to the loan are diametrically opposed to what is good for you. So long as they are satisfied that you will ultimately pay the loan back, they would prefer that the loan remain outstanding for as long as possible at as high an interest rate as possible. It wouldn't matter to them if you used the money to advance your education or buy four tonnes of bubble gum to see if you could fit it all in your mouth at once. Sure, they will often provide you with more money and at better rates if you are buying an asset that retains or increases in value, but that is only because it means that they can use the asset as security to help ensure they get their money back. They don't give a rat's ass if the use of the money works out for you, or what it may do to your longer-term goals; they only care that they will be getting their money back with the agreed-upon interest.

Financial institutions do not have goals that are remotely congruent with yours. They may appear to be working in your interest, but rest assured, they are working in the interest of their shareholders. Many financial institutions do this part of their business very effectively and that is what makes them a great long-term investment.

Distinguishing Between Good Debt and Bad Debt

Good debt is generally defined as money borrowed to invest in an appreciating asset or one that will generate more income than the interest paid to purchase it. The most commonly cited examples of good debt are mortgages for a house or condo, or a loan used to invest in a portfolio of stocks or other financial assets; both are expected to increase in value over the long term. Good debt has the potential to help increase net worth if used in a shrewd and pragmatic manner.

Bad debt, on the other hand, is generally described as money borrowed to spend on something that will depreciate in value or an expense with no enduring value beyond a temporary bump in lifestyle. Bad debt would include things like borrowing money to go on a vacation, buy a 112-inch flat screen television, or to purchase season tickets to the opera. (Actually, any expenditure related to the opera is questionable, borrowed or not.)

The concern I have with these definitions is that "good debt" can easily morph into not-so-good debt. Not all assets expected to increase in value, or produce income in excess of interest expense, will always act according to plan. If you borrow money to invest in the stock market, and the market trudges along sideways, or worse yet crashes, that "good debt" just cost you money, maybe a lot of money. If you use borrowed money to invest in a condo and you immediately get hit with a large special assessment, or city hall decides to build a nuclear plant beside it, or property values correct soon after purchase … that good debt just cost you a lot of net worth.

Another problem I have with the simple labels of good debt and bad debt is that I think categorizing borrowing under the good debt banner is often used as an excuse to spend beyond an amount that would be considered appropriate. For example, borrowing to invest in a house is generally considered to fall under the heading of good debt. I believe that in many cases an investment in a house is a good, supportable decision. But for that to be the case, I believe the house must be suitable to meet the buyer's needs as opposed to grossly exceed them. When a person buys more house than they need, they are committing to a much longer stream of interest payments than would be required for a house that meets their needs. This doesn't strike me as a smart financial move. This is a case of good debt gone bad.

For example, if a three-bedroom 1200 sq. ft. bungalow meets your needs, fits within your financial capacity (plus you have an adequate down payment), and would not unduly delay the achievement of other competing goals, I agree that a mortgage in support of this purchase could qualify as good debt. On the other hand, if this is the extent of the house you need, I do not believe that the mortgage associated with the purchase of a 3,000 sq. ft., six-bedroom, six-bathroom custom-built McMansion qualifies as good debt. The costs associated with a house of this nature do not generally stop with the purchase price, either. Likely this particular house resides in a neighbourhood that implies certain other requirements like the newest SUV (or two), a topiary garden, an in-ground pool and hot tub combo, and a covered barbeque area beside the guest house to host the Little League team at the conclusion of another successful season. All of these costs are additional to the higher maintenance and operating expenses that are also associated with a higher-value property. A "good debt" decision like this will cost the home owner dearly.

In the late 2000s, before the stock market crash, there were many financial sales people (masquerading as investment advisors) pushing leveraged investment programs. A leveraged investment program consists of borrowing money to enhance personal investment capital, usually targeted for the stock market. For some people, leveraged investment programs, used in moderation, are appropriate. On occasion, I have used a very modest amount of leverage in my investment program. However, if you are approaching retirement and are investing your extra cash to help build a nest egg sufficient in size to support your well thought-out and documented retirement goals, likely a leveraged investment program is something that does not suit your situation. It is bad enough if you get hit with a market correction and lose a big chunk of your own money. But if you use leverage, you lose both a big chunk of your own money and a big chunk of borrowed money, which you still owe and have to pay interest on as though it were still there. This debt would fall under the traditional definition of good debt (investing in an asset expected to appreciate in value). In my mind, this is an entirely different category of debt; perhaps "stupid debt" is an appropriate label.

The bottom line is that all debt should be approached with apprehension and scepticism. You need to practice due diligence, understand the potential downside, and be able to absorb any predictable negative outcome without unduly exposing your goals to potential obliteration. It is easy to overlook the downside; just ask anyone who got lambasted in the housing crisis recently experienced south of the border. When they bought, property values were only going up; there was no analysis of the downside risk. Financial institutions were lending money to investors without exercising appropriate/any due diligence. Investors were leveraged to the hilt because they saw the upside and couldn't comprehend the downside, had they taken a moment to consider it. House owners began using the equity they built up in their houses as though they had a personal ATM.

The world these people knew changed instantaneously when credit dried up. For many, their mortgages were upside down (meaning they had negative equity), but they were still able to afford the payments and persevere. For many others, bankruptcy and starting over was the only viable alternative. You never want to place yourself in a position where severe hardship is possible and, in my view, debt is the fast route to financial oblivion if you take a substantial misstep.

I like the revised definition of good debt penned by David Chilton in his excellent book, *The Wealthy Barber Returns*. He writes:

> "Good Debt" should be defined as any money borrowed to buy an appreciating asset where the cost of servicing the loan doesn't affect your ability to save to the appropriate level *and* where the principal will be fully repaid before your retirement. "Bad debt" is everything else.[2]

All debt needs to be considered not in the isolated circumstances of the use being made of the money, but also in terms of the broad picture of your financial plan. Oh, before I forget, you have to read the chapter titled "Dashed Hopes" in *The Wealthy Barber Returns*; it is beyond hilarious.

The safe way to manage debt is to minimize or eliminate it from your life on an ASAP basis, like your grandparents probably did. It is not easy to do, but it is doable if you are organized and constrain your use of debt to appropriate situations and levels. If you aren't organized and don't have the aptitude, wherewithal, and discipline to constrain your use of debt to only those situations where it is appropriate, then you should operate as your grandparents did, on a cash basis (primarily using a debit card to avoid the safety concerns associated with currency).

CHAPTER 14 – CREDIT CARDS

Given what I have said on the subject of debt so far, clearly I must hate credit cards, right? Many financial authors despise credit cards, essentially writing them off as evil. I read one book a while back and as I remember the story the author's daughter was so against the use of credit cards, through his tutelage, that she used this as a mechanism for evaluating potential suitors. (On a date, and he pays with a credit card? Bye-bye, buddy.)

The fact is that I love many aspects of credit cards, have used them extensively, and intend to continue to do so. I love the convenience, I love the free stuff, I love how effective the credit card companies are at detecting fraud and correcting any mistakes that occur, I love the records they provide for my monthly accounting process, I love the safety in that I don't have to walk around with excessive amounts of cash, I love being able to conveniently purchase goods online, and not to be overlooked, I love the interest-free loan. The last one is the key point; if you are not taking advantage of the interest-free loan, then you are paying what I consider to be usurious interest rates. I don't love the interest rates they charge, but the key is, you don't have to pay any interest and yet you can take advantage of all the benefits.

In all of my years of using a credit card, I have paid nary a cent of interest to the credit card company. In all of my parents' and in-laws' years of using credit cards, interest was avoided by paying on time and in full. What is not to like about this opportunity? I paid for the new floors for our house on a credit card and received enough WestJet dollars to avail myself of a free return flight to Phoenix. I tried to buy a car on a credit card (three times actually), but alas, they wouldn't let me. It would have been great. Another free flight to and from Phoenix! The key, though, is to have enough cash available to pay off the credit card balance each and every time the payment date arrives. Under no circumstances would I buy a new car on a credit card if I didn't have the money free and clear to pay for the car in the first place. Similarly, we would not be redoing the floors in our house if we did not have the cash to foot the bill at the ready.

If you do not adhere strictly to the pay-off-the-full-balance-when-due mantra, then using a credit card will be financially destructive and potentially devastating.

As an example of how financially destructive a credit card can become you need look no further than your credit card statement. I am right this moment looking at a recent credit card statement. Their interest rate chart is pretty straight forward because there is only one rate, 19.99%. Substantial indeed! Above that disclosure there is a cute little section that states "If you make only the minimum payment each month, we estimate it will take 129 year(s) and 8 month(s) to fully repay the outstanding balance." Hmm, at that point I'll be well over 180 years old, which is about the time I project reaching my cholesterol target. If you take them up on their offer to fund your purchase for 129 years, well, you are probably destined for bankruptcy at some point and that is what is scary about using a credit card.

However, there is one other key disclosure on this statement that I believe is vital to the successful use of a credit card ... "Your account is currently set up on an Auto Pay plan." So in the end this statement tells me that I owe $14,789.86 (mostly related to flooring), the balance is due on May 26, any balance owing after May 26 will attract interest at a rate of 19.99%, but I am set up to automatically pay the balance before any interest is charged to me. So, assuming I have the money to settle the obligation in my bank account (which I made sure of), I end up paying no interest. I use the credit card company's money for a couple of weeks, pay no interest, and get a bunch of WestJet dollars that I can use for a flight of my choosing. Credit cards work nicely if their terms are respected and spending is maintained within your personal budget. Credit cards are not in and of themselves bad tools; people, however, often use them in a financially destructive fashion.

To sum up my position on credit cards: if you are one of the people who are organized enough and financially able to pay the balance each and every month (through an automatic payment so you don't forget), then a credit card is a good vehicle for your use. On the other hand, if you lack the discipline to pay off the balance each and every month in full, or are using a credit card to finance a lifestyle that you cannot otherwise afford, then they facilitate a quick and easy path to ruin.

In the introduction to this section, I noted that the average Canadian consumer has a balance of about $4,000 on their credit card. If you are carrying that balance from month to month, that is a recipe for disaster.

Credit Cards - A Few Final Thoughts

It is possible to write a whole book on credit cards, but a more boring book to read is difficult for me to envision. So I will offer just a few more random thoughts on credit cards:

- Credit cards all come with long and complex agreements. Before you apply, take the time to read the cardholder agreement. I know, but it is short-term pain.
- Understand and respect the payment terms associated with your card. If you miss the payment deadline interest will accrue from the date of purchase in most instances, not the payment deadline.
- Deciding which credit card suits your requirements best is a daunting task. There are just too many credit cards out there to personally do a fulsome evaluation of them all. Luckily, there are sources that will help you narrow the search. In Canada, while there are other sources, I consult www.moneysense.ca to look at the results of their most recent credit card assessment and to utilize the tools they provide.
- I like the idea of keeping a low-limit credit card to facilitate my online purchases and I use it exclusively for those purchases.
- It is easy to accumulate a lot of different credit cards. Retailers are great at accosting you at the checkout and *trying to save you money* on the purchase you are about to make by having you sign up for their credit

card. A bunch of credit cards leads to a bunch of extra, unnecessary complexity. Your credit score will take a hit if you make a habit of collecting credit cards. Avoid the temptation.
- I am continually amazed at how often credit cards are compromised. While the fraud detection capability of the credit card companies appears to be very effective, and has worked very well to quickly shut down any illegal activity taking place on my card, it is still inconvenient to wait for your credit card to be replaced. While I don't like the idea of having many cards, I do think having two (for people who can use them responsibly) is reasonable.
- There is no reason to let anyone else handle your credit card. Keep the card in your possession at all times. While you are at it purchase a wallet, or other containment device, that blocks the ability to steal your credit card information (RFID).
- Reconcile your credit card statement every month. Be one of those people who take the receipt and actually confirm each transaction recorded on the credit card statement by tying them back to the receipts you have collected. If you see a transaction on your statement that you did not initiate, immediately follow-up with the credit card company. If you are simply not wired to collect receipts and reconcile your statement on a monthly basis, at a minimum, make sure you review the transaction record and question any you feel are not yours.
- Having and using a credit card is the quickest way in which an individual can establish a credit history. If you are in a relationship I believe it is important to establish your own credit history, and credit score, by having a credit card in your own name. My parents both had and used credit cards, but my mother used a card associated with my father's account. When my father died, my mother had no credit history of her own. It made it a little tricky to get a credit card in her name, even though she had been using a card responsibly for decades.
- If you are on a date and he/she uses a credit card to pay the bill, don't judge them on that basis alone. It may be a perfectly reasonable action to take. However, if the relationship becomes serious, make sure you have the *money talk*. Poor debt management is the source of many divorces.

CHAPTER 15 – DEBT ELIMINATION

I am not an idiot. (At least I hope I am not an idiot.) I realize people have debt, often quite a lot of debt. I do not believe people who are in debt are stupid or deficient; the same way that I do not automatically assume that people who have substantial net worth have their stuff together. Clearly, if you have substantial debt, you have made some decisions somewhere along the line that got you into that position; hopefully your debt is manageable. It is my hope too that your go-forward decision-making process is modified to exclude bad debt through better awareness and more thought about other competing goals.

I want you to spend your money where it brings you the most value over the course of your life. This does not mean undue hardship now for easy street later, or easy street now for life on the street later. It is about organizing yourself to achieve what you want out of life, over the course of your life. From a financial perspective, this means that you need to be aware of your financial circumstances and have goals and objectives established that clarify what you want to achieve such that current sacrifice (i.e., saving) seems less like sacrifice and more like what it is: achievement.

If you have debt you want to extinguish or at least get under control, the what-to-do recipe is relatively straight forward from my perspective ... all you have to do is make debt repayment your priority. I am not an expert in this area of financial planning because I don't have a lot of experience with debt. I have made it a personal mission to avoid debt that is not automatically eliminated in the next payment cycle. That said, these are my thoughts on the best approach to eliminating debt.

1. Make spending reduction a priority until debt is well under control. All spending on wants should be severely restricted if not eliminated. Extra cash should be dedicated to debt repayment.
2. Identify all of your outstanding debt. This is first an inventorying exercise; determine what you owe and who you owe it to. Write it down (create a spreadsheet), always keep organized financial records because *knowing* is the key to fixing and/or advancing.
3. Understand the terms associated with each individual debt balance owing, including payment freedoms and restrictions. Record when payments are required and the embedded interest rate.
4. Henceforth, make ALL minimum payments on time.
5. Organize your debt list in accordance with your debt elimination goals. Generally you should be paying off your highest-interest-rate debt first. So organize your list of outstanding debt obligations on the basis of interest rate, starting with the highest rate and progressing sequentially to the lowest rate obligation.

    After making all minimum payments each month, pour all available extra cash into paying off the highest rate debt first, to the extent allowed within the repayment terms. Move down the list to the next highest rate debt and apply any remaining resources until all resources have been so allocated.

    While I believe the focus should first be on paying off high-rate debt, some people gain more satisfaction from paying off some small balances to reduce the sheer number of debt obligations outstanding. From a purely financial perspective, this is suboptimal because you end up paying more interest by leaving the higher-interest-rate debt outstanding for a longer period of time. However, from a psychological perspective, for some people, reducing the number of obligations can be invigorating. If you are more likely to stick with the debt elimination program by reducing the volume of obligations as your priority, then go for it.
6. Celebrate your achievements. Modest celebrations, though! Perhaps a bottle of wine around a fire in the back yard ... burn something

representative of the debt that has now been eliminated (the last statement and/or the associated credit card, perhaps). Relish in your achievement. You are moving in the right direction! There is nothing better than the feeling of gaining or regaining control.
7. Keep focused on debt repayment until all bad debt is gone. I realize that I haven't talked about good versus bad debt to this point in the repayment process. Generally, though, you will naturally focus on bad debt repayment first simply because it tends to be the highest-interest-rate debt. Once you have eliminated the bad debt, then you can begin to focus, in a more measured way, on eliminating good debt.

If you have a number of sources of high-interest-rate debt, you should look into the benefits of a debt consolidation loan. This approach would reduce administrative complexity and may result in a lower embedded interest rate (depending on your credit rating and the nature of any security provided). It also adds structure to the repayment process, which can be helpful in enforcing diligence. There are some potential disadvantages that would need to be understood within your specific circumstances, but it is worth consideration.

If debt is a really big problem, I would suggest visiting a credit counselling service to ensure you arrive at the best course of action to take. When you get to the point where bankruptcy could potentially enter the picture, then your debt repayment priorities could change depending on certain debt characteristics (callable/secured). At that point you really need to talk to an expert in the area.

Post Debt Crisis

One of the key pieces to enduring debt containment is recognizing and fixing the behaviour that led to a debt problem in the first place. If you have a spending problem, then you will need to establish a system that will help you control spending. This may entail moving to a cash only system, eliminating credit cards from your life, closing the home equity line of credit, etc. Gail Vaz-Oxlade has written a number of books on debt management that would be a useful resource for you to consult. Gail's books are generally an easy, informative, and entertaining read.

Kevin O'Leary, in his book entitled *The Cold Hard Truth on Men, Women and Money*, advocates using what he calls a Cold Hard Truth Card.[1] This card, which you carry with you at all times, is to be pulled out and read before each and every purchase made to ensure that the expenditure meets certain specific criteria.

My favourite financial planning academic and author is Moshe Milevsky, who teaches all things wealth management related at York University (Schulich School of Business) in Toronto. One of the statements Moshe makes in *Your Money Milestones* related to the main question you should ask yourself when contemplating going into debt is:

> Will today's purchase, which might be financed by high cost and long-term **debt**, reduce my **future** standard of living by more than the purchase will increase my **present** standard of living?[2]

Going through either of these thought processes (O'Leary's or Milevsky's) before making a purchase will cause you to think of the purchase in terms of the ultimate trade-off you are making. If you do this correctly more often than not, it should modify your spending/saving behaviour for the better.

Credit Report and Credit Score

Every week, at some point, when I am watching television there will be an advertisement (or more likely, several) telling me how I can get my credit score for free. I just finished reading a financial management book written by a millennial directed at millennials and it spent a full chapter, 30 pages or so, talking about all things credit score related. Given the apparent obsession with credit scores, I figured this section of the book would be incomplete if I didn't at least touch on the subject.

How well you handle your credit obligations is a primary determinant of your ability to gain access to credit and it impacts the terms made available to you by lenders. If you have a history of responsible credit use, it seems that lenders are falling all over themselves to entice you into taking out a loan or to increase your credit limit for existing credit sources. If you have a history of failing to use credit responsibly, then you will have more limited credit options and the terms that are made available to you most certainly will not be favourable.

In Canada, there are two main credit bureaus that track, store, and share your credit history: Equifax and TransUnion. The credit bureaus must comply with federal and provincial laws that control the right to access your personal credit information. According to the Government of Canada website,[3] all of the following are allowed to see and use your credit report:

- banks, credit unions, and other financial institutions
- credit card companies
- car leasing companies
- retailers
- mobile phone companies
- insurance companies
- governments
- employers
- landlords

Clearly, your credit information is being used in a whole range of decisions that can impact you, beyond just whether or not to lend you money, so it is a good idea to pay attention to the exposure you assume to credit and how you manage your responsibilities. While I tend to favour designing your financial life such that credit becomes an ever smaller presence, having the option to utilize credit on favourable terms certainly is a comfortable safety blanket to have when/if you need it.

Your credit report contains three main categories of information: personal, financial, and credit history. The credit bureaus do not create the data that is contained in your credit report, rather they collect, compile, and display the information. The information contained in your credit report is sourced from retailers, student loan providers, utility companies, auto dealers, banks, finance companies, and various public records. You can gain access to your credit report for free by following the procedure outlined on each of the credit bureaus websites. If you see any inaccuracies in your credit report information, both of the credit bureaus have a clearly defined process on their websites that you can follow to correct the disclosure.

The process through which a consumer of your credit report requests to see the information is dependent on their purpose and the applicable government regulations. Depending on your province of residence, the requirements range from having the inquirer tell you they are checking your credit report to written consent to allow the enquiry; though there are some provinces that allow certain government representatives access to your credit report without consent or notification. Often any written consent is embedded in the application process. (Make sure you read the fine print to know what you are providing access to.)

Your credit report contains all of the information that is used to compute your credit score. Each of the credit bureaus utilizes a proprietary statistical formula to translate the information contained in your credit report into a three-digit credit score. As a result, your credit score will vary a little bit, depending on the credit bureau consulted. Presumably the core message provided by the credit scores sourced from the two credit bureaus will be similar.

Neither of the credit bureaus provides the details of their credit scoring formula on their website, but the inputs used by the formula to arrive at your credit score are generally inclusive of:

- your history of payment on loans of all types
- the balances you currently owe on your credit accounts
- the relationship between your credit availability and usage
- the length of time your accounts have been operative
- your credit mix
- the number of inquiries on your file (note though, many types of inquiries have no impact on your credit score—employment, insurance, rental, your own inquiries, among others)
- any record of insolvency or bankruptcy
- referral of debts to a collection agency

A numerical weighting process is applied to each of the rating characteristics of concern, the proprietary formula chugs for a bit and cranks out the three-digit number. A lender may use other information additional to the credit score in determining if credit will be granted or not. So if you have a solid credit score, and you have an application for credit turned down, you may want to explore the reasoning further with the lender.

What I find interesting is with respect to some of the information that is not used in determining your credit worthiness according to this scoring system. You will note that your credit report does not include information that you might think of as being relevant to your credit worthiness, such as:

- your income
- purchases that you paid for in full (cash or cheque) without the intervention of a credit source
- information about your personal accounts that involve no debt

If you are not happy with your credit score, the good news is you have ultimate control over fixing it. All you need to do is focus on improving the elements that go into the formula determining the score and over time your score will improve. Some of the things you can do to improve your credit score include:

- pay your bills by the due date
- periodically check your credit report and fix any inaccuracies
- keep account balances below 35% of available credit
- limit your applications for credit
- manage your credit consistently over a long period of time
- it may be beneficial to keep the oldest account on your credit file open to demonstrate a lengthy period of active use

If you are interested in gaining access to your credit report, or learning more about how your credit score is calculated, visit the TransUnion and Equifax websites.

PART V – INVESTING

It is impossible to do a comprehensive job of discussing investing without dedicating several books to its many and varied aspects. Luckily, in order to do a credible job of designing and managing an investment portfolio, you don't need to know more than a few relatively basic principles.

The focus within this section will be on the primary investment categories of equities, fixed income securities, and cash, with a brief touch on alternative investments. Investment alternatives such as hedge funds, managed futures, precious metals, currencies, principal-protected notes, art, convertible debentures, put and call options, segregated funds, labour-sponsored venture capital corporations, flow-through shares, private equity, individual stocks, rental properties, among others, will not play a central role in the discussion. Sorry to disappoint. Many of these types of investments may hold a valuable spot within an individual's investment portfolio, but a successful investment program can be built without detailed knowledge of, or dedicated holdings in, any of these.

It is important to realize that in order to have a successful investment result you don't need to have detailed insight related to the worldwide macroeconomic picture, the micro picture facing Middle Eastern oil, what President Trump will tweet next, or knowledge of the latest new energy source discovered within the depths of the deepest reaches of the Pacific Ocean. If you do have this knowledge, you can use it to fiddle with your investment program at the fringes, but the core of what you are doing should not respond to these details in any significant way.

Previously in the book I came clean with a couple of my investing mistakes. Those mistakes were the result of me tinkering. The tinkering always had an objective, which could have been to find a little more return, reduce income taxes, add more sophistication to my understanding of how an investment worked, or just to show how smart I thought I was. Lots of my tinkering has brought me face to face with the mediocrity I demonstrated in high school. The investing world can be humbling.

Once upon a time, I subscribed to a couple of investment newsletters. Often their advice on a particular stock or investment looked foolproof. In reality, though, more often than not those investments turned out to be either mediocre or outright failures. I no longer purchase any investment newsletters. All advice I read in books, magazines, online, and in the newspaper is taken with a high degree of scepticism, researched more fully if I consider it to present a compelling idea, and virtually never acted upon. AND if there is any action taken, the impact is contained through limiting the size of the investment.

Andrew Hallam, in his international best seller *Millionaire Teacher*,[1] devotes a short, but enlightening, section in the book to investment newsletters and their track records. He points out that there are several organizations that track the results of financial newsletters, and while the information he presents is based on US-domiciled newsletters, I suspect that the conclusions are equally relevant to the Canadian experience. One of the organizations highlighted by Mr. Hallam that focused effort on evaluating the effectiveness of investment newsletters published *The Hulbert Financial Digest*. (This is written in past tense because it recently shut its doors after 36 years of publication.) One of their studies of the recommendations of 160 newsletters found that only 10 of them had beaten the stock market indexes with their recommendations over the preceding decade. Ten ... not exactly a rip-roaring record of success.

Common sense would suggest that if the publishers of a newsletter had sufficient insight to make you wealthy, they wouldn't sell it to you. Would it not make more sense for them to simply use their research to become rich on their own? And if their system was so consistently effective, would they not be a household name because they were among the richest of the rich?

In my opinion, to be a successful investor, you need to understand a few basic concepts, save enough money to build a sufficient investment portfolio, take advantage of time to allow compounding returns to work in your favour, and above all else, stay out of your own way.

Takeaways from Part V

- ✓ Investing is the process of putting capital to work with a view to generating a variety of forms of return. The intention is that the capital plus the after-tax compounded returns will ultimately become sufficient to fund the financial demands of the investor's goals.
- ✓ Investments are categorized into classes that have similar characteristics. An investment portfolio is generally comprised of four primary asset classes: equity, fixed income, cash, and alternative investments; sometimes a fifth asset class, termed variable income, will be identified.
- ✓ The assets classified as variable income can be included in one of the other primary asset classes with equal validity. The purpose in segregating income focused assets into a separate class is to recognize that one of their primary attributes is the generation of cash flow. If cash flow is an important element of an investor's portfolio, as it often is in later-stage financial planning, then segregating this asset class may be a prudent action to take.
- ✓ Equity investments reflect an ownership interest in a business. Equities provide returns primarily in the form of capital appreciation (or depreciation) and dividends. Stock exchanges have evolved over many years to provide an efficient mechanism for buying and selling shares in publicly listed businesses. Stock market indexes provide a snapshot of market performance as well as a useful tool for evaluating relative performance. They also function as an effective design template for equity portfolio construction.
- ✓ Fixed income investments represent a form of loan as opposed to ownership. These loans generally include a periodic payment as well as the repayment of the original principal. The primary source of income from these investments is interest income, though there can be a capital gain or loss if the investment is marketable.
- ✓ Cash tends to be a horrible investment from a return perspective, but provides many other benefits. Cash saves an investor when emergencies and surprises arise. Cash provides a calming effect when the financial markets are going crazy. Cash provides options.

- ✓ Alternative investments tend to be investments that do not fit cleanly within the bounds of one of the other primary asset classes, or they have dominant characteristics that make them more appropriately segregated from other classes. They can offer certain diversification and return benefits to a portfolio, but often are not necessary to achieve intended results.
- ✓ Most investments bring with them a plethora of risks that need to be understood and managed within the context of the overall portfolio. Some of the more common risks include:

  - Business risk
  - Credit risk
  - Interest rate risk
  - Currency risk
  - Maturity and reinvestment risk
  - Political risk
  - Liquidity risk
  - Systematic risk
  - Lack of transparency
  - Complexity
  - Leverage
  - Investment specific risks, etc.

- ✓ Each investor needs to understand their goals and risk tolerance to design an investment strategy appropriate to their circumstances. The primary methods used to manage the risk profile of a portfolio include well-designed asset allocation, proper diversification within and across asset classes, and skillful time-frame management.
- ✓ Many investors are their own greatest obstacle to success. I don't fix my own car because I don't know what I am doing. If you don't know how to invest properly, either learn how to do it and stay out of your own way, or hire the assistance you need to be successful.

CHAPTER 16 – ASSET CLASSES

Within an investment program, there are generally three or four groupings of assets, referred to as asset classes, utilized by an investor:

- equities (comprised primarily of common stocks that are either directly held or indirectly held through an exchange-traded fund or mutual fund),
- fixed income (comprised of guaranteed investment certificates, bonds, and debentures either directly held or indirectly held through an exchange-traded fund or mutual fund),
- cash (currency or a money market instrument scheduled to mature within a year), and
- alternative investments (hedge funds, managed futures, private equity, art, antique cars, tulip bulbs, collectibles, etc.).

These groupings are aggregated in this manner because the investments within each category generally (alternative investments being the exception) tend to embed roughly similar characteristics and therefore act in a similar fashion to a given set of economic conditions or expectations. Alternative investments are simply those that don't fit one of the other three classes.

More recently, some authors have started to recognize another asset class labelled *variable income*. This asset class grabs a number of investments that have traditionally been considered to reside at the fringe of other asset classes. The key feature of this grouping is the emphasis that the securities place on providing regular cash flow. The cash flow is generally not guaranteed as it is with a Government of Canada Bond, but there is some predictability to the timing, if not the exact quantum. The assets captured within this asset class include preferred shares, income trusts (including real estate investment trusts, natural resource trusts, etc.), and certain income-oriented mutual funds and exchange-traded funds.

In my view, variable income is not so much an independent asset class as it is a subset of existing asset classes. As your investment needs change over time, it is natural for your approach to investing within each and every one of the asset classes to be modified, generally becoming more risk averse. Within the fixed income portion of your asset allocation, this would mean moving from longer-term issues to shorter-term issues and from lower-quality issuers to higher-quality issuers. Within the equity portion of your asset allocation, it is natural to move, as time progresses, from more emphasis on growth to more emphasis on dividends and larger potentially more stable enterprises. Personally, I have a section of our asset allocation that is dedicated to variable income investments, but I consider this investment subset to be a portion of my overall equity allocation … it just has a different and specific role to play in our portfolio vis-à-vis the other equities we hold.

While most readers likely have a working understanding of what each of these asset classes is comprised of, I am often surprised by the limited understanding or misconceptions that are held by people that I talk with about investing. So, somewhat against my better judgement, I will delve into the details of each asset class.

In the longer term, I am cautiously optimistic that the public education system will evolve to ensure high school graduates develop better skills in all aspects of personal finance. In my view, this has been a key failing of our education system.

We will return to the broad discussion of asset classes in a later chapter when we consider portfolio construction and more specifically asset allocation.

CHAPTER 17 – EQUITIES

Over the course of time you have no doubt heard someone say, "Be an owner, not a loaner." Likely within moments of hearing that said, you did whatever you had to so that you could find a different conversation to participate in; politely excused yourself, waved to no one in particular across the room and wandered off in that general direction, faked a cramp that required immediate attention, etc. Well, sorry, but that is where we are heading with this chapter because "being an owner" is the key element that distinguishes the equity asset class from the others and, like it or not, this requires us to get into the different forms of business ownership. I will try to get through this in a quick and pain-lite fashion.

Business can be conducted under three main structures: a proprietorship, a partnership, or a corporation. Each of these has different implications from an investment perspective.

A *proprietorship* is owned and run by one person and there is no legal distinction between the owner and the business. A proprietorship represents an investment for that person only.

A *partnership* is a business venture where two or more persons participate in the financial fortunes of the operations (*persons* don't have to be people). Depending on the structure of the partnership, a partner can be either a general partner or a limited partner. General partners are individually responsible for the debts of the partnership. Limited partners generally assume no financial responsibility beyond the capital contributed. The partnership agreement will spell out the rights and obligations of each class of partners. Many tax shelters use a partnership structure.

Last, but not least, a *corporation* is a legal entity that is separate and distinct from its owners. Corporations enjoy most of the rights and responsibilities that an individual has. The corporate form of business structure allows for an efficient change in ownership and therefore continuity of existence beyond the lifetime of the existing shareholder(s). There are two different types of corporations, private and public. Private corporations have charters that restrict the number of shareholders and the right of shareholders to transfer their shares. Public corporations, on the other hand, allow for the free and unencumbered transfer of shares (or stocks) from one owner to another.

Most often, an investor's equity exposure is through the direct or indirect ownership of shares in a public corporation.

One of the key features of the corporate form of business structure from an investor perspective is that of limited liability. Limited liability essentially puts a cap on the amount that can be lost by the shareholder, the maximum loss being the amount they have invested. It is bad enough if you lose your investment due to poor business results or fraud, but at least you know the full extent of the possible loss before you make the investment.

Stock Exchanges

In order for people to purchase ownership interest in public companies, there needs to be a mechanism that allows for the efficient and effective transfer of share ownership. That is the function of a stock exchange.

A stock exchange is simply a facility that supports the buying and selling of the stocks that are listed on that exchange. Each stock exchange has criteria that a company must meet in order to list their stock on the exchange. Once a stock is accepted for listing, it is available to be bought and sold by brokers that are registered to trade on the exchange. Individuals use their brokers to make trades on their behalf and they pay transaction fees to have this done for them.

Not all that long ago, it was quite expensive to trade stocks through a broker due to a rather steep commission structure. As I remember it, my first ever purchase cost me about $600, and since I don't still own that particular stock, it also cost me about the same to sell the position. That represented a substantial hurdle to overcome before making any money. The trade that I made yesterday cost me $9.99 to complete. Another interesting point to note is that the commission fee is payable for each trade, but it is not influenced by the dollar value of the trade. It costs the same $9.99, regardless of whether I am buying/selling 100 shares of stock for $2,000 or 100,000 shares of stock for $2,000,000 (I wish).

According to *Wikipedia*, there are nineteen major stock exchanges in the world, each with a market capitalization of over $1 trillion US dollars.[1] Together, these exchanges accounted for 87% of the global stock market capitalization in 2015. The largest stock exchange in the world was the New York Stock Exchange. The TMX group owns and operates the main exchanges in Canada, the largest of which is the Toronto Stock Exchange.

The larger and best-known Canadian companies trade on the Toronto Stock Exchange (TSX), many smaller and less well-known companies trade on the TSX Venture Exchange. While the companies listed on the TSX represent a wide range of businesses, when taken as a whole, the Canadian market is relatively concentrated in just a few *sectors* (groupings of companies that operate in similar industries). More than half of the market capitalization of the TSX is accounted for by companies whose businesses are classified as either financial or energy.

While Canadian stock markets hold a relatively prominent position in the stock markets of the world, they are dwarfed by the size of the largest markets. The Canadian markets represent only about 3% of worldwide stock market capitalization. These characteristics, relatively small size and sector concentration, are something you need to keep in mind when building the equity portion of your investment portfolio.

Stock Ownership: What Does it Get You?

Owning stock in a company gives you a proportional interest in the success of that company. For instance, if you buy a share of the Royal Bank, you own a piece of the bank, albeit a very, very small piece. If you own even a single share in a company, you have the right to collect your proportionate amount of any dividend declared by the Board of Directors as well as to vote at shareholders meetings on things such as electing the Board of Directors and appointing the auditors. You also have the right to sell any shares you own at any time that the stock exchange is open for trading. Unfortunately, just because you are an owner of the company, you do not get a key to the head office and a direct line to the CEO to discuss your thoughts related to how the company should be run. However, if you can accumulate enough shares, you certainly are in a position to influence what the company does through your voting privileges.

Forms of Equity Ownership

To this point in time we have been discussing equity ownership in terms of the direct ownership of shares in the business. In actual fact, for most people, the equity interest they have in their investment portfolio will come through the purchase of units or shares of a mutual fund or exchange-traded fund. If you participate in equities through these forms of ownership, you do not get to vote, but you will participate in the dividends declared and the change in stock price in the same way that you would if you owned shares directly.

With equity-based mutual funds (MF) and equity-based exchange-traded funds (ETF), you are purchasing an ownership interest in an underlying portfolio of stocks. You do not own the underlying stocks directly, but rather you will own shares or units of the mutual fund or exchange-traded fund that has purchased and holds the underlying stocks. These forms of equity ownership provide you with the opportunity, within a single purchase, to spread your investment across a broad range of stocks with a single transaction. Investing in a number of different businesses and, more generally, investing across different asset classes, is called diversification. Both MFs and ETFs, when properly selected, are an excellent way to gain immediate and broad diversification.

Costs of Equity Ownership

When you purchase a stock directly you need to have a brokerage account and pay for each transaction you initiate through your broker. If you use a discount brokerage account, the cost of all of this is relatively light. As an example, the discount broker I use charges me no administration fees related to any of the various accounts I hold with them and about $10 per trade they execute on my behalf.

If you use a portfolio approach through either MFs or ETFs, then you have an additional layer of costs you are dealing with. Both of these products bring with them management and administrative costs, which are ultimately paid for by the investor through a reduction to the returns earned by the fund. The management expense ratio (MER) describes, on a percentage basis, the extent of these costs. The MER can vary significantly from one fund to another.

First, let's consider ETFs. ETFs trade on a stock exchange in exactly the same way that an individual stock does. So, in terms of expenses, you will have any investment account fees that your broker charges you and transaction fees related to the purchases and sales of ETFs you enter into. In addition, each ETF will have management fees and expenses. Many of the fees associated with ETFs are minimal, often a small fraction of a percent on an annual basis. Some of the more specialized ETFs, though, will have more substantial costs, so it is important that you look at the details of the ETFs you are considering to understand the cost profile.

Most of the mutual funds that investors utilize are classified as open ended funds; units of these funds are purchased from an individual registered to sell mutual funds (no stock exchange is involved in an open end mutual fund transaction). There are thousands of different mutual funds available. In fact, there are more mutual funds marketed in Canada than there are stocks listed on Canadian stock exchanges, if you can believe it.

The costs you assume when investing in a mutual fund tend to be more varied, and often considerably more substantial, than those associated with ETFs. There are some exceptions to this general rule. For example, certain index-based mutual funds have relatively low management fees. Often, though, especially in Canada, mutual funds are encumbered by relatively steep costs of ownership.

It is up to each investor to control the cost structure of their portfolio. As we will discuss later, costs that might appear to be subdued in that the percentages do not appear to be all that substantial, turn out to be huge when considered over the time frame of an investing lifetime.

Stock Market Indexes

It is important to understand what a stock market index is and how it is constructed. There are two reasons I believe this to be important.

1. Stock market indices provide the foundation for understanding both absolute as well as relative performance when assessing how you or an investment manager has performed over a period of time. For example, if you have Canadian equity investments, it is useful to know how the Canadian stock index has performed in percentage terms over time and to compare that to how your Canadian investment portfolio has performed over that same period of time. By calculating your return, you know in numeric terms the return you were able to amass, but when you compare that return to how the market did, you can determine if the performance was relatively good or relatively bad.
2. It is my belief that a core component of most equity investment strategies should involve healthy doses of low-cost indexed investments. Given that one of the key principles you should follow when selecting your investments is to never invest in something you do not fully understand, an understanding of what indexes are is necessary.

There are market indexes designed to be representative of performance in all areas of the investment landscape. There are equity market indexes, bond indexes, managed futures indexes, currency indexes, hedge fund indexes, and there are even specialized indexes that can be as narrowly defined as the North American Medical Marijuana Index. The list of indexes and index-based investment products is extensive.

One index that is often quoted and has an extensive history is the Dow Jones Industrial Average (DJIA), established way back in 1896. You are likely asking yourself, what else happened in 1896? I know I was, so I consulted the world wide web and found the following tasty little bits:

- Wilfrid Laurier was the 7th Prime Minister of Canada (we are now on our 23rd different PM)
- The first modern Olympics began in Greece

- The Tootsie Roll was invented
- Dear to my heart, the first CPAs were awarded their certificates
- And most significantly, the Winnipeg Victorias beat the Montreal Victorias for the Stanley Cup. From what I read, it was during this game that the Winnipeg goalie introduced the first set of goalie pads (and he got a shutout)

Market indexes have been around for a very long time indeed.

The DJIA is constructed to measure a point-in-time value based on the prices of 30 large publicly traded US-based companies. The DJIA index is unusual in the investment world because it is *price weighted*, which, in very simplistic terms, means that each of the 30 component companies are weighted in the index relative to the price of their common stock. The value of the index is determined by adding up the prices of all of the component stocks and dividing that sum by a calculated divisor, which is regularly adjusted to reflect stock splits, spin offs, and a variety of structural changes designed to eliminate their influence. Only one of the companies currently in the index, General Electric, was also a component of the original index. At the time of writing, the companies included in the index had changed 54 times since inception.[2] Thus, while the index has been around for a long time, its composition is ever-changing.

I can hear you asking, how is an index that is based on the share price of only 30 component stocks supposed to demonstrate effectively any relevant move in the equity market of a country that trades thousands of different stocks across a number of different stock exchanges? That is a really good question. Personally, I don't think this particular index is overly useful, but it has been around for a very long time and because of its familiarity it is still widely covered in the business news.

Sticking to the US as an example country, likely the second-best-known market index worldwide is the S&P 500. The S&P 500 index is a capitalization weighted index (meaning that the larger companies of the index have a greater impact on the level of the index at any point in time) comprised of 500 large US companies that trade on the two major exchanges in the US. The specific stocks included in the index change periodically (in most years approximately 25–30 stocks change[3]), the number of changes over any period of time can vary widely. The stocks included in the S&P 500 are selected by a committee, who consider each stock in terms of eight specific criteria. Changes to the index are measured, but not infrequent.

When stocks are purchased to replicate an index under the structure of a mutual fund, the product can be bought in small pieces by individual investors; this is called an *index mutual fund*. When a similar fund is compiled under the legal structure of an exchange-traded fund, it then is listed on a stock exchange and shares of the ETF can be purchased and sold by individuals. This financial product is referred to as an *index exchange-traded fund*. These can be very powerful products for individual investors because they, with a single purchase, provide exposure to the entirety of the index component companies.

We have talked only about two specific indexes to this point, but suffice it to say that there are hundreds of indexes and thus index products that can be purchased. Indexes have made it possible for the average investor to find and buy a low-cost investment that replicates almost any equity market, or combination of equity markets, in the world with a single transaction fee and an embedded expense profile that is often razor thin.

As just one example, a Canadian investor looking for exposure to global stocks that excluded Canadian stocks might consider the Vanguard FTSE Global All Cap ex Canada Index ETF[4] (who names these things?); the description provided on the Factsheet states:

> The fund seeks to track, to the extent reasonably possible and before fees and expenses, the performance of a broad global equity index that focuses on developed and emerging markets, excluding Canada. Currently, this Vanguard ETF seeks to track the FTSE Global All Cap ex Canada China A Inclusion Index (or any successor thereto). It invests directly or indirectly primarily in large-, mid-, and small-capitalization stocks of companies located in developed and emerging markets, excluding Canada.

By purchasing this one ETF that is listed on the Toronto Stock Exchange, an investor is able to gain exposure to about 10,000 stocks from all over the world. The stocks held in the ETF do not exactly replicate the benchmark index, in this case, but they do a very good job of mimicking the index with a reasonably small error. The price for this investment is about $10 for the trade and an annual management expense of 0.27%. Yes, for about a quarter of a percent annually, and a $10 transaction fee, you can purchase exposure to a diversified equity position that includes major stocks from all over the world. Again, this is just one example. All of the major ETF providers (iShares, Horizons, BMO, RBC, Invesco, Vanguard, etc.) have options that include low-cost domestic, international, and/or global equity funds.

Fees and expenses will be more fully explored in chapter 22.

Problems with Stock Market Indexes

As helpful as indexes can be for investors, there are some pitfalls that you need to be aware of. When you buy an index-based fund, you are investing in the stocks that make up the index in the same proportion that they are in the index. So if a stock is a big piece of the index, your exposure is also exaggerated toward that stock. Some indexes have a few stocks that hold a substantially greater profile than the balance of the stocks in the index. For example, in Canada, it is not long ago that we had one dominant company in our index, Nortel Networks. At its peak, Nortel made up almost 35% of the TSE 300 index (the TSE 300 index was replaced by the S&P/TSX Composite Index in 2002). So if you bought a TSE 300-based index product at the time, about 35% of that investment was in Nortel and 65% of the investment was in the other 299 companies. Perhaps this is not the level of diversification you thought you would be getting by "buying the market." There are a number of indexes around the world that are quite concentrated in a small number of stocks.

One other form of concentration that you need to be aware of is that related to companies in the same sector. In Canada, for instance, the stock market is concentrated in three sectors. At the time of writing, financial stocks account for 37% of the market capitalization of the S&P/TSX Composite Index, and energy stocks and materials stocks account for 21% and 12% of the index, respectively. Together, just these three sectors account for 70% of the market capitalization of the S&P/TSX index. In fact, the three largest stocks included in the index at the time I am writing this are all banks. So when it comes to investing strategies based on indexes, it is important to understand how the constituents are determined, how their index weighting is calculated, and gain an appreciation for the extent of turnover (particularly if you are investing in a taxable account).

The indexers and the financial product developers are aware of the biases within many of the indexes that are widely quoted in the financial media. They have responded by developing a number of specialized indexes, and associated index-based products, designed to focus the underlying investment profile differently than the broad capitalization weighted indexes. Many indexes have maximum allocations to an individual stock (capped indexes). Some indexes use equal weighting so you will be exposed to all of the companies in the index, but the weighting of the companies is the same across the board to rectify concentration concerns. So there are options available to effectively quell any index composition concerns you may have.

Risks of Investing in the Stock Market

Go to the website of any mutual fund or exchange-traded fund management firm and download any equity index product prospectus, then look for the *risk of investment* section. It won't be hard to find because it goes on for pages and pages. You will find a very thorough discussion related to the multitude of risks that are associated with equity investing. It is difficult to muster up the courage to go forward with any investment once you are ten pages deep in this risk disclosure. If only you could actually get a decent return from a GIC, all of this could be avoided.

I will take a look at some of what I consider to be the main risks associated with equity-based investments, and offer some insight as to how you can manage these specific risks. You need to recognize though that this is a general discussion and any time you spend looking at the risk disclosure section related to any investment you own, or are thinking about owning, is time well spent. The risk universe is ever expanding and with each product innovation it is inevitable that a new risk will also be born.

"You" Risk. This is a risk that you will not see listed in any investment security prospectus, but it may well be the biggest risk that needs to be managed. Everyone with an interest in investing likes to think that they can add value to a portfolio by picking better investments than the average market investor. Study after study has demonstrated that investors, through their activity, manage to reduce their returns by not being able to keep their sticky little fingers off. With the current discount brokerage options it is now easy to set up an account and become a day trader, or periodic trader, at seemingly low cost with a very low barrier to entry. All I can say is … don't.

I know that all of the very poor investments that have occurred in my past could have been avoided by simply deciding on the appropriate asset allocation, selecting a broad-based ETF reflective of the asset segment, and ignoring the outcome other than to periodically rebalance my holdings.

For most people, if they were to simply get some professional help to design their asset allocation, select very low-cost indexed products, and keep to their investment program, then market gains will be matched minus the very small cost of the investment products used. Presto, you have now beaten many of the great minds at work in the investment universe and eliminated the "you" risk at the same time!

Business Risk. In its simplest terms, business risk is the risk that a company does not perform well, causing an investor to lose money. If you invest in Nortel, your investment does as well as Nortel does. The best way to manage business risk is to diversify. Invest in many different businesses so that you are not overly exposed to any one or a small number of them.

Currency Risk. This is the risk that the currency you are investing in loses value against your home currency. Most of your investments are likely to be denominated in your home currency; it is only foreign-based investments that are exposed. One way to help manage this risk is to diversify your currencies. In that case, the averaging effect may even out across currencies and over time. The alternative is to invest in currency hedged investment products. These investment products will have a program designed to largely offset any gains or losses due to changes in the currency of the investment (these programs never offer a perfect hedge, but an effective program will serve to limit the impact of currency fluctuation). Keep in mind, hedging programs have a cost associated with them and that will be reflected in the performance of the investment. Many foreign investments come in both hedged and unhedged versions.

Political Risk. This type of risk can be described in many alternative ways, depending on the nature of the investment you are considering and whether you are looking at it in a micro or macro context. However, broadly speaking, political risk refers to the risk an investment's return could suffer as a result of political decisions, changes, or instability. This type of risk is well and alive both here and abroad.

In 2006, you may remember this, the Government of Canada seemingly out of the blue announced a 31.5% tax on income trust distributions to take effect in 2011. That announcement, which was not easily determinable in advance of the announcement, eliminated billions in personal wealth overnight once the stock market got hold of the income trust stock prices the day after the announcement. Investors (many of whom were seniors) had been flocking to investments in this category due to tax advantages as well as the need for more income in a low-interest-rate environment and got royally screwed by their own government. I remember sitting in a meeting that day, with a number of high-profile, politically linked types, and they were all taken aback by the announcement and the impact.

When it comes to political risk, while there are a couple of ways you can manage your exposure, eliminating it is not something that can be done via any reasonable actions. The first is to diversify across and within asset classes and jurisdictions. It is impossible to know how political manoeuvring will impact any given investment or investment class, so the first thing you need to ensure is that you are not at risk due to overconcentration. The second way to deal with this risk is through your time frame. If you keep an appropriately long-term vision with your investments that are most at risk to political shenanigans, then you will likely have time to recover, if not prosper, in any new reality that emerges. In the world of investing, time is often the great saviour.

Liquidity Risk. Liquidity refers to the ability to enter or exit a position lickety-split without dramatically affecting the market price. Many if not most stocks have a substantial trade volume on any given day and thus a transaction can usually be made when there is a tight spread (the spread is the difference between the bid and ask price on a security; in a liquid market, the difference is small). If you are interested in Royal Bank, for instance, given that this stock trades multiple million shares on most trading days, the spread is usually a penny or so and there are lots of buy and sell orders generally in the queue. RY (Royal Bank's trading symbol) is a very liquid stock.

The easy way to manage liquidity risk is to invest in securities that have an active and steady market. Another way to manage liquidity risk is to ensure that you have an adequately sufficient time frame before you need to sell any given investment. If you give yourself enough time, you will substantially increase the odds of getting a price that reasonably resembles the underlying value of the investment.

Systematic Risk. This is a risk that is inherent with investing, period. Diversification within an asset class does nothing to help because it is something that affects all investments within the class. It is a cost of entry.

The most effective actions you can take to soothe the impact of systematic risk are to ensure your time frame is sufficiently long to allow you to ride out any downturn, and to ensure that you have sufficient diversification across asset classes. If you are able to keep the investment intact while it experiences a depressed price, and sell only once it has recovered, then you are able to avoid a loss. That doesn't mean you might not have done better by using your money in a different manner, but time does reduce the risk of significant loss due to systematic risk. This is why you need to understand what your cash flow needs are in the near- and mid-term before you commit to an investment that may require a long-term commitment to realize its expected value.

Equity Investment Risk Management

By way of summary, the stock market is something that often pays off over short holding periods but almost always pays off over long holding periods. Most of the risks that are tied to stock market investments can be managed through proper diversification and time frame management. Volatility is the traditional way that risk is measured in financial markets. Diversification reduces volatility by combining assets that have low, no, or negative correlation to one another. Through properly combining different asset classes, it is possible to not only reduce the volatility of a portfolio, but also increase the return of the portfolio; presto, the best of both worlds! By extending the holding period of a portfolio, the day-to-day volatility becomes less important from a risk-management perspective.

If you do a good job of understanding your risk tolerance, then design and implement a properly diversified asset allocation in accordance with your investment time frame, your capacity to absorb the risks inherent in the stock market are greatly enhanced.

CHAPTER 18 – FIXED INCOME

In the current low-interest-rate environment, two of the main asset categories available to investors, fixed income securities and cash, have lost considerable lustre. However, each still plays an important role in ensuring an investment portfolio is properly diversified and prudently structured to move toward goal achievement and protect wealth.

Fixed income securities are generally any type of investment under which a borrower (or issuer) is obliged to make payments of a fixed amount on a fixed schedule. This sounds pretty straightforward. But, as with most everything in the world of finance, volumes can and have been written delving into the unique risk/return characteristics embodied within this asset category and how those characteristics behave within an investment portfolio.

If you feel you want to read more on this topic once you are done with this chapter, a really good, succinct book discussing the bond market has been written by Hank Cunningham, entitled *In Your Best Interest*.[1] Hank does a great job of walking through the breadth of the topic in just over 200 pages.

Fixed Income Investment Products

There are three fixed income investments commonly held within a portfolio:

- Bonds
- Debentures
- Guaranteed income certificates

Each of these securities has the obligation to pay a fixed amount according to a fixed schedule. The associated payments are comprised of interest, which can be paid over time or at maturity, as well as the face value of the instrument at maturity. Bonds and debentures can be held individually or within a mutual fund or exchange-traded fund.

The difference between a debenture and a bond is the manner in which the underlying liability is secured. In the case of a *debenture*, the liability is secured by the general credit of the issuer; whereas, a *bond* is typically secured by specified assets. The use of these terms is somewhat confusing in that virtually all government bonds are actually debentures because they, in most instances, are secured by the government's authority to tax the citizenry as opposed to specified assets.

Marketable vs. Non-Marketable Fixed Income Securities

The distinction between marketable and non-marketable fixed income securities is relatively straightforward. Marketable fixed income securities are those that you can sell prior to their stated maturity date; non-marketable fixed income securities cannot be resold.

The piece of this that is essential for fixed income investors to understand clearly is that, while a marketable fixed income security can be bought and sold prior to maturity, the features of that fixed income security remain constant over the course of its life. The interest rate specified for the security remains the same, the maturity date for the security remains the same, and any special features attached to the security—you guessed it—remain the same. The security remains the same, but it is trading in a market that is constantly changing. Depending on how the market changes, the security will become either more or less attractive to potential investors. The only way the security can remain liquid in this reality is to have its price adjust to the supply and demand characteristics of the market.

If an investor purchases and holds a fixed income security until it matures, they know precisely what the payment stream is designed to look like over the course of the security's life. If, on the other hand, the investor purchases a marketable fixed income security, and they choose to sell it before maturity, the return they realize from the instrument will be influenced by market forces and it may result in a very different value than was originally expected based on the face value and embedded interest rate.

Fixed Income Securities – A Closer Look

While there are several characteristics that are common across the family of fixed income securities, there are also many features that can be unique to any given issue. The most common holdings found in a fixed income portfolio include:

- Federal Government Bonds. The federal government is a huge participant in the bond market. It issues long-term and short-term securities, and real return securities, as well as strip bonds (more on these last two in a moment).
- Provincial Government Bonds. All of the provinces are major players in the fixed income market. They each offer a wide variety of maturities and features.
- Municipal Government Bonds. Many of the large, as well as some of the not so large municipalities also look to the fixed income market and offer a variety of investment options.
- Corporate Bonds and Debentures. Many large, medium, and even small corporations rely on some level of debt financing within their capital structure. The credit worthiness of corporations ranges widely as do the interest rates and features offered within their bond and debenture issues.

- Guaranteed Investment Certificates. Many banks, credit unions, and *caisse populaires* issue GICs as a means of attracting capital that they then turn around and re-lend to their customers or members.
- Zero Coupon Bonds. These are a class of fixed income security that have a different cash flow structure. There is no periodic interest payment; rather, they trade at a discount to their face value. The level of the discount, combined with the term to maturity, allows the investor to calculate the implied interest rate.
- Real Return Bonds. A real return bond is a bond that pays a rate of return that is periodically adjusted to reflect inflation.
- International Bonds and Debentures. These are bonds and debentures emanating from issuers resident in foreign countries—US, emerging markets, etc.
- High-Yield or Junk Bonds and Debentures. These securities are IOUs, issued by non-investment-grade lenders (investment ratings will be discussed shortly).
- Convertible Bonds and Debentures. Convertibles are fixed income instruments that contain a feature that gives the investor the option to exchange the security for shares of the issuer.
- Structured Fixed Income Products. This is a catch-all category that includes securities with a wide variety of features such as mortgage backed securities, structured notes, asset-backed securities, principal-protected notes, etc.
- Fixed Income Mutual funds. These are mutual funds that invest in a portfolio of fixed income securities.
- Fixed Income Exchange-Traded Funds. These are ETFs that invest in a portfolio of fixed income securities.

The fact that fixed income products have in recent years been generating lower returns than they did over the past couple of decades does not diminish the importance of this asset class, nor does it mean that you do not need to develop a well-thought-out investment plan for this segment of your portfolio. In fact, it is quite the opposite. If you do not pay due attention to managing the fees and risks embedded within the fixed income products you select, your overall portfolio performance is likely to suffer noticeably.

In the current low-interest-rate environment, it is no longer possible to simply invest in a fixed income mutual fund, pay a 1.5% (or higher) annual management expense ratio, and realize a healthy return. You now need to work a little harder and pay more attention to the details because it is the details that will determine your success or failure within this segment of your portfolio.

Rating Agencies

One of the general principles of investing is the greater the risk you take, the greater the return potential you should expect. In the world of fixed income instruments, rating agencies look at the financial health of an issuer and determine a credit rating based on their assessment of how likely an investor is to receive the payment stream promised by a debt-based investment.

The better the rating an issuer is able to achieve, generally, the lower the yield they will offer on their debt instruments. This makes perfect sense because if you are very likely to receive what is promised you in terms of interest and principal, you will not require as much incentive to make the loan as you would in a situation where the return promised is less certain. As a result, the interest rate you receive from a federal government bond will be lower than the interest rate you will receive from a bond with similar characteristics issued by a corporation.

There are three main bond rating agencies in Canada: Moody's, Standard & Poor's, and Dominion Bond Rating Service. Each has a slightly different rating system, though they are all designed to convey their assessment of the issuer's ability to repay debt obligations and therein the issuer's credit worthiness.

Table 2, below, illustrates the rating categories used by the three rating agencies. The table does not replicate exactly the terminology used by each agency in describing credit worthiness, nor the full granularity of the ratings, but it does capture the essence. There are generally four "investment grade" rating categories and a variety of more speculative rating categories.

Table 2: Comparison of Rating Agencies and Rating Categories.

CREDIT WORTHINESS	DBRS	MOODY'S	STANDARD & POOR'S
Highest Quality	AAA	Aaa	AAA
High/Superior Quality	AA	Aa1, Aa2, Aa3	AA+, AA, AA-
Upper Medium/Good	A	A1, A2, A3	A+, A, A-
Medium/Adequate	BBB	Baa1, Baa2, Baa3	BBB+, BBB, BBB-
Speculative Lower Grade	BB	B1, B2, B3	B+, B, B-
Highly Speculative	B	Caa1	CCC+
Very Highly Speculative	CCC, CC, C	Caa2, Caa3	CCC, CCC-
Bankruptcy/In default	D	Ca/C	DDD, DD, D

For more information on the precise meaning and differentiating features of the rating categories and subcategories, all rating agencies offer very detailed and informative websites.

As an individual investor, it is very important that you consider not just the interest rate associated with any given fixed income investment, but also the likelihood you will receive the full money stream promised. I personally would never purchase an individual bond or debenture rated below what is considered to be investment grade. When I do venture into the lower rating territory, I use a portfolio approach through a low-cost exchange-traded fund or mutual fund. (High-yield bond funds invest primarily in bonds that are rated BBB and lower.)

In the wake of the subprime crisis, there has been significant scrutiny of the role of rating agencies and the conflict of interest embedded in their compensation structure. Regulations have been strengthened as a result. My personal opinion is that where there is a link between compensation and any rating work being performed, the investor must act with due caution, though to ignore the rating agency opinions in totality would be foolish. If you haven't already, you might find reading *The Big Short* [2](by Michael Lewis), or watching the movie by the same name, to be an interesting adventure into the subprime crisis and in particular the role that the rating agencies in the US played.

The Yield Curve

The yield curve is a graph that visually demonstrates the yield available on fixed income instruments plotted against their associated maturity date. In a normal yield curve environment, the slope of the curve is positive, meaning that the longer the time frame covered by the debt instrument the higher the interest rate it will command. This stands to reason because there is greater risk with a longer-term loan (more can change or go wrong for the lender in a longer time frame), so the interest rate in normal circumstances will reflect this risk/return relationship.

An increasing yield/maturity date relationship is almost always evident with the GICs that are offered by your local credit union. The rate offered on the one-year GIC will almost certainly be slightly less than that offered on the two-year GIC, which will almost certainly be lower than the rate offered on the five-year GIC.

There are times when the yield curve becomes inverted or flat, or portions of the yield curve are inverted or flat (i.e., where shorter-term interest rates are higher or equal to longer-term interest rates). In fact, the yield curve is almost always changing shape to reflect the opinions of market participants regarding a variety of economic conditions and expectations.

I tend not to make dramatic changes to my investment strategy based on what the yield curve is doing. I will, however, direct any new money dedicated to the fixed income portion of my portfolio into shorter terms when longer-term rates do not adequately compensate for the additional risk inherent in longer holding periods. (I just don't see the value in locking-in for several more years if the return differential does not properly compensate for the added term.) Generally, though, there is a sufficiently positive slope to the yield curve to allow me to follow my fixed income investment strategy without modification. (More on that later.)

LARRY WILSON

Risks of Investing in the Fixed Income Market (Boring Alert)

Before getting into the individual risks that an investor in fixed income instruments must consider, I first want to discuss very briefly some of the basic principles of bond price movement and the various sources of volatility inherent in fixed income pricing. I'm sure many of you will feel that this discussion is not brief enough, as the read can be a little tough. I think it is worth slogging through, with apologies at the outset.

I am continually surprised by the general lack of understanding related to some of the basic concepts of finance. For instance, there is an ad running on television currently (for a robo-advisor) that shows a young investor, in somewhat of a panic, because he is unsure of how to approach investing. (I hate how investment firms use insecurity and uncertainty to draw-in business.) The young man who is the subject of this commercial is shown getting advice from anyone and everyone. He clearly is confused and doesn't know who he should be listening to; he maintains a dumfounded look on his face throughout the entire commercial. In one scene of this particular commercial, there is an older gentleman who offers up the opinion "interest rates, they are rising." Just a short sequence later, the same gentleman is suggesting that bonds are the place to invest. Well, if interest rates are increasing, is the price of a bond going to increase? No. Exactly the opposite will occur, all else remaining equal. Maybe this is the point of the commercial, but that pisses me off every time I see it because I think it reinforces the exact wrong relationship between interest rate movements and bond price reactions. Generally, I dislike all commercials. They get in the way of enjoying a hockey game or delay seeing who has been voted off the island, but I really dislike them when they reinforce people's insecurity while trying to attract their business.

As we move more deeply into this topic, it is important to keep in mind what a bond is—it is a capital loan made to an issuer that results in the investor receiving an IOU from the issuer that includes a series of interest payments and a repayment of principal. This loan is made for a specified period of time and the interest rate embedded in the payment stream is set at the time the loan is made.

The nature of the underlying cash flow is important to keep in mind because the interest rate available in the marketplace is not set for any length of time; rather, it is continually changing. With each change in the interest rate in the marketplace, there is a corresponding change in the value of a pre-set series of cash flows. If interest rates in the market increase, then the value associated with a set stream of payments will decrease. On the other hand, if the interest rate were to fall, a stream of payments based on a higher-interest-rate structure will command a higher purchase price. Thus, there is an inverse relationship between interest rate movements and the value of a fixed income instrument, all else remaining equal.

The amount by which the point-in-time value of a set stream of payments changes with a change in interest rates is dependent on the length of time over which the payment stream is scheduled to remain in place, the composition of that stream of payments (how much and when), and the amount of the change in the interest rate. In general, the price volatility of a fixed income instrument increases as:

- The maturity date extends into the future. This means that the interest payment stream goes on for a longer period of time and the time until the repayment of the principal is well out there. The more extended this payment stream becomes, the more the current-day price of that payment stream will respond to a change in interest rates. A longer term means more volatility, which means more risk if you need to sell that instrument before maturity.
- The interest payment element of the stream declines. The lower the interest rate embedded in the fixed income instrument, the lower the importance of the periodic payment stream becomes relative to the principal repayment amount; thus, the longer it takes to repatriate your money, on average. The overall value of the payment stream, being more dependent on the repayment of capital that happens at the maturity date, adds volatility to the investment. So the less dependent your return is on the interest payments embedded within the product, the more volatile the current market price becomes with a change in interest rates.

The measure used within the industry to describe the vulnerability of a fixed income investment to a change in interest rates is referred to as *duration*. Duration is a measurement of how long, in years, it takes for the price of a bond to be repaid by its internal cash flows. It takes into account the relative size of the interest payment stream and the time until you receive the principal repayment promised. The longer the duration associated with your fixed income instrument, the more it will react to a change in interest rates.

A long duration instrument will react violently to a change in interest rates. If interest rates decline, the reaction will look nice on your investment statement and the longer the duration, the nicer it will look. If interest rates increase, the reaction will look bad on your investment statement and the longer the duration of your fixed income portfolio, the worse it will look.

HHHHHHHHHHHHHHHHHHHHH. Oops, just fell asleep with my nose on the keyboard. Sorry for that venture into the deep hole of boring, but I really think it is something that is important to know—perhaps the most important concept you need to grasp when it comes to fixed income investing. I'm sure some of you read through it thinking, *Hey, this is cool*. If not, just be thankful that I didn't get into the math. (But if you are one of the people who thought this was cool, by all means, do some further research into the math!)

When going through the many courses I have taken in my quest to educate myself about all things important in the world of personal financial planning, I had to learn how to do the duration calculations with my trusty little non-programmable calculator. Who knows, maybe getting this calculation right was the deciding point that won me the gold medal in the Canadian Securities Course. I used some of the prize money from that win to buy a membership at the short-game (golf) facility close to my place of work so I could go over at lunch and work on my sand saves. Similar to the concept of duration, the farther I find myself bunkered from the hole, the more infrequently I am able to manage an up and down and the more volatility I see in the end result. With practice, I figured I would be able to tame that volatility a little and become more predictable from the sand. Sadly, it wasn't to be. I am still just as likely to skull it across the green and into the water, as always … but I digress.

There are five main sources of risk that generally reside within the fixed income segment of a portfolio. Given the wide array of different fixed income products, each risk will be more or less influential depending on the characteristics of the particular security. The five main risk areas include the following.

Interest Rate Risk. As we have already discussed, the market value of a fixed interest product is inversely related to interest rate movements. What that means is an increase in interest rates will, all else remaining equal, reflect negatively on the market value of a fixed income security, and a decrease in interest rates will, all else remaining equal, positively affect the market value of a fixed income security. The longer the duration of a fixed income investment, the greater the reaction to a change in the prevailing interest rate will be.

Credit Risk. This is the risk that the party to whom the capital was lent does not pay the interest and/or principal in accordance with the terms of the fixed income security. The rating agencies, through their evaluation of credit worthiness of various borrowers, provide their opinion as to the degree of certainty an investor can place on the payment terms of the security being respected throughout its life. Fixed income products sourced from issuers with lower ratings have to compete harder for your investment dollars by increasing the embedded interest rate they offer.

Currency Risk. This risk is present if your fixed income security is denominated in a foreign currency.

Maturity and Reinvestment Risk. This is the risk that the interest rate will be lower when you receive cash from a holding (interest payments or principal upon maturity) and therefore are not able to reinvest the funds in another security with terms that are as favourable as the investment from which the interest or principal payment flowed.

Liquidity Risk. Liquidity risk is the risk that there isn't a market for a fixed income instrument willing to pay a fair price at the time the holder wants to sell it. Some fixed income instruments, like GICs, are designed to be illiquid. For most bonds and debentures, there is a huge secondary market willing to take an issue off your hands, even if you have a sizable holding. However, if you are holding a debt instrument from a less-well-known issuer, or it has characteristics that are not appealing to market participants looking to buy, then it is possible to run into a situation where it is difficult to get a fair price. In 2008, in the midst of the asset-backed securities saga, there was no market for certain debt instruments because no one could determine what a fair value was for them. Liquidity dried up.

Fixed Income Investment Risk Management

In my opinion, the best way to manage the risk inherent in the fixed income portion of your portfolio is to develop and stick to an investment policy that is designed in recognition of the various risks and responds to them in a prudent and consistent fashion. As with any form of investment, you will never eliminate risk altogether, but you can manage the risk in a manner that is suitable for your personal situation.

My approach to fixed income investing includes the following elements:

1. Focus the fixed income portfolio on the purchase of several individual investment grade bonds or debentures with the intention of holding them to maturity. (You can do this with GICs, too, but GICs are limited in that they have short lifespans, and while your intention is to hold to maturity, no liquidity.)

    - By using several investment grade bonds, credit risk is reduced through diversifying the holdings among issuers, thereby reducing the level of dependence on any one security or issuer.
    - The use of individual bonds held to maturity allows an investor to know exactly what the maturity value and interest payments (if any) will be with certainty in the absence of a credit event. If an investor's intention was to sell the security before maturity, they would be exposed to several types of risk. If, rather than individual bonds, a mutual fund or an exchange-traded fund is purchased, that security never matures; thus, you have no certainty around what the value of the investment will be when you need it.

- Fees are kept to a minimum. Buying a bond and holding it to maturity results in paying a commission upon purchase, and nothing more over the course of the holding period.
- If there is a need to sell a bond before the maturity date, for any reason, the bond market is extremely liquid for investment grade securities. If a sale is undertaken, then the investor is exposed to what the market is willing to pay for the security at the time of the sale, but it is always an option.

2. Focus on a slightly lower rating of investment grade bonds to gain a yield advantage.

   - Given the extremely low yield offered by federal government bonds one strategy is to avoid them in favour of provincial or municipal bonds or sometimes those of a major financial institution or utility.
   - Personally, I never invest in individual bonds rated BBB or lower.

3. Use strip bonds as the foundation of the investment program (and hold them to maturity). This works best in a registered account.

   - Strip bonds are bonds that have just a single payment, which takes place upon maturity. This eliminates reinvestment risk across the holding period as there are no cash flows that need to be reinvested. This also means that the fluctuation in value of the holding can be substantial because there are no interest payments to smooth out the impact of changes in interest rates. Remember the discussion about duration? A strip bond's duration exactly equals the length of time until maturity because there are no interest payments. This makes them more volatile, a feature that can be managed by ensuring that the investor is not in a position where they need to sell the holding before it matures. Thus, while marketable strip bonds can be sold, the intention and investment plan is designed to hold each and every bond to maturity, thereby locking-in a result at the time of purchase.

- Clearly, if you rely on cash flow from your bonds, then you may choose a different strategy that generates a more regular, less lumpy, flow of cash.

4. Invest primarily in domestic currency bonds. Any investment in foreign currency bonds would be designed to meet cash flows that are expected to be required in that foreign currency.

    - Exposure to currency fluctuation is eliminated by matching the currency inflows to expected currency usage.

5. Use an investment grade bond ladder (supplemented, where appropriate, with GICs).

    - A bond *ladder* is simply a strategy whereby an investor determines the total value they want to invest in fixed income instruments, the period of time they want the fixed income portfolio to cover, and selects regularly spaced maturities of roughly equal value over that period of time. When a holding matures, it is reinvested in the longest part of the maturity spectrum defined in the ladder strategy (because at that point the longest-term investment in the portfolio has moved forward by an equivalent period of time).
    - Personally, I use a ten-year ladder, which means I have bonds of approximately equal value maturing every year over a ten-year period. When the one-year bond matures, it is reinvested in a ten-year bond … and this process goes on consistently over time. This allows me to take advantage of the higher rates offered by a normal yield curve.
    - This strategy also ensures that I have a bond, or series of bonds, maturing every year, which takes the guesswork out of interest rates and smooths out the average interest rate embedded in the portfolio.

6. Use investment grade real return bonds for a designated proportion of the portfolio to provide an element of inflation protection.

- Use a low-cost ETF or MF; it is much easier than purchasing individual real return bonds. *Low cost* is essential.

7. If high-yield bonds offer rates far superior to investment grade bonds, a predetermined maximum weighting of the fixed income allocation of the portfolio can be dedicated to a high-yield bond MF or ETF.

    - Because of the risk associated with high-yield bonds, proper diversification is essential. Investing in a low-cost MF or ETF makes sense, in this circumstance.

8. Never invest in structured products such as principal-protected notes.

    - These securities are marketed as a financial instrument that will make your dreams come true with low risk. Generally, all they do is shelter you from exposure to meaningful gains because their structure is laden with fees. Don't do it. If it sounds too good to be true …

So that is my fixed income strategy in a nutshell. The core component of the strategy is a ten-year investment grade strip bond ladder. This is supplemented with a meaningful allocation to both real return bonds and high-yield bonds through low-cost ETFs.

CHAPTER 19 – CASH

The cash asset class consists of currency and liquid short-term securities that have a highly predictable and stable market value. It includes essentially anything that can be converted into face value in short order.

When it comes to cash, there are two distinct investment aspects that need to be taken into account: cash as an emergency fund and cash as an asset allocation classification.

Cash as an Emergency Fund

The extent of emergency you need to be prepared for ranges from the not so expensive to the very expensive. An event that can be funded through adjusting how you manage your excess cash flow for a short period of time is not a big planning concern. Things that are unexpected and slightly expensive, like a red light camera ticket, bailing your first-born out of jail, the deductible for an insurance policy claim and all of the many and varied surprises of a modest quantum are just "life." You should strive to organize your financial affairs such that your budget is able to absorb these little surprises in short order.

Financial emergencies that you need foresight to handle—such as a new roof for your house, a new furnace because yours went for a crap in the middle of winter, your basement floods and you find out that the source of the water or water-like substance (nooooo, not a water-like substance!!) is not covered by your home owners insurance policy, etc. These are events that call for a reasonably substantial pile of cash and need to be dealt with quickly.

Then there are the big financial emergencies, like losing your job, suffering a substantial uninsured or underinsured loss, having your significant other do something incredibly stupid that leaves your finances in complete and utter disarray, etc. This level of emergency can call for a much larger resource allocation.

So should you plan for a new-roof-sized fund or the walk-to-the-elevator-we'll-send-your-stuff-later-sized fund? Do you need to accumulate a couple grand, ten grand, or forty grand? If we knew the answer to this question, the planning becomes much easier, but we don't.

My approach to the emergency fund conundrum is as follows:

1. Use insurance prudently to eliminate the need to worry about certain types of emergencies. Generally those things with low likelihood of occurrence but high financial consequence are where you should consider insurance. Death, disability, fire, theft, health, and employment are the sorts of things where you should consider inviting insurance into your financial strategy.

    One of the most important activities you can undertake that acts as a form of insurance, and doesn't involve a recurring premium, is to continually enhance your marketable skills. If you are readily employable, then the income risk inherent with any job is much more manageable in a timely fashion. If you are not readily employable, and have a high risk of job loss, this should factor heavily into how big of an emergency fund you target.

2. For many of the smaller-scale financial emergencies I believe the *live within your means* philosophy should provide sufficient coverage. The more able you are to engage a lifestyle that can be scaled to a change in your means, the more flexibility you allow yourself to adapt as challenges present themselves. If you insist on living close to the edge, your need for emergency fund access is much greater.

    If you structure substantial expenses into your lifestyle—such as excessive lease payments because you have too much vehicle, high mortgage payments because you have too much house, any of a variety of other consumer debt repayment responsibilities, memberships at expensive clubs, etc.—your ability to adapt becomes much reduced. Organizing your lifestyle to have excess cash flow is a wonderful safety blanket to have in place.

3. Over time, save up $5,000–$20,000 that is kept in a readily available form of investment. (The size of the fund really depends on the nature of your particular exposures.) This fund would be invested in something accessible, like a cashable GIC, a high-interest savings account, or something along those lines. This pot of money is sufficient to help with situations like the hot water tank springing a leak, the water main break that happens on your property, your dashboard lighting up the day after your warranty expires, etc. If you have a more substantial risk profile, then you need to establish a more substantial emergency fund.

   But, if (this is a big "if") you can truly identify what qualifies as an emergency and have the means and willpower to quickly pay back a loan, then you could rely on a smaller-sized fund and do #4.

4. Arrange for a line of credit sufficient to cover off the likely maximum value of an emergency you feel is within the realm of planning applicable to your circumstances.

   A good idea to ensure there is sober second thought related to accessing this line of credit would be to have a trusted friend or family member act as a secondary signing authority over the account to ensure they agree with your definition of *emergency*. You and your trusted clear-thinker should have a heart-to-heart before setting up the loan facility to decide the parameters that define what constitutes an emergency. This pre-thought ensures that you are on the same page before a crisis hits and the thinking process gets murky and/or emotive. I'm not sure that everyone has a friend or family member that would be willing to take this on, but if you do, it would likely be a useful avenue for ensuring your rationalization process is authentic.

One point to emphasize is that you really need to be disciplined when it comes to the definition of what constitutes an emergency. For example:

- Going on vacation is never an emergency, no matter how cold winter becomes or how unbearable your boss is acting.
- Attending a destination wedding does not constitute an emergency.
- Finding money for Winnipeg Jets season tickets is not an emergency.
- Buying a show horse (or whatever they are called) because your daughter wants to be an equestrian is not an emergency.

All of these non-emergencies need to be dealt with in the normal course of your financial planning and their relative importance must be driven by the goals you have set out in your plan. That means you save enough to pay for them outright and when you have the cash, and when the priority is on that particular expenditure, you consume your reward. At that point in time, you have earned the right to spend because you have done so with appropriate thought and planning. Have a blast.

Often, I read about the idea of building an emergency fund equal to six to twelve months of salary or living expenses. That is a pile of wealth just sitting there, doing little to improve your financial standing. I fully agree with the need to make arrangements so that you are able to deal with emergencies when they arise, but saving up tens of thousands of dollars and investing it at an extremely low interest rate seems like a drastic step to take. It may be the right step in your circumstances, if your risk profile demands, but a year's worth of salary isn't necessary for everybody.

The decision with regard to an emergency fund and cash in general is a very personal one, and is dependent on your specific circumstances. You need to consider the nature and likelihood of the risks you have to manage, the stability of your employment, and the size and nature of your net worth. Is it realistic that you could lose your job, or is that highly unlikely? Do you rent your place and are therefore less concerned about those house-related surprises? Are you the kind of person who would rationalize that a trip to the Dominican Republic is in fact an emergency? (After all, your great-great-grandmother-in-law via your first wife is buried there.)

The bottom line is that if you are at risk, then you need to design an appropriate strategy to deal with your liquidity obligations. Part of that may be an emergency fund in cash, a line of credit, or simply available wealth readily convertible into cash sufficient to offset any emergency that is reasonably likely to arise. Ultimately, getting yourself into the position where your net worth is sufficient to manage any emergency that comes your way (when combined with a well-designed insurance plan) is what your goal should be.

To summarize, there is no reliable formula to define a specific dollar amount everyone should retain as an emergency fund. The fund you decide on must be tailored to your situation. You need to look at the non-insured risks confronting you and define a strategy that can respond in a timely and fulsome manner. This is a great discussion to have with a fee-for-service financial planner if you find it perplexing.

F*ck Off Fund[1]

This is a special form of emergency fund. Both of my children have started one of these funds ... but we call it a freedom fund.

It is absolutely essential that you give yourself financial options in the event that you find yourself in an abusive or otherwise unmanageable relationship, be that with your significant other, your employer, or some other situation. Even strong independent men and women can find themselves backed into a corner, with limited options, if they do not have readily available, short-term financial means. When building your approach to an emergency fund, make sure you take a very personal inventory of your exposures and think through the "what if" scenarios. Have a plan and design the financial capacity (cash and credit) to implement the plan should the unthinkable happen.

My wife was friends with a married couple, and one day the husband walked out of the marriage, completely blindsiding his wife. She never saw it coming, never. So when thinking of the "what-ifs," it is a good idea to think outside of the box and be financially prepared.

If you have taken an inventory of the risks in your situation and see the potential for needing to make a big move if your work or personal relationships take a turn, then it is vital that you have a financial cushion available to allow you to turn your plan into action in short order. You don't want to find yourself in a position where you need to accept what is happening to you because you don't have the financial wherewithal to make a change. Your f*ck off fund will give you options that you might not otherwise have.

Cash as an Asset Allocation Category

It is my belief that if you have a sufficient investment portfolio, or sufficient net worth that you can readily turn into cash within a short period of time, then you likely do not need to allocate a specific portion of your portfolio to cash. Having said that, I don't need to allocate any portion of my investment portfolio to cash, *but I do anyway*. I like to have cash available in the event that a really good investment opportunity comes along. I also like to have cash for the reduced volatility that it provides to my portfolio. It suits my level of risk aversion to have a reasonable amount of our family net worth in cash.

Defining and holding cash as a strategic portion of your asset allocation is a personal decision and it needs to be thought of in terms of your overall financial situation. If you are at higher risk of needing cash due to your position in life, then you should decide how much to hold and stick to it (this may be described by a specific dollar amount or more generally as a percentage of your investment portfolio). If you can make do with a line of credit, and have other assets and cash inflows that provide the capacity to replenish the line of credit very quickly, then this approach may work for you and an allotment of cash via your designated asset allocation may not be necessary.

My target is, and always has been, to keep 5–10% of my portfolio in cash. As conditions warrant, I may go on either side of that, but not without having thought through my reasoning. For many people, this is too much wealth to allocate to an asset class that will not produce much, if any, real return. With current interest rates where they are, and inflation where it is, if taxes are applicable to earnings on your cash, you will most certainly be looking at a negative real return on this asset class.

Cash is the investment category that provides a feeling of security for most people; that is its value as opposed to a financial return of value. When deciding on an appropriate allocation for cash, it is important to try to put your feelings aside and look realistically at your financial needs and risks to define the right cash balance. From that point, you can then consider the psychology and increase your holding if it makes sense to you. One thing you don't want to do is work yourself into a situation where you need cash and don't have sufficient liquidity designed into your options.

Your cash allocation holds a unique position in your portfolio. It is an investment class, but as such it offers little return potential. However, cash is very useful and valuable as a form of insurance and source of peace of mind; as such, it deserves a considered plan.

CHAPTER 20 – ALTERNATIVE INVESTMENTS

Most of the investment possibilities included within this asset class are probably not for you. I was originally going to ignore alternative investments but given how much effort is devoted to trying to get people to invest in them, I thought I should give them a little space. This is a tricky asset class to discuss because the individual investments included within this broad classification do not necessarily have much in common with each other and their risk and return characteristics are also asset specific.

An alternative investment is an asset that tends not to fit neatly within one of the conventional asset classes. Alternative investments include a wide variety of things such as private equity, hedge funds, managed futures, commodities, currencies, derivatives contracts, art, precious metals, rare coins, wine, antiques, venture capital, real estate, infrastructure, distressed securities, and a variety of other odds and ends. Many, if not most, of the alternative investment category assets possess characteristics that make their appropriateness for the general investing population (i.e., non-expert) questionable.

One of the key principles that every investor should abide by is to stick to investments they fully understand. The average investor generally does not have a sufficient understanding of most investments that fit under the alternative investment banner nor the capacity to engage the specialists that do. The average individual investor is at a huge disadvantage when it comes to investing in much of this asset class.

The most famous hedge fund collapse that I am aware of was that of Long-Term Capital Management. It was run by some of the best and brightest financial minds in the world. It boasted no less than two Nobel Prize-winning economists who were members of the Board of Directors. How could their strategy possibly go wrong with all of this highly decorated, prime grey matter designing their investment strategies and computer models? Well, after a few years of very successful operation, along came an ill-timed big bet on Russian government bonds and the losses mounted to the point where a bail out had to be orchestrated by the government of the United States. Can you realistically expect yourself to assess this type of investment?

Alternative Investment Risks

Keeping in mind that this is a broad category and the risk characteristics can be very different from one investment to the next, a quick summary of several key risk areas that you are likely to experience within alternative investments includes the following.

Complexity. These investments tend to be hard to understand and when it comes time to file your taxes, you will likely venture into lines on the T1 and supporting schedules that were previously only thought to be there for visual effect. Read all of the available marketing and securities materials, understand them, and carefully consider if the investment is right for you. If you don't understand something about the investment, before you invest, figure it out.

Lack of Liquidity, part I. With many of these investments, especially if they are packaged in some sort of wrapper like principal protection, there is no active secondary market. This will often mean you can't sell the investment before maturity. If you are considering an alternative investment, be sure to take a hard look at the liquidity profile of the investment and what your needs for liquidity could be to see if there is a match.

Lack of Liquidity, part II. Even if there appears to be a secondary market, you need to critically consider if it will be there when you need it. There are lots of listed investments that have very little sales volume and a considerable bid/ask spread. If there are redemption privileges associated with the investment, keep in mind that the underlying assets need to be sufficiently liquid to allow redemptions. For instance, there are many instances where funds are pooled and invested in assets that are in and of themselves illiquid (a few large properties, a series of venture capital projects, etc.). In cases like this, it is not uncommon for a promoter to freeze redemptions if there are too many requests for the managers to honour at any given time. They are forced to do this because they cannot sell the underlying assets to meet the redemption requests.

Lack of Transparency. Many investments within this space are made available to *accredited investors* only. Where this is the case, the nature of the information provided to prospective investors is less fulsome than it is for more broadly marketed investments.

Commissions and Other Embedded Costs. Where commissions are high, your chances of making money diminish. Make sure you understand the commission/cost structure before you make any commitment; controlling fees is a big determinant of the ultimate success of any investment.

Leverage. Borrowed money will magnify results on both sides of the return equation. Even if your contribution is from capital that you have accumulated, that does not mean that the underlying investment is not relying on significant leverage. If leverage is involved, and you are locked into an investment because it is illiquid, how do you think you will feel if you start to see the value of the investment slide and you have no viable option to get out?

Where an Alternative Investment is Appropriate

Having issued the above warnings, there are certain types of alternative investments that are more widely appropriate than others, as well as certain situations where an alternative investment option may fit nicely into an investment portfolio for an average investor.

1. If you are in a position of specialized knowledge.

    Advanced knowledge gets you past many of the risks discussed above and allows you to determine, more accurately, what the odds of success are and what potential failure would look like. If that picture is clear to you and the asset fits into your investment strategy, then it may be reasonable to participate.

2. If you can afford to lose the whole balance you are intending to invest in the asset without it unduly impacting the achievement of your goals.

    When people invested in Long-Term Capital Management, they envisioned indefinitely collecting the excess returns that the fund delivered in the first few years. According to *Wikipedia*,[1] the fund returned 21%, 43%, and 41% respectively in each of its first three years. (Wow! Sign me up!) However, they followed that successful start with a loss of $4.6 billion in a period of four months when their strategy hit a "snag." The fund was eventually liquidated.

3. If you invest in one of these assets using an experienced manager and the form of security you are investing in is liquid, then you can reasonably consider an appropriately sized investment in the sector.

    Certain infrastructure mutual funds or ETFs fit this profile. Many real estate investment trusts (REITs) fit well within an individual's investment portfolio. If you are investing in REITs, make sure you consider how much you have already invested in real estate to ensure you remain properly diversified. For example, REITs are perfect for renters who want some exposure to the real estate market.

    Keep in mind, though, there have been a number of MFs and ETFs that venture into the waters of alternative investments that have not made a go of it. Unless the natural gas ETF, managed futures ETF, or other specialized offering attracts enough ongoing interest to make it profitable for the sponsor, it will be wound up and you may get little warning. When one of these funds gets wound up, it is almost certainly after a period of significant underperformance and is likely the exact wrong time to sell, but that is exactly what you will be doing.

4. If the investment you are considering will not cause you to be too concentrated.

If you have an investment that captures the Canadian equity market, for instance, you already have exposure to precious metal producers, agricultural commodities, REITs, engineering firms whose fortunes and stock prices live and die with infrastructure projects, etc. The exposure through a stock investment is not exactly the same as direct exposure to an underlying project or commodity, but generally there is a strong positive correlation between the two investments.

That's about it. Your investments can do fine without participating in the vast majority of this asset class in any significant way additional to the exposure you will already gain through the diversified equity portion of your portfolio. If you feel that you must proceed, do so in a measured way with due care and caution.

CHAPTER 21 – PORTFOLIO CONSTRUCTION AND MAINTENANCE

When building an investment portfolio, there are two important strategic decisions that need to be made:

1. How to divide the total investment value between asset classes
2. The specific investments to be utilized within each asset class

People make all kinds of mistakes at this stage of the investment process. It really is too bad to screw up at this point because the most difficult part of the investing equation has already been achieved … investment capital has been accumulated.

You have at this point conquered, at least to some extent, the compelling urge to spend. Maybe you have selected an adequate ride that gets you from point A to point B instead of leasing a G-Power Typhoon (I'm told it's an expensive Beamer). Perhaps you kicked a habit or two and have a stream of cash flow that is no longer destined for the bottom line of Altria, Guinness, Starbucks, or McDonalds. You might have done the math and determined that allocating $1.5 million to a 900 sq. ft. condo and its ongoing sizable maintenance fee made less sense for you than renting an equivalent-sized bachelor pad while you remain open to considering job opportunities in less expensive areas of Canada,

Europe, and Asia. It is making these kinds of decisions, the ones that impact your immediate lifestyle, that can easily trip you up and be the most difficult of the financial challenges to overcome. Compared to the challenge of actually accumulating investment capital, the task of devising a credible investment plan is relatively easy.

One key concept that an investor must get a handle on when devising a suitable investment portfolio is *diversification*.

Diversification

In order to be properly diversified, you need to hold a number of different stakes both within and across asset classes. If you don't pay attention to both pieces of this, you could be placing yourself in an unnecessarily precarious situation. Proper diversification acts like a financial life preserver by reducing reliance on any one piece of your investment portfolio.

Diversification within Equity Holdings

As previously covered, there are three popular ways to gain equity exposure within a portfolio:

1. Direct stock ownership
2. Equity-based mutual fund ownership
3. Equity-based exchange-traded fund ownership

If you favour direct stock ownership, proper diversification requires that you purchase stocks that reflect the global economy, crossing both sectors and countries. While this is possible, it will involve considerable work both to set up and manage. For most people, this path involves too much time, effort and expertise to properly design, implement, and maintain.

An efficient and effective way to achieve diversification in the equity portion of a portfolio is to utilize broadly diversified (index-based) mutual funds or exchange-traded funds. I favour exchange-traded funds because they are generally, and often significantly, less costly than mutual funds.

Most of the advice I have read over the years related to equity diversification suggests that a Canadian investor divide their equity allocation into three roughly equal-sized segments: Canadian equity, US equity, and international equity. Given that the Canadian equity market represents less than 3% of world market capitalization, and is highly concentrated in just a few sectors, substantial investment in global equity markets makes sense.

As an example of how a well-diversified equity portfolio can be established with the purchase of just two exchange-traded funds, an investor can look to the Vanguard or iShares families of exchange-traded funds (or one of the other large ETF management companies, for that matter). Both of these fund families offer a global equity fund that is reflective of a recognized and well-diversified market index. (This would take care of both the international and US portions of the investment—roughly half of the global fund is invested in US stocks.) The cost to purchase the ETF would be approximately $10. The management expense ratio (MER) associated with the global equity-based fund is under 0.3% annually (closer to 0.2%, actually). Both fund families also have a Canadian-based index fund, reflective of the capped capitalization-based S&P/TSX index, that can also be purchased at a transaction cost of $10; the MER associated with either of these funds is less than 0.1%.

Presto, you have purchased a position that is well-diversified across global equity markets, with just two transactions that cost you about $20 to buy and about a quarter of one percent annually to maintain.

You couldn't have done that a couple of decades ago!

Diversification within Fixed Income Holdings

With fixed income investing, you could follow the same sort of formula as above to gain diversification through either mutual funds or exchange-traded funds. However, as I previously stated, my preference is to invest in fixed income products that actually mature. Almost all fixed income mutual funds and ETFs never mature; thus, you don't know what their value will be when it comes time to sell. It is also my personal opinion that it is not as important to diversify fixed income holdings globally. Generally, you will be spending the currency of your home country, so investing in bonds or GICs from your home country that have an appropriate credit rating, and which will mature in accordance with your need for cash (or in a staged fashion over time), is a prudent course to follow.

The key to this piece of your portfolio is to invest across the yield curve, and to ensure that you actually get your money back, both in periodic and maturity payments (if you are using regular bonds/debentures), or at maturity (if you are using strip bonds/debentures) by focusing on investment grade products. This approach shields you from many of the significant risks that come with fixed income investing. In the current interest rate environment, fixed income products are not great at building wealth; their value is in protecting wealth. In order to preserve their wealth protection role, it is imperative that the investor sticks to guaranteed or investment grade offerings.

Many people like to follow this strategy using GICs. This will certainly work, but you need to keep in mind that CDIC insurance is only good for GICs that are of a five-year or shorter time frame. Also, only the first $100,000 is eligible for insurance, so you may need to involve more than one supplier in order to maintain a fully insured ladder. Note, though, that some credit union deposits, including GICs, may be covered by an unlimited insurance program, depending on your province. In Manitoba for instance, the Deposit Guarantee Corporation of Manitoba provides an unlimited guarantee on all deposits, including accrued interest. One of the problems with using a GIC ladder is that it will focus on the short end of the yield curve, from one to five years. In the current interest rate environment, that isn't a big problem, given the flat yield curve, but when the yield curve is more steeply sloped, it is likely that you will want to stretch your ladder out to cover a longer duration, and add exposure to higher interest rates available through longer-term bonds.

As a complement to a bond/debenture ladder, it is also prudent to dedicate some of the fixed income allocation to real return bonds and high-yield bonds to gain further protection from inflation and improve yield. Unlike the above strategy, where individual bonds are purchased, I favour using a portfolio approach for both of these investments (through a low-cost index-based ETF). Diversification is vital for high-yield products and is instantaneously achieved through an indexed investment approach. Real return bonds are much easier to invest in with a pooled product; therefore, an ETF is an easy way to gain the exposure sought.

Diversification Across Asset Classes

Diversification across asset classes is achieved by setting and respecting a personalized asset allocation policy appropriate to your circumstances. The concept is simple: hold a proportion of your investment portfolio in each of the main asset classes to ensure you are not overexposed to the risks unique to an asset class. Equity, fixed income, cash, and alternative investment valuations respond to stimuli in different ways and with different degrees of vigour.

One of the most important ideas that I feel must be emphasized at this point, and it is so obvious that it sounds stupid, but it is very important that you realize it: *you only have one portfolio*. You may have a number of different investment accounts, but taken as a whole, they represent one portfolio. Your asset allocation needs to be considered within the context of one portfolio. It is amazing to me how this simple concept gets lost within many investment programs.

I read book after book that lay out individualized asset allocation strategies for a RRSP, for a RRIF, for a TFSA, for a regular investment account, etc. (Don't worry, we will talk in detail about each of these accounts later.) Considering your asset allocation in pieces such as this is simply not appropriate. You need to consider your asset allocation based on your financial position, your goals, your risk tolerance, and your time horizon—your personal situation. After you have determined how you want your asset allocation to be constructed and maintained, only then do you have to determine the best way to manage the tax consequences and it is this that will direct how you determine what goes into your RRSP, your RRIF, your TFSA, and your unregistered investment account. You do not set an asset allocation for each account and invest according to that. Asset allocation decisions need to be designed on a portfolio basis, and then you use your accounts to strategically manage the tax consequences.

I know, investment planning is difficult enough on its own without the tax considerations—you can thank the government for the outrageous complexity of the tax system our country has. For most of us, our largest single expense across the whole of our lives will be the federal and provincial income taxes we pay. For my family, the second-largest expense category is not even close to what we have paid in income taxes. As such, income tax considerations become a vital part of a comprehensive financial plan.

Diworsification

The investment industry loves to invent new terms, many of which are not necessary. I kind of like this one, though: diworsification. This represents a situation where an investor, likely driven by a desire to diversify, ends up with a portfolio that is full of duplication and has become unwieldy to manage.

It is relatively easy to have this happen over time without even realizing you are doing it. If you are one of the people who rush out every RRSP season and buy last year's best-performing mutual fund because that is what your fund guy has recommended, you will end up with many different mutual funds that have a significant amount of overlap in their holdings. More is not always better.

Your goal should be to invest in enough different stuff to be properly diversified. You don't increase your diversification much when you buy five different mutual funds that all have eight of ten of their top holdings in the same stocks. When you do this, you add complexity with no real benefit. One investment that holds the market is in and of itself diversified.

A Word on Risk

Ultimately, risk should be thought of in terms of the likelihood of loss. Within the investment industry, though, risk is often considered in terms of the variability of valuation implicit within an investment as measured by its standard deviation. In my opinion, the fluctuation in value of an investment is not a big deal unless you need to sell or the sight of the valuation swing is likely to make you do something stupid. (And history has shown that, on average, that is exactly what it does with many investors.) Investors tend to react when there is a big move in the valuation of an investment; often, the action taken turns out to be exactly the wrong thing to do. So if variability in asset valuation is something that will influence what you do, then you should likely take a more conservative approach to investing and you should also use a fee-for-service investment advisor who can act to help you control any self-destructive tendencies you have.

My preference is to think of risk in terms of time rather than in terms of volatility. Equity investments are more volatile and thus are often viewed as being the most risky. However, over time, equities outperform all other asset classes across virtually all longer time frames. So if you don't need your money for, say, 25 years, then your view of the day-to-day volatility of your portfolio should be very different than if you require the money in the near term. If you need your money next year, then investing that money in equities would be foolish because short-term volatility could kill the value with such a short time frame. On the other hand, if you don't need the money for a couple of decades, then the day-to-day volatility is essentially meaningless and you can switch your focus from volatility to long-term return expectations.

Determining an Appropriate Asset Allocation

All of the above blubbering on about the different asset classes, risk, and proper diversification is intended to help form the foundation for the design of a target asset allocation that is appropriate for your situation. Your asset allocation is something that should be critically evaluated on an annual basis and each time there is a significant change to your personal circumstances.

The key to the asset allocation decision is finding the proper balance, which maximizes your chances of meeting the financial elements of your goals within your personal risk tolerance. Being absolutely comfortable with the investment approach you have taken in all markets is very difficult to achieve. In order to work toward understanding the right asset allocation, we are blessed to have available to us all of the hard work that has been done by those who have struggled with this question before us. The internet is a wonderful thing in that it provides us with information and tools that are very useful in our quest to define an appropriate asset allocation.

Where I suggest you start is by completing a couple of the risk assessment questionnaires that are readily available on the internet. I would select questionnaires offered by large, respected financial institutions or financial planning firms. (Maybe try a robo-advisor or two.) All of the questionnaires run through a series of alternatives designed to determine both your position in life and your attitude toward risk. They will ask you questions that are specific to your financial and personal situation (how old are you, when do you plan to use the investment income from your portfolio, how stable is your income, how do you expect your income to change over time, etc.), as well as behaviour-based questions that are designed to determine how you would act in certain situations. At the conclusion of the questionnaire, they will provide you with an assessment of what this means in terms of your attitude toward risk and how that translates into an asset allocation.

For many of the questions, the answer will seem obvious to you, but for some, you may have a couple of different perspectives based on what you read into the question. If there are a number of questions where you fall somewhere in the middle of a couple of the answers, do the questionnaire twice and see how it impacts the end result.

One more thing I have observed that can serve to limit how well the questionnaires work is the tendency for people to try to answer the questions with what they think is the right answer as opposed to *their* answer. Don't do that. Answer each question as honestly as you can. There is not a right and wrong answer; there is just your answer. Try to put yourself in the situation of the question to understand your emotions before you answer because when this happens in real life, emotion will be involved. Either put some numbers to the situation or think back to what you actually did when something similar happened in your investing past.

For example, say you have a $500,000 investment in index-based equities, and the market drops 35%—that means you are now looking at an investment statement that shows a revised value of $325,000. That kind of paper loss in real life can play with your head. In real-life terms, you just lost a sum that might have been sufficient to put your kids through university and buy them their first car. Now all you have is a piece of paper that feels like it is telling you what an idiot you have been. Don't hide from what you would actually do in the situation, if it were to occur. If you answer the questionnaire saying you would take the opportunity to invest more money in the devastated equity portion of the portfolio, this action is interpreted by the questionnaire to mean that you don't mind the risk and therefore it would suggest you invest aggressively. Be truthful in answering the questionnaire; don't try to be someone you are not, because when it happens, you are who you are, not the person you pretended to be when you answered the questions.

My recommendation is to do a few of these questionnaires and then look at the average asset allocation suggested. If you are like me, you may find that there is a difference between what it says the appropriate asset allocation is for you and the asset allocation you have in place. That doesn't mean that you immediately run out and change your asset allocation to what the questionnaire says. It means you need to think through what that is telling you. The questionnaire does not have a full view of your goals and aspirations. You may be able to meet your goals by investing differently than the questionnaire suggests. Perhaps you are willing to take more risk according to the risk assessment questionnaire, but if you don't need to in order to meet your goals, then why would you?

Additionally, you may find that you can't possibly meet your goals by investing in the manner suggested by the questionnaire. In this case, you need to take a hard look at your goals and decide what is achievable within the risk profile that you can comfortably take. In my view, investing more aggressively than you are comfortable with is seldom an appropriate path to follow and it will be highly likely to cause you to take inappropriate action at precisely the wrong time. You are human and you will react as a human; however, the more you know about investing and the more thought you have put into your financial plan, the more likely you are to approach the academically correct response.

I am not someone who likes to apply rules of thumb, but as a part of thinking through what is an appropriate asset allocation for your situation there is one that I like to apply as a check on what is *on average* reasonable. That rule of thumb is that you invest in fixed income and cash instruments to a percentage that equates to your age. So if you are 40, then you would invest about 40% of your portfolio in fixed income and cash with the remaining 60% dedicated to equities. If you are 60 years old, you would invest about 60% in fixed income and cash, with the remaining 40% allocated equities. The theory is that as you age, you should reduce the risk within your portfolio, thereby becoming more conservative.

In general, I agree with the premise of this formula, though it is too simple to accurately capture what is right for everyone. If your investment allocation significantly deviates from this rule of thumb, it is not necessarily wrong, but your personal situation should explain the difference. If you have enough money to meet your goals without taking on any risk, then perhaps it is reasonable to have no money invested in equities. If you have enough invested in bonds to meet all of your incremental income needs for several years into the future, then maybe it is appropriate to have all of the balance of your investments in equities. The asset allocation needs to be constructed with your specific circumstances in mind.

In the end, what is right for you is likely not something that is as formulaic as the results of the risk questionnaire and/or the rule of thumb dictate. If you have a lot of experience with investing and understand how you react to the curve balls that the investment world will throw at you, and have a good understanding of the financial implications of your goals and objectives, then I believe you can make the asset allocation determination yourself.

If, on the other hand, you are inexperienced with the investment world or have a history of reacting in the wrong way to market stimuli, then I think it would be a good idea to work with a qualified investment advisor to arrive at the best asset allocation for your situation. The advisor would be there to help guide you through the inevitable surprises and shocks that will materialize.

Over a long period, equity investments will almost certainly return more than any other asset class, and likely by a wide margin. Over a short period, the return from equity investments is variable and extremely uncertain. Thus, while you will want to use stocks to help achieve your longer-term financial goals, you will want to lock-in any wealth required to meet your near-term requirements and goals. The asset allocation decision needs to be considered in terms of the unique elements of your personal situation.

Your asset allocation is the most important investment decision you make. It is not a decision to be taken lightly.

Portfolio Management

Once you have gone through the process and defined an appropriate asset allocation, it is likely that you will have to make some adjustments to your current holdings. If you are moving to a more conservative asset allocation, my preference is to get there with prudent expedience. If you are not faced with switching fees or substantial tax implications, likely it is best to do it all at once. If there is a tax or transaction cost associated with the alteration, then a more measured approach will have to be planned and taken. Alternatively, if you are moving to a more aggressive asset allocation, then a staged sequence of transactions is a reasonable approach to take. Dollar-cost averaging (essentially, investing consistently over a period of time) is a long-accepted strategy.

Once you get to your new asset allocation, a funny thing happens. The relative market value of your investments change and you are once again out of sync with your strategy. So long as your actual asset allocation is reasonably close to the target allocation, the divergence is not a big deal. There are a couple things you can do to maintain an approximate match. First, as new money is available for investing, you can direct it to the asset class that is underrepresented. (Essentially, you are buying low through this approach.) Second, once a year or so, you can sell an amount of the asset class that has relatively outperformed and use the proceeds to buy the underperforming asset class in order to re-establish the target asset allocation (buying low and selling high). This process is called *rebalancing*. It is important to rebalance your portfolio periodically because it will get out of whack. It should be done annually or when the gap becomes substantial.

CHAPTER 22 – THE IMPACT OF INVESTMENT FEES AND COSTS

The importance of cost minimization has been mentioned a number of times, but a case for the strength of that importance has not yet been vividly displayed. So let's take a short but deeper dive into this subject to better understand the insidious impact of excessive management fees and expenses.

Have you had the opportunity to walk down Bay Street in Toronto? Whenever I am in Toronto, I make it a point to take in the vibrancy and energy of downtown and, in particular, Bay Street. Bay Street is the Wall Street of Canada—seemingly all of the important financial stuff that occurs in Canada filters through Bay Street. Most of the major financial players have a presence there in one of the ostentatious sky-scrapers clad in marble with the high volume foyer filled with tailored suits, expensive haircuts, and colourful socks visible between the pant cuffs and relentlessly polished shoes. The management fees, expenses, and various other forms of payment—either remitted directly or, more likely, deducted from your returns—pay for all of that.

Let's presume you are looking for a broadly diversified Canadian equity investment to employ in your retirement account, and you plan to hold that investment (say $100,000) for a period of 25 years. You are familiar with the FP Canada Standards Council Projection Assumption Guidelines that suggest the long-term rate of return that should be assumed for such an investment is 6.1%

(before fees). In terms of investment options, your friend told you about an indexed ETF that he uses in his investment strategy and your mutual fund sales guy, Melvin, has a product that he considers to be ideal for your circumstances. In terms of fees, this is what the two options look like:

1. Index-based exchange-traded fund MER 0.06%
2. Actively managed Canadian equity mutual fund MER 2.94%

Melvin took you out for lunch to expound on the virtues of the actively managed fund. You know that 2.94% is higher than 0.06%, but think that 2.94% isn't really all that much. Even though the lunch was good, you told Melvin that you wanted to think about it before making a decision (always a wise move). When you got home, you pulled out your calculator to determine how much more that higher MER would cost you over your expected holding period.

Your first calculation was to determine how much a $100,000 investment that returned 6.1% would be worth at the end of your 25-year holding period—in essence you pretend that there were no fees or expenses. Once you purchase the necessary batteries for your high school business calculator and refresh your understanding of how to clear the memory so that you can get an accurate calculation, you come to the following result:

Investment	$ 100,000
Projected return	6.1%
Value in 25 Years	$ 439,425
Increase in Value	$ 339,425
Cost of fees	$ 0

Nice! Sign me up!

Next, you take a look at the low-cost exchange-traded fund and do the same calculation. You adjust the projected return to reflect the 0.06% MER of the ETF and arrive at the following:

Investment	$ 100,000
Projected return	6.04%
Value in 25 Years	$ 433,254
Your account gain	$ 333,254
Cost of fees	$ 6,171

Hey, not bad. You were a little surprised that this cost you $6,171 (154 less trips to the theatre with your loved one to see movies that help you get in touch with your feelings), but nothing in life is free after all. You recognize that this option will also require that you set up an account at a discount broker and pay $10 to buy the investment and again $10 to sell it 25 years later … not a whole lot of work and minimal cost. You consider this to be very doable.

But you have been working with Melvin for a few years and he did buy you a nice lunch. So you take a look at what Melvin's alternative would cost you, using the exact same approach.

Investment	$ 100,000
Projected return	3.16%
Value in 25 Years	$ 217,662
Your account gain	$ 117,662
Cost of fees	$ 221,763

How does that lunch taste now? Do you think it was worth $221,763? How is it that you put in all the capital, and your gain turns out to be a fraction of the implied cost of the fees? That is where the tall buildings on Bay Street come from: fees. The fee seems so small when it is bandied about in percentage terms, but when you considered it as a percentage of your expected return … it is not so small all of a sudden. Also, the fees are certain to occur; your return is not certain.

Looked at slightly differently, in this example, you have one option that provides 98% of the pre-fee earnings to you, and another that provides only 35% of the pre-fee earnings. In the first instance, you keep $333,254 of earnings, and in the second you keep $117,662. The expected gross return is the same in both instances; the only difference is the fee and expense differential. Huh, kind of makes you think, doesn't it?

Lest you believe this is an unfair or misleading example, the MER figures were taken from a popular ETF available through Vanguard (though you can find a similar offering, sometimes even slightly cheaper, with several of the large ETF providers) and a Canadian equity MF that has attracted well in excess of a billion dollars of investment capital (all sold by a mutual fund guy). These are real-life numbers!

The next argument that Melvin would likely make is that his fund has professional management, and the manager is really smart and has the opportunity to outperform the index. In truth, the fund manager probably is really smart, but it is improbable that he/she will outperform the index by more than the fees charged for an extended period of time. In fact, in the case of these two specific funds, the manager did outperform the index ETF in one of the four calendar years that both had been in existence, but underperformed by a considerable margin in the other three. In addition, the managed fund also had a deferred sales charge attached to it that would kick in if the investor wanted to sell the fund within seven years, excessive switching fees, and short-term trading fees—more potential fees and more complexity to keep track of.

There are a lot of ETFs and MFs available that cover all of the major investment groups (domestic and international equity, fixed income, alternative. and variable income investments). Many of the index-based ETFs have microscopic MERs, but there are also some index-based MFs that boast low MERs. Expenses and fees really matter; it is imperative that you pay close attention to all of the fees associated with your investment program because Melvin won't be worrying about them on your behalf. Melvin needs the big fees to feed *his* retirement account and pay for his colourful socks.

It is now possible to assemble an entire investment portfolio on one's own that is very to extremely low cost. For example, using three ETFs from the Vanguard Canada family, you could set up a portfolio invested in equal parts Canadian equities, international equities, and bonds with an embedded MER of about 0.16%,[1] plus $60 to purchase and later sell the three investments. If it is too much work assembling this yourself, Vanguard also offers several different portfolio ETFs that invest directly in established proportions of their own ETF family for a total management fee of 0.22%. (The MER will be a wee bit higher than this.) The portfolio ETFs will look after the rebalancing piece making the investment process even more hands-off. Again, Vanguard is just one ETF provider; there are others where a similar low-fee opportunity exists and most of the large ETF companies are also offering portfolio ETFs with similarly small or even slightly smaller MERs.

Assuming the projection returns espoused by the FP Canada Standards Council, the three ETF portfolio above would provide its owner with 95%[2] of the total projected gain (over a 25-year investment period). If an investor instead went to Melvin, who found an option that had a 2% MER, the investor would only receive 48%[2] of the total projected gain associated with the investment. This is not a fair allocation—high fees hurt and hurt a lot.

For those of you who are not enamoured with the idea of determining which funds to use and in what proportions, but who see that fees and expenses are a significant hurdle that cannot be ignored, there are still options you can use to realize lower costs. The first is to hire a fee-for-service financial planner who will help you determine an appropriate asset allocation and recommend the low-cost ETFs or MFs for you to use. In this case, you would still need to set up an account and consummate the transactions on your own (easy to do). A second viable option is to set up an account with a low-cost robo-advisor. This will cost you a bit more, but significantly less than many other options. The nice thing about the robo-advisor route, too, is that you can automate the whole process (with preprogrammed periodic contributions) and it will rebalance the portfolio for you on a scheduled basis.

If you want to read more on this subject an excellent book was written by Larry Bates called *Beat the Bank*.[3] Mr. Bates also has a very useful website that does fee-based return calculations for you and offers references to other useful calculators and sources of personal financial planning information.

PART VI – WHERE TO HOLD INVESTMENTS

If there were no income taxes to consider, it really wouldn't matter which type of account you chose to hold your investments in. You would simply have to decide on an appropriate asset allocation and invest—easy. What a wonderful world that would be … the Winnipeg Jets would make a deep run in the playoffs annually, Canada would win the World Junior Hockey Championship, donuts would be a health food, ahhh a wonderful world, indeed.

Alas, we do have taxes and tax impacts that need to be considered as we design our investment approach. We will begin this discussion with a look at the different types of investment accounts.

- **Tax-Free Savings Accounts (TFSA).** Tax-paid cash is transferred to the TFSA and used to invest in eligible securities. (I refer to the cash used in a TFSA as "tax-paid" because it is cash that has already run the gauntlet of taxation—it is after-tax cash.) No tax is paid on investment income when earned in the TFSA. No tax is paid on withdrawals from the TFSA.

- **Registered Retirement Savings Plans (RRSP).** Tax-deferred cash is transferred to the RRSP and used to invest in eligible securities. (I refer to the cash used in a RRSP as "tax-deferred" because it is cash that will, when deposited to the RRSP, create a tax deduction that will later become taxable when it is withdrawn from the RRSP—the tax gauntlet has been avoided temporarily but it will be run in the future.) No tax is paid on investment income earned while in the RRSP. Tax is paid on withdrawals from the RRSP.

- **Registered Retirement Income Funds (RRIF).** A RRIF is essentially a continuation of an RRSP and the tax implications are the same regarding income on investments and withdrawals. One major difference from the RRSP is that a RRIF has a minimum withdrawal that must be made on an annual basis.

- **Non-Registered Investment Accounts.** Tax-paid cash is transferred to the account and used to purchase investments. Each form of investment income is taxed according to the rules contained in the *Income Tax Act*. There is no tax sheltering.

Along with these personal savings accounts, there are two other very important sources of income that are likely to have substantial impact on revenue streams at some point and therefore savings and investment strategies.

- The first of these revenue streams results from government programs. With the Canada Pension Plan (CPP), Quebec Pension Plan (QPP), and Old Age Security (OAS) programs, you have absolutely no investment management responsibility. Rather you just need to be familiar with the benefit programs, how the benefits are determined, and any benefit risks that might be relevant to your situation.
- The second of these revenue streams is not universal, but it will affect many, registered pension plans (RPPs). Participation in an RPP can also evolve into participation in the locked-in version of an RRSP and/or RRIF if an employee ceases participation in the RPP.

I have been trying to avoid it as much as possible, but in the final chapter of this section there will be a short discussion about income taxes, insofar as they relate to investment income.

Boring Alert

One of the first rules or writing is not to bore your reader. Believe it or not, I am aware of this. Unfortunately, rules around the various forms of investment accounts, and the wide variety of government programs in operation, do not provide a setting that allows for the excitement of having Batman swoop-in to save the day. I have yet to see Batman do his taxes in any of the movies, but I suspect he does them. That piece gets edited out. Even though this section of the book may not provide scintillating reading, it is nonetheless important to the extent that it applies to you.

Much of Part VI gets rather technical due to the nature of the material being discussed. In personal finance, to be successful, it is important that you build general awareness of the topics that aren't central to your current situation, but a more informed stance related to those plans and programs that are directly applicable to your immediate financial circumstances. For those pieces of this part of the book that have limited current relevance to you, give them a quick scan to help build a foundation of general awareness without getting bogged down in too much detail. For the other pieces that are directly aligned with your situation, a more thorough understanding should be your objective.

Always remember, no one cares more about you living your dream than you … do the work!

Takeaways from Part VI

- ✓ Once you get to the point where you have investing decisions to make the hardest part is done—you have managed to save some money. Way to go! You now need to put that money to work through a properly structured investment program that uses the correct accounts suitable to your personal circumstances.
- ✓ There are a number of different account options available. The high-level decision boils down to can/should I use a tax-sheltered account or a regular investment account; and if I use a tax-sheltered account should it be a "retirement" account or a tax-free savings account.

- If you have room to invest in a tax-sheltered account, and capital available to invest with a substantial time frame before its planned use, in most cases you should place the investment in one of the tax-sheltered options. Time, combined with tax-free compounding, is a formidable combination.
- If you have available contribution room in both a TFSA and a RRSP, then you need to consider what your planned use is for the funds in order to select the best account. If you make a withdrawal from your TFSA, the contribution room will be restored the following calendar year; conversely, if you withdraw funds from your RRSP, that contribution room is lost forever. If your use of the money is well down the road, then you will need to think about what your current tax rate is versus your expected future tax rate to determine if you are better to use a TFSA or a RRSP.
- When you are planning your retirement income, make sure you do not lose sight of government benefits (Canada/Quebec Pension Plan, Old Age Security and possibly veterans benefits) as well as any registered pension plan or pooled registered pension plan you may be the beneficiary of. While you may not think of these sources of funds as investments, per se, their contribution to your future cash flow will likely have a very real impact on your investment strategy.
- When it comes time to convert your various plans into income, there are quite a number of decisions you will be required to make. Ensure you consider the implications of each program fully before making a decision.

    o RRSPs can remain intact until the end of the year you turn 71. At that point, you will need to take the cash, convert it to a Registered Retirement Income Fund or annuity, or some combination of the three. Both RRIFs and annuities have a suite of benefits that should be fully evaluated. Only in very limited circumstances does taking cash make sense.
    o Government pensions offer a variety of cash flow options that need to be evaluated. If you expect to live a good long time then often it is best (mathematically) to defer receipt of benefits to take advantage of an enhanced payment stream. However, there are

many factors that can make it a better choice to take the money earlier in the option window provided. There is no one-size-fits-all solution here.
- Employer pensions, like long-distance runners, come in all shapes and sizes. (If you don't believe the runner bit, you should go to the start line of a local marathon and see for yourself, people are amazing—the winner will almost assuredly be tall and thin, but the finishers will be all shapes and sizes.) The only way you will know the extent to which you can rely on your pension for income is to gain a fulsome understanding of the benefit profile and any options you have under the plan. Some defined benefit pension plans will provide sufficient income for the recipient to meet all of their needs, wants, and desires. More often, though, a combination of accounts will need to be utilized to provide the means for retirement bliss. Don't blindly rely on your employer pension plan; you could be in for a rude awakening.
- TFSAs and non-registered investment accounts can also form a significant piece to the retirement puzzle. For example, a young adult that focuses on their TFSA as a savings strategy could, all else remaining equal, accumulate a value well into seven figures by the time they retire. TFSAs are also very useful in that withdrawals from the account do not impact the availability of many other benefit programs.

✓ The *Income Tax Act*, like Jason in the *Friday the 13th* movies, has a resiliency that demands respect. You likely will not outwit it, so it is best to understand how it works so that you can survive within its rules. Like Jason, the taxman will get his due; it is up to you to ensure that the impact is measured, not lethal. As it stands currently, the average Canadian experiences their tax freedom day in June … June!

You should understand:

- How the progressive taxation system is designed, from both a federal and provincial perspective.

- How taxation works in the case of your registered accounts in terms of both your contributions to and withdrawals from.
- How taxation of the various forms of non-registered investment income (interest, dividends, and capital gains) works and impacts your net return.

✓ Don't use complexity as an excuse for not determining what plan of action makes sense for you. A successful investment program, combined with a prudently designed strategy that takes advantage of the various programs and accounts in a tax-effective manner, enhances the likelihood that you will be financially placed to live your dream.

CHAPTER 23 – TAX-FREE SAVINGS ACCOUNTS (TFSAs)

Almost everyone who is eligible should make it a priority to invest in a TFSA regularly to the full extent of the contribution limit.

The TFSA is a savings program designed for Canadian citizens (who have attained age 18 and have a valid social insurance number) to set aside tax-paid money in a tax-free environment. What that means is you don't get a tax deduction for depositing money in a TFSA the way you do with an RRSP, but you will not pay any tax on the earnings from that money while it is in the plan, nor will there be any tax applied when you take the money contributed, or the associated earnings, out of the plan.

In practical terms, within the current rules, this program could be used by our children to accumulate substantial investment portfolios, in excess of $1.5 million by the time each retires, and this would be money that brings with it no additional tax encumbrance.[1] The most recent statistics published on the Government of Canada website (2018 statistics, inclusive of the 2016 contribution year) show average unused TFSA contribution room of $27,653 and an average TFSA fair market value of $17,286, per individual. Clearly there is room for improved use of this valuable program.

The TFSA should be a major factor in investment and retirement planning for millennials and future generations. Unfortunately, it is, and will become even more so, a major planning hurdle for the government as it will be used by Canadians to reduce their tax exposure. Thus, in my opinion, there is a longer-term risk to the program. With each passing year, the balances Canadians devote to the TFSA will become more substantial and the impact to the federal and provincial treasuries will correspondingly become more acute.

How the TFSA Works (Boring Alert)

I will try to cover off the main elements of the TFSA program, recognizing that you do not need to understand all of the details in order to make a well-informed decision. The CRA does a very good job of walking through the intricacies of the program in well-organized reference materials available through the Government of Canada website. These aren't novels that have drama and suspense to keep you engaged start to finish; rather, they are reference materials organized to help you find the details you need when you need them (and the program details will change over time).

I will run through the important elements in bullet points to minimize any pain.

1. Administrative Aspects

    - Banks, insurance companies, trust companies, and credit unions (most financial institutions) offer TFSAs.
    - A TFSA is not an investment. A TFSA is akin to a virtual filing cabinet, envelope, safe, or even wine cellar in that it provides the vessel within which something of value is held.
    - In order to open a TFSA, a person must have a valid social insurance number (SIN) and have attained the age of majority in their province of residence.
    - As soon as you turn the age of majority for your province, you are eligible to open a TFSA. You start to accumulate contribution room the year you turn 18.
    - You do not lose your TFSA contribution room if you do not use it. It will accumulate and be available for future use.

- TFSAs operate on a calendar-year basis. New contribution room is available on January 1.
- The TFSA dollar limit is not prorated in the year an individual turns 18, dies, or changes residency status.
- There is no scheduled date by which a TFSA must be wound up.
- Generally, federal income-tested benefits and credits you receive will not be reduced as a result of income you earn inside a TFSA, or by any amount you withdraw from a TFSA. This characteristic makes a TFSA an ideal investment vehicle for lower-income Canadians.
- You can have as many TFSAs as you like, but your TFSA contribution room must be respected cumulatively across all your accounts.
- You can transfer funds from one TFSA to another. But this should be done using the direct transfer capability of your issuer.
- TFSAs are a very effective avenue for achieving income splitting. So long as your spouse or kids qualify to have a TFSA, a higher-income earner can contribute to a family member's TFSA. But (there is always a *but*) if one contributes to the TFSA of someone else, the money is now theirs to do with as they wish and the contributor has no control over what is done with it.
- When you set up the TFSA, make sure you name a successor holder and/or beneficiary, whichever best suits your situation. If your situation changes vis-à-vis your partner arrangement, review your designations to ensure they accurately reflect your ongoing wishes.
- A successor holder can only be a spouse or common-law partner. The significance of this designation is that the successor holder, upon the passing of the TFSA owner, essentially steps into the shoes of the deceased assuming ownership of the account complete with ongoing tax benefits.
- You will want to double check to ensure that you indicated the successor holder option correctly when you set up your account. If you were an early adopter of the TFSA, chances are good that your provincial legislation was not formalized at the time you established your account and you may not have had the option to name a successor holder at that time.

- If upon death the investment portfolio is distributed to a beneficiary, rather than to a successor holder, then the tax-free benefits are eliminated going forward for the new owner.
- TFSA issuers report all transactions made related to your TFSA(s) to the Canada Revenue Agency. The CRA keeps track of each individual's contribution room.

2. Contributions to a TFSA

- There are a couple of main points related to contributions that differentiate the TFSA from other savings and retirement accounts:

    - You do not need to have earned income. All individuals receive the exact same contribution room every year, so long as they meet the account eligibility criteria.
    - Contributions made to a TFSA are not deductible for tax purposes.

- Your TFSA contribution room, at any given point in time, is dependent on four figures:

    - Your TFSA dollar limit for the year, plus
    - Unused TFSA contribution room from previous years, plus
    - Withdrawals made from the TFSA in the previous year, minus
    - Contributions made during the year

- The annual TFSA dollar limit for each year since inception is as follows:

YEAR	TFSA DOLLAR LIMIT
2009	$5,000
2010	$5,000
2011	$5,000
2012	$5,000
2013	$5,500
2014	$5,500
2015	$10,000
2016	$5,500
2017	$5,500
2018	$5,500
2019	$6,000
Total	**$63,500**

- The annual TFSA dollar limit is indexed by inflation, but for administrative simplicity, is rounded to the nearest $500.
- The type of investments allowed, called qualified investments, are similar to those permitted in an RRSP and include: cash, mutual funds, securities listed on a designated stock exchange, guaranteed investment certificates, bonds, certain shares of small business corporations, etc.
- "In-kind" contributions can be made to a TFSA. However, there may be tax implications associated with the asset being transferred that need to be explored due to the deemed disposition rules.
- If you make a withdrawal from your TFSA, the amount you withdraw will create additional contribution room. However, the additional

contribution room is not credited to your account until the calendar year following the withdrawal.
- Within the TFSA guide[2] produced by the CRA, there are several examples of how to calculate available contribution room in a number of different scenarios. If you are having trouble with this concept and how the formula works, you should consult the guide to ensure you do not inadvertently make an over-contribution.

3. Withdrawals from a TFSA

- You are free to make a withdrawal from your TFSA at any time, so long as the specific investment can be converted to cash and the account provider you have selected does not have any restrictions.
- Any amount withdrawn from your TFSA that is "normal" in character will be added back to your TFSA contribution room at the beginning of the next calendar year. If you are simply taking money out of your TFSA to spend or invest, in almost every circumstance the amount withdrawn will be added back to your contribution room at the beginning of the next year.
- When you make a withdrawal—and this is the thing of beauty that accompanies the TFSA—there is zero, nada, zippo tax impact.

4. Taxes and TFSAs

- Generally, income and gains earned on investments held in a TFSA are just that, tax free. They are tax-free while held in the account and they remain tax free upon withdrawal from the account.
- Over-contributions to a TFSA will attract tax. Follow the rules associated with contributions and withdrawals and tax issues will not arise.
- If, at any time in a month, you have an over-contribution (called an Excess TFSA Amount) you are liable to pay a tax of 1% on your highest Excess TFSA Amount in that month.
- When an over-contribution is deemed to be intentional, then the CRA will tax the profits of the over-contribution at 100%. There is simply no advantage to be gained by trying to bend the rules.

- It goes without saying that you should eliminate any over-contribution ASAP to reduce the tax impact. If a non-qualified investment or prohibited investment is made in a TFSA, it is recommended that you visit a tax professional to help you sort through the implications.
- Where TFSA taxes are applicable, a whole new world of paperwork is opened up to you. A TFSA return (form RC243) must be filed.
- In order to have a tax liability waived, you will need to write a letter to the CRA to explain why you made the mistake and how it was a reasonable error, as well as the steps you have taken to rectify the situation.

5. Types of TFSA Plans

- The type of plans available for TFSAs can best be described by the nature of investments that are allowed to be held. The assortment of investments allowed within any account is determined by two things:

    - The investments available through the issuer, and
    - The investments that are allowed under legislation.

- Issuers tend to offer a number of different plans that are designed to hold a subset of the investments permitted by legislation.
- It is up to the consumer to select the issuer. In my opinion, this decision should be guided by three key criteria:

    - The scope of assets allowed,
    - The fees attached to the account, and
    - The issuer.

- In terms of the scope of assets, it is important that you give yourself sufficient investment options to formulate the type of portfolio that fits within your asset allocation strategy. The account I use gives me the opportunity to invest directly in stocks, ETFs, bonds (government and corporate), GICs, and virtually anything I would want to access at reasonable transaction costs, with no account costs.

- The issuer is important because you want a provider that can meet most or all of your investment (TFSA, RRSP, RRIF, RESP, non-registered account) and perhaps banking needs, with low embedded fees. The fewer relationships you enter into, the less complexity you build into your financial footprint.

6. Other TFSA Points of Interest

- In the event of a marriage or common-law partnership breakdown, TFSA assets can be directly transferred from the plan of one spouse or common-law partner to the other.
- With respect to US-sourced dividends, TFSAs are not covered by the Canada/US tax treaty. This situation is different than that of RRSPs and RRIFs that are covered by the treaty. Given this, you may choose to hold any US-based investments in an account other than your TFSA.
- While the types of investments permitted inside a TFSA are extensive, not all shares of small business corporations are eligible. If you meet CRA's definition of a *connected shareholder*, the stock associated with that small business corporation would not be eligible. The penalties associated with non-qualified or prohibited investments can be substantial.

Tax-Free Savings Accounts – A Final Word

I love TFSAs!

TFSAs are flexible, tax-effective, and universally available to all Canadian residents who are both 18 and meet provincial age of majority requirements. TFSAs have the added benefit that they will not impede the receipt of the majority of government benefits and credits. TFSAs allow for the accumulation of substantial investment balances, in a tax-advantaged environment, which makes them ideal investment vehicles for all ages, but especially younger generations, who have more time to benefit from tax-free compounding. They are a wonderful complement to the RRSP and RESP options that are also available to serve savings goals.

Like all savings vehicles sponsored by a government initiative, the rules can get relatively complicated when you dig into the nooks and crannies. The federal government has published a fairly user-friendly TFSA guide for individuals.[2] If you want to read a book dedicated in its entirety to TFSAs, Gordon Pape has written a book, now in its 4th edition, dedicated to the topic, titled *Tax-Free Savings Accounts: How to Profit from the New TFSA Rules*.[3] It is an easy read (that is, once you get past the history piece), though parts of it are not up to date with the current rules—one of the hazards of writing a book. Mr. Pape even gives you a test at the end to ensure you understood some of the more salient points. I enjoy tests.

CHAPTER 24 – REGISTERED RETIREMENT SAVINGS PLANS

Ah, yes, retirement, an oft stated but little understood goal. Having just recently started mine, I consider myself to be a veritable rookie, and having an extra 2000–2500 hours a year is awesome!

Beyond the additional pleasure travel I have been able to enjoy, retirement has given me the opportunity to spend more time with my two beautiful children, though they are kind of beyond "Dad" time these days. They do still appreciate a ride to school, and that is how I start many of my days. Fitting in exercise and eating better is much easier. I think I have only pulled out the iron once this year, and that used to be a considerable time commitment in the old work days. For me, retirement is largely about doing some of the simple things I didn't have time to participate in while working. Best of all, I am no longer waking up in the middle of the night thinking about potential solutions to the issues that were ever-present at work. If something doesn't get done today, no biggie, manana.

RRSPs are just one of the vehicles available to most Canadians designed to help fund their retirement. RRSPs have applications that go beyond funding retirement, but their primary purpose for most of us is to help accumulate funds to be spent living our retirement dreams.

Sadly, the statistics suggest that RRSPs are not being availed of to the extent possible. There is over $600 billion[1] in available RRSP contribution room,

$600,000,000,000; that is a bunch of zeroes. RRSPs provide an excellent opportunity that is being missed, to a large degree, by many.

As with the TFSA, this book will not discuss all of the features of the RRSP that may be relevant to your situation; indeed, that is a whole book unto itself. While I hope to cover most of what you need to know in this text, if you want to read a book dedicated to RRSPs, there are several good ones out there. One of my favourites is written by Bruce Sellery, entitled *The Moolala Guide to Rockin' your RRSP*.[2] I like it because it covers the basics thoroughly, offers practical advice that is broken down into actionable pieces, and is presented in a manner that makes a dry subject relatively entertaining. (As you know by now, I am easily entertained.) Mr. Sellery doesn't provide a test at the end of his book the way Mr. Pape did for the TFSA (and in his book on RRSPs, for that matter), but he does take you through a bunch of assignments as you think through how an RRSP applies in your circumstances, requiring your noodle to become actively engaged within your personal context.

How the RRSP Works (Boring Alert)

Like the TFSA, an RRSP is not in and of itself an investment. You don't buy a RRSP. You open an RRSP and then place investments in it that are temporarily protected from the ravages of taxation. Once the account is open, you contribute pre-tax assets to it, let them grow on a tax-free basis while they are held within the RRSP, and include any withdrawals from the account in your taxable income in the year the withdrawal takes place. From an income tax perspective, when the contribution goes into your RRSP, you get a tax deduction, and when a withdrawal occurs it is included in your taxable income. You do not avoid tax in the end, but rather you defer tax on both the contribution and the investment earnings and you control when tax is ultimately paid. All-in-all, this is a good deal to take advantage of.

How much your RRSP is worth at any point in time is a function of how much you contributed to it and how the investments you selected have performed. If you have $100,000 in an RRSP invested in a GIC paying 1.5% annually, at the end of five years, your RRSP will be worth $107,728, and at the end of 20 years you would have accumulated $134,686. If, instead, you invested in a balanced portfolio that returned 5% over that same five-year period, the value of your RRSP would be $127,628, and after 20 years the value would rise to $265,330. If, instead, you invested in the stock of a gold exploration company that somehow found a substantial vein and their stock appreciated 20% per year, in that circumstance you would have an RRSP worth $248,832 after five years, and after 20 years the value would accumulate to over $3.8 million. On the other hand, if you invested in a gold exploration company that had the plot of land that just missed the vein and its stock lost 20% per year, then you would have an RRSP valued at $32,768 in five years and if that pattern of ineptitude continued for 20 years, you would have just over $1,100 left in your RRSP. So it goes with investing; the $3.8 million outcome is quite attractive, but if you decide to take that approach, you invite the possibility of the $1,100 outcome.

As can be seen from the above, your fate is very much in your own hands when it comes to how much capital ends up in your RRSP. The government has given you the rules around which the investment program must function, but it is how much you invest (within the program limitations) and how you invest (within the bounds of the qualified investments) that will determine how successful you are in building an adequate nest egg.

1. Administrative Aspects

    - If you are a Canadian citizen, have a valid Canadian social insurance number, had *earned income* last year, and are not over 71 years of age, you are eligible to set up and contribute to a RRSP. While there is no age limit on the low end defining when you can begin an RRSP (as soon as you have *earned income,* you are eligible to open an RRSP), there is an age limit on the back end. The year you turn 71 is the last year you can make a contribution to a RRSP and the accumulated funds must find a new home by the end of that year. You can, however, continue to make a spousal contribution until December 31 of the year your spouse turns 71 (more on spousal RRSPs in a later section).
    - As with the TFSA, you can open as many different RRSPs as you like. However, keeping things simple and reducing costs support limiting the number of accounts an investor should open and maintain.

- The RRSP—all registered plans, in fact—gives you the opportunity to name a beneficiary or beneficiaries.
- All RRSPs are registered with the CRA, who keep a record of the transactions you initiate related to your RRSP (contributions and withdrawals) as well as all information relevant to the contribution limitations and carry-forward provisions.
- As long as investments remain in the RRSP, all earnings generated accumulate without attracting tax.
- All assets held in an RRSP must be what are termed *qualified investments*. The list of investments that are *qualified* is extensive and includes: cash, GICs, government and corporate bonds, securities listed on a designated stock exchange, and many more. A full description of qualified investments is available in *Income Tax Folio S3-F10-C1 Qualified Investments*.[3]
- There are tax penalties to be paid if you include non-qualified or prohibited investments in your RRSP.
- It is perfectly legitimate to make an RRSP contribution and choose to defer taking a tax deduction until it is most advantageous (i.e., carrying the contribution forward and deducting it in a year when you experience a higher marginal tax rate). Unused contributions are carried forward and reported on your notice of assessment for future use.

2. Contributions to an RRSP

- Similar to TFSAs, contributions to an RRSP can be made either via cash or "in-kind." Before making an in-kind contribution, ensure that the tax consequences of any deemed disposition are evaluated.
- RRSP legislation contains a formula that determines exactly how much you can annually contribute to your plan, and allows for any contribution room that is not used in a year to be carried forward for future use. The calculation, generally, involves the following:

    ○ Start with your carry-forward contribution room from last calendar year's notice of assessment, then add

- 18% of prior year earned income (or the RRSP limit, whichever is smaller), then deduct
- Your pension adjustment (if any) as reported on your T4 slip, then deduct
- Any contributions you have made since last year
- The result is your remaining contribution limit

- The easy way to figure this number out is to not figure it out. The Canada Revenue Agency will do the calculation for you and tell you what the number is on your notice of assessment, which they will send to you a very short time after you file your tax return.
- In order for a deduction to be available for use when completing an income tax and benefit return, the contribution must have been made within 60 days of the year end following the taxation year.
- The CRA does allow an over-contribution of up to $2,000 before penalties kick in. This is different than for the TFSA, where there is no over-contribution allowance.
- You are assessed a tax of 1% per month on excess contributions, and you get to fill out a new return called the T1-OVP (not exactly a wooo-hooo moment). It goes without saying that, as soon as you find out you have made a contribution that exceeds your contribution limit by more than the allowed $2,000, you should take steps to eliminate the excess amount.

3. Withdrawals from a RRSP

- From a legislation perspective, an RRSP holder can make a withdrawal from a regular RRSP (i.e., one that is not locked-in) any time. In order to do so, the holdings themselves must be in a form that can be extracted from the plan (and any withdrawal rules associated with your plan must be respected), but there are no restrictions embedded in legislation.
- When you withdraw an amount from an RRSP, there is no provision for that amount to be available for subsequent redeposit to the account (except in the case of the Home Buyers' Plan and the Lifelong

Learning Plan, which require withdrawn funds to be redeposited or alternatively included in income over a period of time). When money is taken out of the RRSP, the contribution room that it represented is gone forever.
- When you withdraw funds from an RRSP, the balance will be added to your taxable income in the year of withdrawal. This is the case in all but a very few exceptions, including the following:

    - You are withdrawing unused contributions (in a limited number of circumstances). If you find yourself in this position, review publication T4040(E)[4] available on the Government of Canada website to determine if you can extract your unused contributions without tax consequences.
    - You are making the withdrawal under the terms of the Home Buyers' Plan (HBP), or the Lifelong Learning Plan (LLP), programs that we will discuss later.
    - The "withdrawal" is actually direct transfer to another plan.

- When you make a withdrawal from your RRSP, withholding tax is applied based on the value withdrawn. However, keep in mind that the amount withheld is not likely the true final tax impact that you will be assessed. In effect, the withdrawal will be taxed at your marginal tax rate in the year of withdrawal.

4. Taxes and RRSPs

The RRSP is designed to defer tax payment from the time of the contribution until *later*. Within limits, later is defined by you. If you have retained your RRSP intact until you turn the age of 71, by the end of that calendar year, you must choose one of three available options for the RRSP assets. You can either, or in any combination that makes sense for you:

- Cash in the assets and pay tax on the balance all at once.

- Transfer all or a portion of the RRSP balance into a Registered Retirement Income Fund (RRIF). Tax will be paid as withdrawals occur over time.
- Transfer all or a portion of the RRSP balance to an annuity, where the annual annuity payment will be subject to tax.

While the investments are held in the RRSP, the tax deferral covers taxes that would have been paid on the earned income that has been deposited into the plan as well as the interest, dividends, and capital gains that are earned on the investments.

5. Categories of RRSPs

There are three broad categories of RRSPs: group plans, individual plans, and spousal plans (#6 below).

- Group Plans. Group plans, if available, are offered by your employer. Each group plan has different terms, conditions, and investment options, but generally a contribution is made by the employee and a matching formula is applied, resulting in an additional contribution made by the employer. The employer also often picks up much of the cost of the plan, resulting in a more efficient RRSP than an individual can arrange on their own. If one of these is offered by your employer, you should talk to human resources to understand the details and determine if it makes sense to include this as part of your retirement plan. If there is an element of employer contribution that would otherwise be lost, the plan likely has a place in your retirement strategy.
- Individual Plans. With individual plans, there are really two distinguishing factors that come into play; the amount of support or guidance you receive and the depth and breadth of investment alternatives that are available to you. Nowadays you can open an individual RRSP at pretty much any financial institution. However, not all plans are created equal.

In my opinion, when you select a plan you want to ensure that the RRSP you select is cost effective and accommodates a substantial variety of investments, including all or most of those that you are likely to use going forward. While you can switch from one RRSP to another, it is easier not to, so if you reduce the need for a future change, you will have made your life just a bit easier.

In addition to the breadth and depth of investment options, it is also important to consider the nature of investment guidance that makes sense in your situation. You will want to ensure that the advice you foresee yourself ultimately needing is available within the financial institution you select or, when the time is right, seek the help of a fee-for-service financial advisor. With a fee-for-service advisor, you have the option of implementing the advice yourself through a discount brokerage account or to opt for a full-service account, where the advisor implements the advice on your behalf.

6. Spousal or Common-Law Partner RRSP

A spousal RRSP is simply an RRSP where contributions are made by one spouse (or common-law partner) for the benefit of the other. Generally, the Canada Revenue Agency frowns on division of property for the purpose of splitting income such as this, but they have specifically made an allowance for the spousal RRSP. Given that we Canadians are faced with graduated tax brackets, any opportunity provided that allows a more even realization of income between spouses represents an opportunity to reduce the overall family tax burden. Less tax equals more disposable income. More disposable income equals more double fudge brownie delights from DQ, yummy.

The contributing spouse uses their own contribution room to fund a spousal RRSP; each person's contribution room is set by formula, and how they choose to use it (for their own or a spousal RRSP) is entirely their call. The end result of a contribution to a spousal RRSP is that income is reduced for the contributing spouse in the year the deduction is taken and taxes will ultimately be paid by the receiving spouse when a withdrawal is made at some point in the future. If this is done with accurate foresight, there will be an overall reduction in taxes paid by the couple.

If you are using a spousal RRSP, be sure to respect the holding period requirements. These requirements dictate that if the receiving spouse makes a withdrawal from the spousal RRSP and a spousal contribution has been made in that calendar year or any of the previous two calendar years, the withdrawal (or the portion equivalent to the amount of the contributions in that time period, if less than the withdrawal) will be attributed back to the contributing spouse, effectively negating the whole point of the exercise. If the spousal RRSP is converted into an annuity or RRIF on retirement, so long as the withdrawals are no more than the legislated minimum required, then no attribution applies if it otherwise would have.

Spousal RRSPs are not as important to retirement income planning as they once were due to the ability to split eligible pension income. However, if you have a good understanding of how you and your spouse's retirement income are likely to compare, there can still be a benefit.

7. Home Buyers' Plan (HBP)

In my opinion, the RRSP should be viewed almost exclusively as a one direction investment account—money goes in, gets invested, and is retained until the fund is converted to a retirement income stream. That was the original intent of the RRSP program and the rules have been designed to encourage an RRSP to be used in this fashion. One possible exception would be to participate in the Home Buyers' Plan and that is only the case if home ownership is the best answer for an individual's situation, which, as I tried to argue earlier, is often not the case.

The HBP allows qualifying individuals to access up to $25,000 (proposed to increase to $35,000 in the 2019 federal budget) for the purchase of a qualifying home. Participants must then either repay the amount borrowed or include the amount in income over a period of years. That is the program in two sentences, but of course there is more to it than that.

As with all government programs, make sure you review the current provisions on the Canada.ca website (search HBP). The rules have a tendency to evolve, and there may be details applicable to your specific circumstances that are not covered here.

Key aspects of the HBP, as it stands at the time of writing, include:

- You must be a first-time home buyer. But, under the rules of the program, you can be considered a first-time home buyer more than once. (Politicians can do magic.) You are considered a first-time home buyer if, in the four-year period (starting January 1 of the fourth year before you withdraw the funds), you did not occupy a home that you or your current spouse or common-law partner owned. The 2019 federal budget also proposes to extend access to the HBP to individuals who experience the breakdown of their relationship (married or common-law).
- The RRSP you intend to use cannot be a locked-in RRSP or a group RRSP, in most circumstances.
- You must buy or build a qualifying home and comply with time frames and dates specified by the Canada Revenue Agency.
- You must be a resident of Canada at the time of the withdrawal; the home purchased must also be in Canada.
- The maximum amount a qualifying individual can withdraw is $25,000 ($35,000 under the 2019 budget proposal)—no withholding tax will be applied to a withdrawal under the program. If there is more than one qualifying individual, this maximum loan can be multiplied.
- Contributions to the RRSP must have been held for at least 90 days prior to the withdrawal under the HBP. If you have made contributions to your RRSP in the 89 days prior to the withdrawal, at least the total of those contributions must remain in your RRSP after the withdrawal is made.
- The home cannot be owned for more than 30 days before the withdrawal is made.
- Form T1036 must be completed for each eligible withdrawal (*Home Buyers' Plan (HBP) Request to Withdraw Funds from an RRSP*).

- You must file an income tax return starting the year you make your first HBP withdrawal, even if there is no other reason you would have to file a return.
- The Canada Revenue Agency will provide you with an HBP Statement of Account each year you are a participant in the program.

The HBP was designed to be a temporary mechanism to help first-time homeowners with the purchase of a home. As such, the amount you borrow under the HBP must be either repaid or included in your income. The repayment period begins the second year after you withdraw the funds and runs for the sooner of 15 years, or until you have returned the full value of the loan. If a payment is missed or one is made but it is less than the repayment amount required, then the balance by which the payment was short is included in income for the year the payment was scheduled. Also, if you miss or short a payment, that amount represents lost RRSP contribution room forever.

If you are planning to use the HBP, you need to ensure that the investments within your RRSP are either cash or cashable. Another point to keep in mind relates to the time horizon of your investment. If you are planning to use the HBP, you should be structuring your investments with an appropriate time frame in mind. For instance, you don't want to be holding common stock in your RRSP only to have the market crash immediately before you want to extract the HBP-targeted funds.

The amount you are repaying does not impact your deduction limit. You can repay the balance borrowed as quickly as you like, but there will be a minimum payment required every year until the balance has been repaid in full. (Schedule 7 is used to designate the amount of your contribution attributable to repayment.) If you turn 71 during the repayment period, there are specific rules and options you will need to consider that we will not get into here.

A Couple of Thoughts on the HBP

If you have determined that a house is the right shelter option for your family, and you have identified the amount of house that suits your situation (i.e., it does not exceed your needs and is within your means), then using the HBP is not something I would argue too much with you about. If you have the funds accessible within your RRSP, you have a plan to meet the repayment schedule and your savings targets remain intact, then the program may be helpful.

Going forward, I would encourage any participant in the program to continue to maximize their RRSP contribution as makes sense within their financial plan. At the very least a participant should ensure that they make the minimum contribution to satisfy the HBP requirements. When contributing more than the minimum that is to be paid back, I would continue to designate the HBP repayment at the minimum required amount and use any contribution over and above that amount as a deductible RRSP contribution. In fact, I would not repay faster than the minimum until I had maxed out my RRSP contribution and my TFSA contribution.

8. Lifelong Learning Plan (LLP)

I am a believer in continually upgrading one's marketable skills. One of the keys to a viable financial plan is a substantial and sustainable income. At the root of a substantial and sustainable income is a skill set that is both current and marketable.

That said, very few people use the Lifelong Learning Plan, and I doubt that will change any time soon. If you find yourself out of work, in need of skill enhancement, and you have available investments in an RRSP, then you may want to take a look at what this program offers.

The LLP operates in a fashion similar to how the HBP is designed. In order to qualify for participation, you must meet four qualifying conditions:

- You must own an RRSP
- You must be a resident of Canada
- You must be either enrolled or approved to enroll by March of the following year:
  - On a full-time basis
  - In a qualifying educational program
  - At a designated educational institution
- You must not be in the repayment period associated with a prior LLP withdrawal

The LLP allows you to withdraw up to $10,000 in any one year, to a total of $20,000, while participating in the program and is designed to support either yourself or your spouse/common-law partner. Similar to the HBP, there are limitations related to the duration contributions must have been held in the RRSP to be eligible for use, and there is a repayment schedule that must be complied with or the withdrawal will be included in your income and the contribution room lost.

In the case of the LLP, you have ten years to repay the amount borrowed, usually beginning with the fifth year after your first withdrawal under the plan (though there are a number of situations where the repayment requirement begins sooner). The plan is designed to allow your participation in it as often as you like. However, you will have to wait until the year after you bring your LLP balance to zero in order to start the process again.

If you participate in the LLP, it is a requirement that you file a tax return every year until you have repaid all of the LLP withdrawals (or included them in income). You will receive an LLP Statement of Account with your notice of assessment each year. If it sounds like this program might be beneficial in your situation, look into the details on the Canada.ca website, or scan a copy of RC4112 (E).[5]

RRSPs – A Final Word

The RRSP is a government initiative that is well placed to help most Canadians achieve a level of financial independence that will serve them a healthy dose of comfort as they move into and through their retirement years. It is true that for some the TFSA may be a better plan to use, and for others their registered pension plan may be sufficient to meet their financial requirements, but the RRSP has a significant role to play in most retirement plans. Everyone in my family, and throughout my network, has planned to use a combination of options, including RRSPs, TFSAs, non-registered investment accounts and, in many cases, registered pension plans.

The CRA has many resources available on the Government of Canada website that provide up-to-date RRSP guidance. One of the key documents that you should reference is publication T4040(E).[4] Again, while the CRA has attempted to make the document readable, it isn't what you would describe as a real page-turner (but it can serve as input to a great evening with your loved one ... after a quick read of a hard copy, you can use it to get the kindling burning for a nice bonfire in the backyard, paired with a cool bevy, stars and the odd mosquito).

I love RRSPs.

CHAPTER 25 – RRSP CONVERSION OPTIONS

The tax benefits associated with a RRSP, while long lived, will eventually fade into the sunset. By the end of the calendar year in which an RRSP owner reaches age 71, the RRSP must be wound up.

There are three options to consider for this transition. The order in which they are presented is from least to most popular:

a) Dissolve the RRSP and take the cash

> If you do this there is an immediate realization of tax at your marginal rate. Our tax system is designed to attack income received in blobs with vigour. In almost every instance imaginable, this would be a sub-optimal course of action to take. If you have a hankering to do this, please seek out an informed second opinion so that you can be talked out of it.
>
> There may be an opportunity to take a modest amount of value directly out of the RRSP in a tax-lite manner in some circumstances, but it is almost assuredly unwise to dissolve a substantial RRSP via this method.

b) Registered annuity

The annuity option provides a guaranteed source of income well into the future, if not for life. No further investment decisions need to be made with respect to any funds allocated to an annuity; that part is on cruise control. You simply sit back and receive regular and ongoing payments for the duration of the annuity contract. It all sounds so relaxing, doesn't it?

The down side with most annuities is that when the term is up, or when you die, unless you have purchased a guarantee, there is no residual value. This point is significant enough to deserve some emphasis—if you purchase an annuity that does not have any guarantees and expires when the annuitant dies, there is no estate value. Your beneficiaries receive nothing from that portion of your wealth. This risk is something you have to balance against the other side of the equation, the potential to outlive your money in the absence of an annuity or annuity-like income flow.

In my opinion, everyone should attempt to guarantee a certain amount of their income in retirement. I like the concept of arranging for guaranteed future income at a level sufficient to cover non-discretionary expenses at a minimum, if not a bit more to allow for some surprises. Most Canadians will have a portion of their retirement income guaranteed through government programs (CPP and OAS) and if they are lucky through a defined benefit pension plan (assuming the plan is on stable financial footing). These sources may or may not be sufficient to meet the non-discretionary expense level, or whatever level of guaranteed cash flow you consider to be appropriate in your circumstances. If not, then there is a solid argument to be made for using an annuity to make up the difference.

The concept of an annuity is quite simple to understand. A pile of cash (or a series of instalment payments) is deposited with an insurance company, who will provide ongoing cash flow according to contracted terms. When the pile of cash used to purchase the annuity comes from an RRSP, the annuity is called a registered annuity. There are lots of features that can be designed into the funding and cash flow elements to meet an investor's particular needs and desires, which make it a somewhat complex product to purchase. In fact, special licencing is required in order to sell annuities.

The timing associated with the purchase of an annuity is also an important consideration. Interest rates have a significant impact on the cost of an annuity, but even more impactful is the age of the annuitant when the annuity is purchased. Because of the uncertainty associated with the best time to purchase an annuity and the impact this decision has on the investor's future cash flow, it is likely best to take a diversified approach to any annuity purchase. Let me explain.

The investor should first decide on the value of assets to be directed to the annuity option and then make the purchase in stages over a series of years. From an age perspective, all else remaining equal, an opportune time to begin this purchase stream is about the time the RRSP needs to be wound up in the annuitant's early 70s. So while some of the assets may flow from your RRSP to an annuity, it is likely that some of your RRSP would first be converted to a RRIF and later used to purchase the remaining annuity allocation you have planned.

If you are considering including annuities in your retirement income planning you should set aside some time to learn more about them. Moshe Milevsky wrote a book titled *Life Annuities: An Optimal Product For Retirement Income*[1] for The CFA Institute Research Foundation, which you can download from their website. This book, along with many others written by Moshe, should be required reading (*Your Money Milestones*[2] and *Are You a Stock or a Bond*[3] immediately come to mind as must-reads for people interested in personal finance).

When the time comes to purchase an annuity, or begin a string of purchases, an annuity broker should be consulted so that the market is appropriately canvassed for the best rates available. Keep in mind, when you are purchasing a long-term product such as this, you will need to consider not just the merits of the product but also the credit rating of the insurer and the nature of the insurance provided in relation to the product. Assuris is a not-for-profit organization that protects Canadian policy holders, should their insurance company go bankrupt, but there are limits on the coverage you will need to educate yourself on.

c) Registered Retirement Income Fund (RRIF)

The RRIF tends to be the most popular choice for at least a portion of a RRSP balance. A RRIF operates very much like a RRSP, with a couple of key differences:

- The first main difference is that there is no ongoing contribution made to a RRIF; the only inflow of funds is via direct transfer from an RRSP, a registered pension plan (RPP), a pooled registered pension plan (PRPP), a Specified Pension Plan (SPP—something only available in Saskatchewan), or another RRIF. We will talk more about RPPs and PRPPs next chapter.
- The second main difference is that a RRIF requires that at least a certain minimum amount be withdrawn (beginning the year after the RRIF is established) on an annual basis. Thus, while the majority of the investment portfolio continues in a tax-deferred environment, there is an element of taxable income realized in a scheduled manner. While a minimum withdrawal is specified, for non-locked-in retirement accounts (see employer pensions chapter), no maximum withdrawal limitations are stipulated. Thus, while there is less flexibility than with a RRSP, there is still considerable income flexibility provided by the RRIF option. Tax withholding applies for any withdrawal from the RRIF that is greater than the minimum required withdrawal.

The types of investments eligible for a RRSP are also eligible within a RRIF; this helps make the transition from a RRSP seamless. The minimum payment factor can be based on either the RRIF owner's age at the beginning of the year or the age of their spouse or common-law partner. (It makes sense to base the minimum payment on the lower of the two ages.)

Notwithstanding the virtues of an annuity for a portion of retirement income, there is a strong argument in support of using a RRIF as the primary recipient of your RRSP contents in many situations. A RRIF provides great flexibility, tax advantages, control over investments, and estate-planning benefits, and while there is the requirement for a minimum payout on an annual basis, which you may not need, there is lots of flexibility for those periods where you require more funds to cross some items off your bucket list. After all, the whole reason you saved to begin with is to be able to fund a series of goals; many of those goals involve the use of capital. Go for it!

On an administrative note, when a RRSP is converted to a RRIF, a new beneficiary designation needs to be filled out. The *Income Tax Act* considers the RRIF to be a brand new plan, so any beneficiary designations made under the RRSP will not automatically carry over to the RRIF.

The Government of Canada website does a great job of discussing all of the RRIF intricacies that you need to be aware of. Make sure to give it a scan when you are considering your options.

CHAPTER 26 – EMPLOYER PENSIONS

If your employer offers a pension plan, lucky you! A well-designed employer pension plan is often the foundation of a solid retirement plan, and in fact *may* be all that is needed to fund the retirement lifestyle that the plan member is after. I have seen both very generous pension plans as well as some that appear to be virtually useless. If you simply assume that your pension plan will take care of you, you could be in for a rude awakening when the first pension payment arrives.

Many employer-sponsored plans are pretty much hands-off from the perspective of the member—the member contributes what they are told and someone else worries about the investing and the administration. More and more, however, the plan member is being asked to make crucial choices that can make or break the effectiveness of the pension in meeting their retirement needs. The more hands-on the plan is, the more crucial it is that plan members take an active role in understanding their responsibilities and fully engage themselves (or their representatives) in the decisions that have been delegated to them.

This discussion is necessarily general in nature because the specific provisions of a plan will have a dramatic impact on how it works and the overall value to the employee. This book will not delve deeply into the federal tax laws or the federal/provincial pension laws that govern pension plans (too boring) or eligibility requirements (too varied).

There are a few common elements worthy of mention before getting into a discussion of the main categories of employer pensions:

- One of the key benefits of employer pension plans is that the employer makes contributions to the plan—free money (yee haw). This often is a substantial element of employee compensation and it does not lead to an immediate tax obligation the way that salary does. When considering an offer of employment, be sure to give any pension benefit (or lack thereof) due consideration.
- Registered pension plan assets are often protected from creditors.
- Most pension plans have an element of employee and employer funding. If the plan has employer matching, as a general rule, you should seriously consider maximizing your participation to at least the level of contribution that is matched (you might as well get as much free money as you can).
- Vesting refers to the point in time where employer contributions belong to the employee regardless of their continuing employment. In many cases vesting is immediate, but you should understand how this works in your specific situation. Talk to your human resources representative to get the full story. It is especially important to understand vesting details if you are considering a job change.
- Generally, once vested in a plan, pension assets cannot be accessed prior to retirement; they become what is referred to as "locked-in." Some provinces have provisions to un-lock a specified value of benefits under specific circumstances, but these circumstances are usually quite restrictive.
- Employer pensions will impact available RRSP contribution room. Your employer will report a pension adjustment on your T4 slip. It is designed to be representative of the value you accrued under your employer pension plan over the course of the year.

There are several forms of employer-sponsored pensions available. The less common forms of employer-sponsored pension plan that we will not talk about in the following section include: individual pension plans, deferred profit sharing plans, supplementary employee retirement plans, target benefit plans, and the various hybrid and combination plans. If one of these plans applies to your situation, I would encourage you to visit your human resources representative to learn all you can about the plan provisions and how you can maximize your benefit.

The forms of employer pensions that are discussed include:

- defined benefit pension plans,
- defined contribution pension plans, and
- pooled registered pension plans.

a) Defined Benefit (DB) Pension Plans

A defined benefit pension plan is a plan where the benefit to be received in retirement is set, via formula, in advance (i.e., the benefit is *defined*). Normally the formula is based on a percentage of earnings (often 2%), multiplied by the number of years worked at the employer. There are a number of different ways that the earnings figure can be defined (final average earnings, best average earnings, career average earnings, etc.), and the chosen earnings definition can have a significant impact on the ultimate cash flow provided by the pension.

Many defined benefit plans are contributory, meaning the employee is responsible to contribute a set percentage of salary to the plan. The employee contribution is tax deductible. The *Income Tax Act* limits the maximum annual pension that can be paid by a defined benefit plan (subject to annual indexation), so highly paid employees are likely to have their benefits restricted.

Generally, in the world of pensions (depending on the provisions of the specific plan), defined benefit plans have the reputation of being the best. The main reasons for this include:

- Investment risk resides with the employer. The pension formula is set in advance and the performance of the underlying investment pool does not matter from the beneficiary's perspective; they are insulated from capital market gyrations.
- The beneficiary has no investment management responsibility. Pension funds are managed by professionals who are responsible for ensuring the contributions to the plan are effectively managed to cover the obligations of the plan.

- Pension income is predictable. The pensioner knows what they will receive on a regular basis and can plan their expenditures around this cash flow with a high degree of certainty (assuming the plan remains viable).
- Often these plans have some form of indexing associated with them alleviating, at least partially, inflation concerns.

There are also a couple of unique risks associated with this form of pension plan to be aware of:

- The pension plan features are not unalterable. There is a risk that plan features could be watered down through changes over time. So while there is more certainty with this type of plan when compared with most others, that certainty is not absolute. The upside of this is that the benefit provisions could also be enhanced over time.
- The solvency of the employer and, even though the assets of the pension plan are segregated from the employer, the financial condition of the plan itself could have an impact on pension income. Federal and provincial pension regulations contain funding and third party evaluation requirements that pension plans must adhere to with a view to managing this risk, but these provisions are not foolproof.

b) Defined Contribution (DC) Pension Plans

Defined contribution plans are considerably different than defined benefit plans; just one word is different in the name, but there is a world of difference in how the plans work and how the risk is divvied up between the employee and the employer.

DC plans, as the name implies, specify the level of contribution to be made to the plan by each of the employee and the employer. The *Income Tax Act* places a limit on the combined employee and employer contribution (18% of earned income up to a maximum dollar amount that is coordinated with the RRSP dollar limit). Thus, there is certainty as to the contributions made to the plan, but that is where the certainty ends.

With a DB plan, the retiree knows the cash flow the plan will provide because their benefits are based on a formula derived from known variables. With a DC plan, the level of income that can be funded in retirement is directly related to how effectively the investments perform while in the fund. Not only is the employee dependent on the effectiveness of the investment strategy for the ultimate value of their pension, but they are also responsible for choosing the investments from the menu provided by the plan administrators. With DB, the investment risk is assumed by the employer; with DC, the investment risk is shouldered by the employee.

Upon retiring with a DC plan, the employee will choose either an annuity to provide a regular stream of income or they will transfer the funds into a locked-in retirement account. If the investments perform well and the contribution formula is sufficient, then the result of a DC plan can be very good for the retiree. The problem with DC is that you just don't know in advance if this will be the case or not.

You may be thinking that a DC plan works in a manner very much like that of an RRSP, and there certainly are a lot of similarities. Some of the benefits associated with a DC plan include:

- Employer contributions are often part of the deal ... free money is always a good thing!
- The menu of investment options is usually substantial, allowing for a well-diversified portfolio to be constructed and maintained. Often, there will be a management fee advantage over options generally available to an individual investor.
- If the investments perform well, a DC plan could provide a higher benefit than that of a DB plan.

There has been a considerable move away from the provision of DB plans to DC plans in recent years. Employers have recognized that there is a very real financial risk in providing a fixed stream of benefit payments. My brother-in-law worked for an organization that decided to change their pension plan from DB to DC. All new employees were required to go with a DC version; existing employees were given the choice to stay with DB or move over to DC. My brother-in-law saw the value in the assumption of risk by the employer and stayed with the DB option. He is now very happy golfing daily with a clear understanding of his retirement income.

c) Pooled Registered Pension Plans (PRPP)

A PRPP is a relatively new retirement savings option that is currently available in pockets around the country, though it appears to be just a matter of time until it will be available coast to coast. Federal legislation (with associated regulations) came into force December 2012, providing the framework for these plans. At that time, PRPPs became available to organizations that came under federal jurisdiction as well as for employees and the self-employed in the Yukon, the Northwest Territories, and Nunavut. Anyone working for a provincially regulated organization has/had to wait for their province to pass enabling legislation. The provinces have been moving at different paces and not all provinces have enacted the necessary legislation. As at the time of writing, Alberta, Ontario, BC, Quebec, Nova Scotia, and Saskatchewan had made PRPPs available, and Manitoba was in the final stages of completing the necessary arrangements to offer the plans.

Each province is likely to have some unique elements within their PRPP legislation, so it is important that anyone considering involvement do some investigation to understand the details applicable to their situation. That said, key features generally associated with the PRPP include:

- The PRPP has been designed to make pension plans more generally available for individuals, including those who are self-employed. They are a less-costly choice for employers to use and have certain features that may make self-employed individuals favour them over the RRSP.
- PRPPs are administered by a financial institution as opposed to the employer. This makes them less burdensome for employers to offer than other forms of pension plans.
- Members, it has been asserted, will benefit from lower administration costs because they will be participating in a large pooled pension plan.

- There are portability improvements over other types of pension plans. Ease of portability is a huge advantage for anyone who takes a more transient approach to employment.
- Contributions made to a PRPP are limited in the same fashion as contributions to RRSPs and other registered pension plans. Contribution limits are cumulative across all pensions.
- Contributions made by an employer are not an immediate taxable benefit to employees. The benefit is eventually taxable when received as pension income. Contributions made by the employee are deductible on the employee's tax return.
- Employer contributions are optional, and employee contribution rates are flexible. Provincial regulations may differ from the federal approach and from province to province.
- The financial institution will decide on the specific investment options that are made available. Members will have the responsibility to direct how their contributions are to be invested. The federal regulations provide a default option to be applied if no specific choice is made by the member (a balanced fund or a portfolio option that takes into account the member's age). The federal regulations also contain certain restrictions and/or requirements related to the investment options to be available. Provinces will likely have similar requirements.
- The *PRPP Act* limits withdrawals that can be taken before retirement. Similar to other RPPs, the funds in your PRPP are generally locked-in.
- The level of retirement income that can be funded by a PRPP is dependent on the funds accumulated in the plan. Payments from PRPP are taxable and considered to be *pension income* for pension income splitting purposes and the pension income amount.
- For federal PRPPs, employees are automatically enrolled upon satisfying eligibility requirements. The employee is then given the opportunity to decline participation if they so choose. The provincial programs that I have reviewed also contain this provision. It will be very interesting to see if this simple idea (making someone opt-out if they don't want to participate as opposed to opt-in if they do want to participate) will make a difference in continuing enrolment. It is almost like the

government is resorting to trying to trick us into providing for our retirement. If that is what it takes, and it works, I am all for it.

The extent to which PRPPs catch on has yet to be seen, given their limited history. To the extent that these plans encourage more employers to offer pension plans, and employees to save for the future, they will be a blessing to those affected. Given that PRPPs are optional (even though the requirement is opt-out as opposed to opt-in), I am a little sceptical that they will have a substantial impact on the retirement planning landscape. I truly hope my scepticism is unfounded.

If you are interested in learning more about PRPPs, further information is available on the Government of Canada website.[1]

CHAPTER 27 – GOVERNMENT PENSIONS

When it comes to government pensions, beneficiaries do not have any asset management responsibility and the benefit levels are predefined. In the case of the Canada Pension Plan (CPP), the benefit formula is relatively complicated; whereas, in the case of Old Age Security (OAS), it is relatively straightforward. However, there will be a number of decisions you have to make that will impact what you receive and when you receive it. You need to be aware of what you are entitled to receive from each program, understand how the various associated benefits work, and account for the relevant benefits as a component of your financial plan. While some believe that the days for these programs are numbered, it is my wholehearted belief that both the CPP and the OAS programs will continue to exist, and provide benefits to Canadians well into the future.

If you live in the beautiful province of Quebec, the CPP will not apply to you; rather, the Quebec Pension Plan (QPP) will be in play. The retirement benefits provided under the two plans are virtually identical at the time of writing, and the QPP mirrors many of the provisions of the CPP. However, there are some significant differences between the CPP and QPP. For example, the governance framework, contribution requirements, and levels are different between the two programs; as well, the QPP has some innovative options with respect to phased retirement. Thus, while the guts of the programs are very similar, and most of the benefit elements of the programs are the same, there are differences.

The balance of the chapter will be limited to discussing provisions of the CPP. If the QPP applies in your situation, most of this discussion will be applicable, but you should explore the differences between the two plans to ensure they are properly accounted for in your planning.

Sustainability

The investment assets of the CPP are segregated from government accounts and are managed by investment professionals. In the words of the CPP Investment Board (CPPIB) website:

> …the assets of the fund are managed in the best interest of the Canadian contributors and beneficiaries who participate in the Canada Pension Plan. These assets are strictly segregated from government funds.[1]

I don't know about you, but that gives me a warm and fuzzy feeling inside. The website goes on to emphasize that:

> The CPPIB Act has safeguards against any political interference. CPPIB operates at arm's length from federal and provincial governments with the oversight of an independent, highly qualified professional Board of Directors. CPPIB management reports not to governments, but to the CPPIB Board of Directors. The CPPIB Board approves investment policies, determines with management the organization's strategic direction and makes critical operational decisions.[1]

In my view, this is a very strong governance structure.

The governance structure will only matter, though, if the fund and the associated operating formula are sufficient to support the financial promises made by the plan. The most recently published *Chief Actuary's Report*[2] *(November 2016)* paints a very rosy picture for the CPP. Among the observations included in the report were:

- The CPP is sustainable for 75 years and beyond.
- Despite Canada's aging demographics, none of the investment income is expected to be needed to help pay pensions until 2021, at which time only a small portion of the investment income will be used to pay pensions.
- The CPP fund is expected to grow throughout the 75-year period covered by the report.
- By 2035, the assets of the fund are projected to be $747 billion.

The chief actuary conducts a review of the CPP every three years, so if there is a material change in the outlook, it will be discovered in a relatively timely fashion. There may be some adjustments to the program over time to recognize changing conditions, but there is no reason I can see to believe that the current governance structure will not successfully maintain the sustainability of the plan.

When it comes to the sustainability of the OAS, the situation is a little less clear, at least to me. There is no segregated fund used to meet program obligations; rather, the continuing viability of OAS is dependent on general tax revenues. While OAS payments were once universally available to all qualified Canadians, there is currently an OAS recovery tax (clawback) process in place that impacts higher-income recipients. When a taxpayer's net income exceeds a threshold level of $77,580 (2019, adjusted annually), the income in excess of this level will result in a 15% recovery tax. As a result of the recovery tax, once net income reaches a level of slightly over $125,000 (2019), the whole of the benefit is lost.

In my opinion, while it is highly likely that the OAS will continue for those who need it, it is also likely that the affordability of the program will drive changes to the benefit formula. It is my hope and expectation that any changes made to the OAS will be implemented in a measured way, with substantial lead time, to allow for proper planning. The retired Canadian demographic is too important to the re-election hopes of politicians to be disrespected by substantial and sudden program alterations (the intersection of empathy and self-interest is a strong combination).

The most recent changes to the OAS, in fact, have been to reverse planned program alterations that would have made the program less lucrative for retirees through delaying eligibility dates. I am not sure if that was prudent or not, but it certainly did garner some votes, maybe even more than the shirtless pics our Prime Minister has become known for.

While the future of both the CPP and OAS programs cannot be described as unequivocally certain, for anyone currently in or approaching midlife, it is my view that it is valid to allow for their continuance in financial planning assumptions. As with all other variables, though, it makes sense to pay attention as the future unfolds and the rules evolve.

Limitations of this Discussion

The CPP and OAS programs are both complex government initiatives. They are subject to alteration at any time as the government of the day initiates policy changes. Indeed, the CPP is currently undergoing a substantial change, which will impact both the contribution side of the equation for employees, employers, and the self-employed, as well as the benefit side of the equation for those who are qualified to receive program spoils.

The Government of Canada website, www.canada.ca, is replete with very detailed and current information on all aspects of the programs, as well as any program changes that are in the implementation stages. If you have any questions about the programs, how they operate, the qualifications for and benefits you can expect, visit www.canada.ca (search for CPP or OAS) for current information.

CPP and OAS Income Levels

Canada Pension Plan

The CPP was originally designed to replace 25% of career average pensionable earnings (CAPE). The maximum monthly pension available from the CPP in 2019 (at age 65) stood at $1,154.58[3] (annual $13,854.96). Payments are indexed to changes in the Consumer Price Index, adjusted annually. However, what your pension will ultimately be valued at is determined by a complicated formula. It is based on the length of your contributory period, the amount you made/contributed to the plan each year during that time, when you decide to take your pension (early, late, or at 65), whether or not you had a period of time when you were receiving disability benefits, the application of low-earnings drop-out provisions, the applicability of the child rearing drop-out provision, etc.

The end result of applying the formula is that the average CPP pension received is well below the maximum. As at the time of writing, the average CPP monthly retirement benefit for new beneficiaries was $723.89[3] (annual $8,686.68) according to the Government of Canada website (May 2019). Even though the average payment for new beneficiaries is a fraction of what the maximum payment is set at, CPP is a consequential piece of most pensioners' retirement income profile.

If you want to learn more about how the formula works in order to maximize your CPP payment, the federal government has lots of information available on its website. If you want an estimate of the retirement pension that you can expect, you can either request one be done for you (visit a Service Canada Centre) or log into your online account at My Service Canada. These estimates are just that: estimates. The closer you are to retirement, the better the information they provide, but make sure you look at the underlying assumptions to ensure they are appropriate. If your situation does not closely align with the estimate assumptions, it could differ quite substantially from an individual's actual result.

If you want to go full nerd and figure out your benefit under various scenarios using your own pencil, Doug Runchey has written a detailed article that walks you through how to calculate an accurate estimate of what you will receive from CPP.[4] Doug also offers a service where he will do customized number crunching for a fee (I would describe it as a reasonable fee, and it varies by the breadth of information you request of him—www.DRpensions.ca).

The CPP is changing. Bill C-26 will make a number of substantial changes to the CPP, designed to enhance benefits. According to the Government of Canada website, the provisions of the Bill will increase CPP retirement, disability, and survivor's pensions. The enhancement will be fully funded through increased contributions and will only impact you if, as of 2019, you are making contributions to the CPP. The level of impact you experience, related to the quantum of benefits received, will depend on how much and for how long you contribute to the enhanced CPP. Once fully implemented, the enhancement will see the CPP target become the replacement of 33% of average work earnings (up from the current 25% target), and the maximum work earnings covered will also be meaningfully increased from the current levels.

The enhancement will have a marginal impact on working Canadians who are currently well into their careers, but it will have a considerable impact on young Canadians just entering the workforce. The hope is that the change to the CPP will help to fill the gap for those who do not have a workplace pension, and thereby reduce the incidence of families at risk of not saving enough for retirement. There is a lot of information available to you on the Government of Canada website that details the operative elements and benefits of the enhancement. In addition, the Department of Finance put together an interesting read entitled *Backgrounder: Canada Pension Plan (CPP) Enhancement*[5] for those who are so inclined.

If you are a resident of Quebec, it was announced in November 2017 that the QPP will undergo an enhancement process similar to the CPP.

Old Age Security

The maximum monthly OAS pension available for the April – June 2019 period stood at $601.45[6] (annual $7,217.40). Payments are indexed to changes in the Consumer Price Index, adjusted quarterly. Whether you qualify for a full or partial OAS pension depends on your Canadian residency history and status. If you are 65 or older, and a citizen or legal resident in Canada for 40 years after the age of 18, you are eligible, subject to clawback, for the full pension (there are other criteria that also may allow you to receive the full pension—please refer to the Government of Canada website for details). If you are not eligible for a full pension, you may be eligible for a partial pension if you are 65 or older, lived in Canada as a citizen or legal resident for at least 10 years after turning 18, or you have lived in Canada for one full year and there is an international social security agreement applicable to your situation. (Again, the internet is your friend in researching the details; it is beyond the scope of this book to get further into the qualification details.) If you lived in Canada as a citizen or legal resident for at least 20 years since age 18, you are eligible to continue to receive your OAS payment, even if you move to another country. (If you do not meet these minimum residency requirements, the OAS payment will stop after six months.)

Other Benefits of the CPP and OAS Programs

In addition to the base retirement pension provided under the CPP and OAS programs, there are a number of additional benefits designed into each. The qualification criteria and details related to these benefits are intricate and will not be discussed further here. If disability, low income, or death are either present or have occurred in your immediate family, these program elements should be researched further on the Government of Canada website.

Canada Pension Plan, Other Benefits:

- Disability benefits – for contributors with a disability and their dependent children.
- Survivor benefits – includes survivor's pensions, the children's benefit, and the death benefit.

Old Age Security Other Benefits (all are income-tested/dependent):

- The Guaranteed Income Supplement (GIS)
- The Allowance
- The Allowance for the Survivor

Other Characteristics of CPP and OAS (Boring Alert)

As with most government programs, there are a number of moving parts that make the application of these programs dependent on the specific circumstances of the individual. What follows is a list of some program elements that may be important to your situation:

Canada Pension Plan

- The "normal" age for receiving CPP is 65.
- If you start your pension before age 65, your pension will be reduced by 0.6% for each month prior to your 65th birthday. You can take your

pension as early as age 60, in which case your pension will be reduced by 36%. Keep in mind, though, if you take the early option and accept the reduced pension, you will be getting the pension for a longer period of time (up to 60 extra cheques, though they will be for a lower amount each). Depending on how long you live, and how smoothing your income over time impacts your tax situation (among other things), this may or may not prove to be a good deal for you.

- If you start your pension after age 65, your pension will be increased by 0.7% for each month of delay. You are allowed to delay receiving CPP up to age 70, at which time you will be eligible to receive a 42% increase over the pension you would have received at age 65. Again, depending on how long you live, and on how deferral of income affects your tax situation (among other things), this may or may not turn out to be a good deal in your circumstances.
- You can begin receiving CPP while you are working.
- A post-retirement benefit (PRB) is earned by Canadians who are receiving a retirement pension from the CPP, and continue to make contributions to the plan. If you are under age 65, both you and your employer will continue to make contributions to the plan that go to funding your post-retirement benefit. Once you achieve age 65, so long as you remain under age 70, you have a choice as to if you (and your employer) continue to make CPP contributions to enhance your post-retirement benefit or not. The PRB will be added to your CPP retirement pension even if you are already receiving the maximum pension.
- There is no benefit to starting your CPP after age 70. CPP benefits will not be paid retroactively beyond 12 months.
- You must apply to begin receiving your CPP benefits. However, the 2019 federal budget is proposing proactive enrolment for contributors who are 70 or older in 2020.
- The formula used for calculating your benefit includes a couple of different drop-out provisions; if these provisions apply to your situation, they will increase your pension.

- The general low-earnings drop-out provision eliminates 17% of your lowest-earning months during your contributory period (up to 8 years). This provision is automatically applied.
- The child rearing drop-out provision takes into account low earning years associated with being the primary caregiver of children who are under 7 years of age. **The child rearing drop-out provision is not automatically applied; it is up to you to request it when you apply for CPP benefits.**

- Spouses and common-law partners who are both at least 60 years old can share their CPP retirement pensions, potentially reducing income tax.
- Certain CPP benefits can be combined, though the total benefit will be subject to capping in accordance with the rules.
- CPP benefits are taxable.
- Benefits can be received outside of Canada.

Old Age Security

- A full OAS pension is payable at age 65. There is an option for deferral; if you choose to defer, then the amount you receive will be increased by 0.6% for each month of deferral (to a maximum of 36%). Taking the option for deferral will impact your eligibility for other OAS program elements (GIS and Allowance); research this impact further if you are eligible for these benefits.
- There is an automatic enrolment process for OAS, though it does not apply for everyone (you will be notified if it applies to you). If auto enrolment does not apply to you, an application will be necessary. Even if the automatic enrolment process applies in your situation, you have the option of benefit deferral if you so choose.
- The OAS pension is taxable and there is also an OAS recovery tax (often referred to as the OAS clawback). If you are over the income threshold ($77,580 in 2019), then you repay the OAS pension at a rate of 15% of income above the threshold.

LARRY WILSON

Significant Decisions Related to CPP and OAS

As outlined above, there is some flexibility designed into each of the programs and with flexibility comes the need to choose among available alternatives. We will focus on a couple of the more significant decisions that need to be made with respect to CPP and OAS. Keep in mind that the answer that best addresses your specific needs can be determined only after considering your circumstances; there is no universal best answer to these questions.

When is the best time to start CPP?

For most people, the decision as to when to begin receiving CPP is not an easy or straightforward one. If a pensioner opts to receive CPP at the age of 65, they will receive 100% of the benefit they have earned. However, a CPP recipient has the option to receive their pension earlier than age 65 or later than age 65, with their benefit being adjusted accordingly.

Early enrolment involves a penalty of 0.6% for each month before age 65 the pensioner decides to take their CPP benefit. In this scenario, the pensioner receives more cheques, but each cheque is for a reduced amount and that reduced value endures for the balance of the pensioner's life. If on the other hand the pensioner decides to defer CPP until beyond age 65, they will receive an enhanced cheque to the tune of 0.7% per month of deferral, with a maximum deferral of 60 months. These larger cheques too will run for the duration of the pensioner's life.

Thus, the decision is one of receiving a reduced cheque by up to 36%, but getting more of them, or receiving an enhanced cheque by up to 42%, but receiving fewer of them. The correct mathematical decision is not known with certainty until you die ... just a little too late to be helpful.

In my situation (the result will almost certainly be different for you), after considering all of the variables included in the pension calculation, the best time for me to start collecting CPP so as to maximize the total amount I receive works out to be as follows:

> If I don't live past age 71 – I should start collecting at age 60
>
> If I live past age 71, but not past 74 – I should start collecting at age 61

If I live past age 74, but not past 76 – I should start collecting at age 62

If I live past age 76, but not past 79 – I should start collecting at age 63

If I live past age 79, but not past 81 – I should start collecting at age 67

If I live past age 81, but not past 83 – I should start collecting at age 68

If I live past age 83, but not past 85 – I should start collecting at age 69

If I live to at least age 86 – I should start collecting at age 70

(This information was calculated by Doug Runchey (www.DRpensions.ca))

One of the exercises you can undertake to estimate how long you can expect to live is to search the web for *life expectancy calculators* and work through a couple of them. Alternatively, the Projection Assumption Guidelines of the FP Canada Standards Council[7] include a probability of survival table (from the 2014 *Canadian Institute of Actuaries Canadian Pensioners' Mortality Report*) which can be used as a reference. According to this table, I have a 50% chance of living to at least age 89, a 25% chance of living to at least age 94, and a 10% chance of living to at least age 97. So, from a strictly mathematical perspective, considering nothing other than maximizing the CPP I collect, it probably makes sense for me to delay applying for CPP.

Life expectancy is one of the key variables to be considered, but there are several others that may be influential in your decision, including:

1. What are your cash flow needs?

    If you need the cash flow to sustain a modest but healthy lifestyle that would otherwise be compromised, I fail to see why you would wait.

2. Will additional income from CPP impact other assistance you are receiving or will receive?

    Your choices related to CPP can impact benefits received under the Guaranteed Income Supplement or the OAS clawback, as examples. You need to review you income profile, and program details, to assess any impacts.

3. What is your income tax profile, and how does the timing of the addition of CPP impact your tax situation?

   CPP benefits are taxable, so they will impact your overall tax situation when you decide to start receiving them.

4. Are there elements of the CPP benefit formula that you need to consider?

   Your contributory period begins the month after you turn 18 and ends either when you turn 70 or when you begin your CPP pension. If you stop working early, you are adding a number of zero earnings years to the calculation of the CPP benefit.

5. Are you concerned that CPP won't be there for you if you wait?

   As previously stated, I think the risk of CPP failing or something else happening to cause a significant and sudden change to the core of the program, is minimal.
   You might also want to consider the availability of survivor benefits should both you and your spouse be eligible to receive CPP. Survivor benefits will only serve to top up the surviving spouses CPP benefit to a maximum; if you are both holding out to get a larger CPP benefit, then the survivor benefit may be negligible and represent a lost opportunity should either of you pass early in the payment period.

6. Do you have other investments that could be used early in your retirement that serve to better meet your retirement income needs across the breadth of your projected retirement time frame?

   Frederick Vettese wrote an article for the *Financial Post* titled "Why you should wait until you are 70 to collect CPP benefits"[8] that is well worth a read. I read it this morning while eating a baby apple pancake at the Original Pancake House. In fact, I have read three of Mr. Vettese's books and found them to be well worth the time spent going through them. I also recommend the giant apple pancake (or its baby cousin) for anyone who is visiting Winnipeg—so very good!

In the article referenced, Mr. Vettese makes the mathematical case, in the circumstances of Mario, that he should delay taking both CPP and OAS to bulk up both of those benefits while using his RRIF income. In this case the math is sound (he is an actuary, after all), but there are some other considerations that the article does not discuss, such as legacy-related issues, which may or may not be a significant consideration.

Mr. Vettese has also recently published a book, entitled *Retirement Income For Life*,[9] which does a thorough job of running through how a couple can optimize their retirement income through strategically utilizing the various sources of income available to them. I enjoyed the read ... though I did read it on the balcony of my cruise ship in the Baltic Sea. Everything was enjoyable on that balcony!

So then, when should you plan to start taking CPP given the options available? Unfortunately, it is not possible to offer a generic answer to this question. Each person must consider their own situation in terms of the variables discussed in order to arrive at a well-founded answer. There is no assurance that it will turn out to be the best answer because the best answer will not be known with certainty until your executor is hunting for your will.

If your situation is complicated, I think this is a really good question for you to explore with a fee-for-service financial planner within the context of your retirement cash flow projections and in full view of your goals and the other variables specific to your situation.

When is the best time to start OAS?

Far more people qualify for maximum OAS than is the case with CPP, but not everyone will be able to keep their full OAS benefit as a result of the clawback, unless they first do some clawback planning.

You will recall that OAS is available to qualified residents at age 65 and there is an incentive of 0.6% per month of deferral up to the age of 70. So if you defer taking OAS until you are age 66, you will receive 7.2% more than at age 65, and so on up until age 70 when you will receive 136% of the age 65 benefit. The cost of each year of deferral is 12 OAS cheques. If you defer the full five years, you will receive an enhanced benefit for the rest of your life, but you will receive 60 fewer cheques than you could have if you had started when you turned 65. Without considering anything else, it would make sense to defer receiving OAS if you are going to live a long time. The age at which deferral pays off is relatively easy to calculate—your financial planner can help you out with this if you are mathematically challenged.

However, there is more to this decision than just this simple bit of math. In my view, the most significant additional considerations include:

1. Do you believe that general tax revenues and government philosophy will support the continuance of the OAS program in its current form?

    I have already stated that I believe any changes to the program will be made in a measured way with sufficient warning that they can be adequately designed into your planning process as and when they are announced. If you are more sceptical than I, and I certainly don't blame you if you are, then you might want to consider taking the benefit on an ASAP basis, but only after thoroughly considering the planning you may have to do around the clawback.

2. Do you need the money now to support your lifestyle?

    If you are 65 and you need the money, take the money. I am guessing that if you need the money, then the clawback is not an issue for you.

3. What impact will other sources of income have on your ability to retain the benefit?

    As soon as other sources of income cause you to have annual net income for tax purposes greater than the threshold level ($77,580 in 2019), you will lose OAS to the tune of 15% of net income in excess of the threshold (with net income of just over $125,000, all OAS will be clawed back). The way you reduce or eliminate the impact of the clawback is to manage your net income to the level of the threshold. There are a number of ways you can do this, all of which need to be tailored to your specific circumstances. The most common options include:

- Time your application for CPP to best manage the impact on your net income, with the clawback in mind.
- If you are married or living common-law, you can consider sharing the CPP with your significant other.
- Take advantage of the opportunity to split eligible pension income allowed within the *Income Tax Act*.
- When you are considering the crystallization of a capital gain (i.e., selling an asset that has appreciated in value outside of a registered account), take into account the impact the transaction will have on net income and the clawback.
- Use your RRSP deduction claims wisely. You have flexibility to claim the deductions in the manner that best minimizes your overall tax liability.
- Plan RRSP withdrawals carefully to ensure you are managing any clawback impact.
- Plan your RRSP conversion to a RRIF or annuity with the clawback in mind.
- Take full advantage of TFSAs. None of the income realized in a TFSA will be reflected in net income for tax purposes.

While there are quite a number of variables to consider when deciding on the right strategy to employ regarding the OAS benefit, and you won't know if you did it just right until you are dead, that doesn't mean that you can't put yourself into a position where you are highly likely to make approximately the most of what OAS has to offer. Give it some thought, consider all of the variables, and only then make your decision. Once the decision is made, treat yourself to a milkshake and don't second-guess yourself. (You can never go wrong with a milkshake ... unless you happen to be lactose intolerant.)

CHAPTER 28 – NON-REGISTERED INVESTMENT ACCOUNTS

Given all of the registered account options, and their associated tax benefits, many if not most people won't do a lot of investing in a plain ordinary non-registered investment account. However, if you successfully organize your life to live well below your means, it is highly likely that you will, at some stage, require one of these accounts.

The key characteristics of non-registered investment accounts include:

- The cash flow that enters a non-registered account is after tax. This means that it has already run the tax-grab gauntlet and represents what is left after the government has taken its piece.
- The investments held in non-registered accounts are restricted only by account-based limitations. Most financial institutions offer a number of different accounts; the key features that distinguish one account from another are:

    ○ the level of service provided – which ranges from do-it-yourself all the way to having access to a professional advisor (online, over the phone, or in person),

- the fee structure – which can include any combination of account-based fees, service fees, commissions, and/or transaction fees, and
- the scope of investments available – which can range from accounts that limit the investor to GICs offered by the financial institution all the way to a full array of marketable securities or maybe even a suite of proprietary investment products.

- The investments will generate income that will be taxable in most instances. How taxation of investment income works is complicated and forms the subject matter of the next chapter.

Non-registered investment accounts are important for people who have already exhausted the tax-deferred investment options available to them. Once you have funded government programs (i.e., paid your taxes), met all of your spending requirements (including debt repayment), funded your registered pension plan, your TFSA, your RRSP, and met your CPP requirements, the remainder of your income (if any) will flow to either a bank account or an investment account. If you are doing all of these things, you are well ahead of the game. Congratulations!

If you have selected your registered investment accounts well, then it is highly likely that the financial institution you are currently using will have a suitable non-registered investment account option available. In the interest of keeping things as simple as possible, this should be the first place you look when establishing a non-registered investment account.

The key aspects to look for in a non-registered investment account include:

1. Cost Minimization.

   I can't emphasize too strongly how important it is to control your investment cost structure.

   - The account should have no meaningful administration costs once a rather low minimum balance is established and maintained.
   - The account should have competitive, low transaction costs associated with the types of investments you intend to use in the account.

- If there are professional services available for you to use, they should match your requirements, and be priced to fairly compensate for the service you are receiving.

2. Sufficient Investment Options.

    Make sure the scope of the account can accommodate the potential growth in your needs. Most large financial institutions offer a variety of accounts that can meet your investment option needs as they change over time. When the financial institution has a product mix that grows with your needs, often it is relatively pain free and cost effective to switch within their suite of offerings.

3. Administrative Ease.

    It is easy to open a new account with many different providers. As the volume of accounts increases, the administrative burden also increases. I would advise against making your financial life any more complicated than necessary.

MoneySense.ca will periodically undertake an assessment of the various account providers, looking at their cost structure, the availability of investments, access to advice, and quality of other investment resources. I would suggest that you take a look at their most recent analysis and consider it when you are looking for an account or assessing the quality of the accounts you currently have. I wouldn't make a habit of chasing the new best account, but you should ensure that you have account options that meet your needs in a cost-effective manner.

Your non-registered investment account should be managed in a manner that is coordinated with your registered accounts. The asset allocation that you determined offers the right risk and return characteristics for your situation needs to be implemented across the breadth of your portfolio. The investments that properly fit within the registered accounts and those that fit within the non-registered accounts will be primarily driven by the tax implications of the holdings and/or access requirements.

The investments that are likely to cause the greatest tax impact should be held in a tax-sheltered account, and those that are likely to have a lesser tax impact should be held in the non-registered account to the extent that they can't be accommodated in a tax-sheltered account. I have seen many instances where an asset allocation is replicated in all of the different accounts held by an investor; this is just plain silly. Do what you can to manage your tax cost by properly using your different accounts.

My wife and I each use the same discount broker for the majority of our investments, registered and non-registered. In terms of account administrative costs, our RRSP accounts cost us nothing, our TFSAs cost us nothing, and our non-registered accounts cost us nothing. The same investments are available in all of these accounts, including virtually anything we would ever want to invest in from very low MER mutual funds, to exchange-traded funds, bonds, GICs, stocks, etc. The transaction fees are also slight in all of the accounts, ranging from zero to reasonable. No advice comes with our accounts. When I want advice, I purchase it separately.

CHAPTER 29 – INVESTMENTS AND TAXES (SORRY)

The newspaper this morning informs me that today is tax freedom day.[1] Hmmm, the year is almost half over and I am just now starting to bring in cash for my family. Enlightening, isn't it? June 10, 2018, was the preliminary estimate for tax freedom day for Canadians as a group, as calculated by the Fraser Institute. It turns out, though, that I should feel a little better than the average Canadian because the tax freedom day for Manitobans was actually June 3 … there we go, much better (not). I guess we should all move to Alberta; Albertans have been swimming in tax-free income since May 22.

The idea behind tax freedom day is to figure out the calendar date by which the average Canadian family has fulfilled their global tax obligation for the year. The level of taxes we pay as Canadians is what requires all relevant personal finance books to consider how taxes impact various forms of income and how best to organize your registered and non-registered investment portfolios. Taxes are, for most of us, far and away our greatest single area of expense. The grand total we pay is well concealed because most every transaction and source of income involves a tax of one type or another. Awareness can help you to manage the cost. Awareness is what tax freedom day is all about.

For the remainder of this chapter, we will look at the income tax system in general and then more specifically at investment income associated taxation. The problem I face in writing this section is that, with the exception of a select very few people, there is nothing more painful than reading about income taxes.

One of the things I found interesting when articling at KPMG was that the tax practitioners as a group tended to have some of the nicest, smartest, most quick-witted, and interesting personalities in the entire firm. These people were able to take one of the thickest, most difficult to read and understand Acts ever created and still maintain both their sanity and sense of humour. Come to think of it, though, on a per capita basis, the greatest number of motorcycles resided in the tax group—perhaps they felt deep down that life was not worth living.

Taxes are inescapable and, frankly, they are necessary if we are going to continue to live in one of, if not the best, and most generous countries in the world. That said, taxes in Canada are onerous and while I absolutely believe that everyone should pay what they owe, I think that is *all* they should pay—what they owe, not a cent more. This requires that you know enough about the tax system to organize yourself to pay as little as possible while fully respecting your tax obligations as dictated by the rules.

Income Tax Brackets in Canada

Canada has what is referred to as a progressive income tax system, meaning the more taxable income you earn, the more income tax you pay, and as your income increases, the percentage that is taxed away increases in periodic increments. As a result, each dollar of your income is not taxed at the same rate; there are a number of thresholds where the next dollar of income will result in you advancing to the next tax bracket where a higher marginal rate of tax is demanded. Getting into the next tax bracket, so long as you have done what you can to pragmatically and legally reduce your taxable income, is a good thing. Yes, it does result in you paying more tax in total, but it also means that you have more money in your pocket. That next dollar of income, contrary to what some believe, will not result in more tax than a dollar.

I often hear people suggesting that they don't want more income because they will pay more tax … that, in and of itself, doesn't make any sense. I can see where you might choose to draw the line as to how much time you spend earning income because the additional net dollars you receive do not adequately compensate you for the time they take out of your life. In fact, that is what I have essentially said by retiring early. I decided to leave money on the table so that I could spend more time the way I most wanted to, with my friends and family (and, strangely enough, writing this book). For someone to say I don't want more income because it will just increase my taxes, well, that is simply demonstrating that they don't understand how the tax system works. So let's take a quick look.

Both the federal and provincial governments rely heavily on income tax to fund their many and varied programs. Some of the tax revenue they bring in comes back to you in OAS, some in services (military, healthcare, infrastructure, etc.), some in social programs, and some in the expense accounts of our senators. (I just couldn't resist.) It costs a lot to offer the quality of life that we Canadians have been blessed with.

The federal government has adopted an income tax regime that currently has six different rates of tax, each depending upon the level of taxable income reported by a taxpayer. Taxpayers progress through these tax brackets as their taxable income increases, with successively higher levels of income attracting a higher rate of tax than the layers before. The first taxable dollar receives the exact same tax treatment for each and every Canadian (at least at the federal level); the tax treatment received by the last dollar of taxable income depends on how many taxable dollars came before it.

Taxpayers tend to have a number of different sources of income such as from employment, government benefits, retirement plans and accounts, non-registered investments that pay dividends, interest and capital gains, rental income from revenue properties, income from business, etc. All of these sources of income are combined, certain deductions are applied, and you are then left with a number called *taxable income*. Taxable income is the number used to calculate the tax obligation. Each year all taxpayers calculate their tax obligation, which is compared to the sum of tax that has been withheld by various sources over the course of the year and either a refund or balance owing results. It all sounds so simple.

The first bracket of taxable income results in no tax being paid at all. The next bracket results in $0.15 of each dollar being paid in federal tax. Once a taxpayer gets to a level of income slightly over $200,000, they will have reached the highest tax bracket and will have to part with $0.33 for every dollar earned above that level on account of federal income tax.

Federal Tax Brackets[2]

Table 3: Federal tax brackets and rates, 2018 and 2019.

2018 BRACKETS	2018 RATES	2019 BRACKETS	2019 RATES
Up to $11,809	0%	Up to $12,069	0%
$11,810 to $46,605	15%	$12,070 to $47,630	15%
$46,606 to $93,208	20.5%	$47,631 to $95,259	20.5%
$93,209 to $144,489	26%	$95,260 to $147,667	26%
$144,490 to $205,842	29%	$147,668 to $210,371	29%
Over $205,842	33%	Over $210,371	33%

As you can see from the above table, the tax brackets change from year to year. They are indexed to reflect inflation.

Provincial Tax Brackets[2]

Each province has implemented its own income tax regime. The basic structure is similar to that of the federal government, but the rates are different from province to province, the brackets are different from province to province, and the approach to surtax and tax credits are also provincially unique.

Table 4: Provincial tax brackets and rates, Manitoba 2019.

2019 TAX BRACKETS	2019 RATES
Manitoba	
Up to $9,626	0%
$9,627 to $32,670	10.8%
$32,671 to $70,610	12.75%
Over $70,610	17.4%

In Manitoba, as you can see in the above table, there are only four tax brackets. The tax rate starts at a relatively low level of income and progresses to the highest rate at a taxable income total of only slightly over $70,000.

In the below table, you can see how Alberta has decided to design its income tax strategy. Rather than four tax brackets, they have six. Tax becomes payable at a higher level of income than in Manitoba. In fact, at every level of taxable income, an Albertan pays less tax than a Manitoban. Those poor Albertans have lower taxes, mild winters, two NHL and CFL teams, mountains, oil … why would anyone want to live there?

Table 5: Provincial tax brackets and rates, Alberta 2019.

2019 TAX BRACKETS	2019 RATES
Alberta	
Up to $19,369	0%
$19,370 to $131,220	10%
$131,221 to $157,464	12%
$157,465 to $209,952	13%
$209,953 to $314,928	14%

2019 TAX BRACKETS	2019 RATES
Over $314,928	15%

So that is basically how the income tax system is designed—the more taxable income you bring home, the more income tax you have to pay. Not only that but, periodically, when you earn more income, you jump up a tax bracket, meaning that not every dollar of income is taxed at the same rate.

There are two different tax rates that every Canadian has and should be aware of: their average tax rate and their marginal tax rate. The *average tax rate* represents the amount of tax you paid on the average dollar of income (total income taxes/total income). The *marginal tax rate*, on the other hand, is the tax rate paid on the last dollar of income. People often confuse their marginal tax rate with their average tax rate, which results in them thinking that they pay a much greater percentage of their income in income tax than is actually the case.

When you combine the federal tax rates with the provincial tax rates, this is what it looks like:

Table 6: Combined provincial and federal tax brackets and rates, Manitoba 2019.

2019 TAX BRACKETS	2019 RATES
Manitoba	
Up to $9,626	0%
$9,627 to $12,069	10.80%
$12,070 to $32,670	25.80%
$32,671 to $47,630	27.75%
$47,631 to $70,610	33.25%
$70,611 to $95,259	37.90%
$95,260 to $147,667	43.40%
$147,668 to $210,371	46.40%

2019 TAX BRACKETS	2019 RATES
Over $210,371	50.40%

Table 7: Combined provincial and federal tax brackets and rates, Alberta 2019.

2019 TAX BRACKETS	2019 RATES
Alberta	
Up to $12,069	0%
$12,070 to $19,369	15.0%
$19,370 to $47,630	25.0%
$47,631 to $95,259	30.5%
$95,260 to $131,220	36.0%
$131,221 to $147,667	38.0%
$147,668 to $157,464	41.0%
$157,465 to $209,952	42.0%
$209,953 to $210,371	43.0%
$210,372 to $314,928	47.0%
Over $314,928	48.0%

While it is clear that tax rates differ, and even differ quite significantly from one province to the next, income tax management is important for each and every Canadian. Income taxes are substantial all across the country. According to the Fraser Institute in a recent research bulletin,[3] the average Canadian family now spends 43.1% of their income on taxes (all forms of tax) and 35.6% on basic necessities (food, shelter, clothing, etc.). Wow.

Taxes and Investment Income

Of necessity, the discussion here will be limited to the more salient points that are generally applicable to the average investor. If you want to dig further into the subject of taxes as they relate to investment income, I would recommend a visit to any of the national accounting firms' websites, or purchase one of the annual tax publications that delves into the details of personal income taxes. One of the books I purchase annually is KPMG's *Tax Planning for You and Your Family*.[4] It does a thorough job of discussing the key elements of personal tax in a readable, though somewhat technical, manner. A more reader-friendly publication is written by Evelyn Jacks entitled *Family Tax Essentials*.[5] This book takes a more conversational approach to personal income tax, which may or may not be more to your liking.

If you hold investments in a registered retirement account (RPP, RRSP, RRIF) it makes no difference from a tax perspective what form of income is earned by the investment. All income earned while within the envelope of the applicable registered plan is sheltered from immediate taxation. The impact of tax is only felt when a withdrawal is made (or payment received).

A TFSA is a little different from a tax perspective. The money invested in a TFSA has been taxed before being deposited; any income earned within the TFSA is not taxed further either within the account or when it is withdrawn from the account.

One common element of all registered accounts is that there is no distinction as to the nature of the income earned by your investment portfolio: capital gains, dividends, and interest. In the case of non-TFSA-registered accounts, taxation happens at your marginal tax rate and is applied to the whole of any withdrawal (i.e., tax is applied to capital and income earned alike). In the case of a TFSA, no additional income tax impact is experienced because the money deposited into the account in the first place was on an after-tax basis and any/all income earned while within the account is tax-sheltered.

With respect to investments that are held outside of a registered account, income that is generated is taxable in the year earned (in the case of dividends and interest), or in the year realized (in the case of capital gains). In order to not miss a chance to make things even more complicated, the government has made a distinction as to how the various forms of investment income are taxed. In fairness, there are good reasons for the different tax rates, but the end result to you and me is simply a more advanced state of complexity.

In the world of taxable investment income, there are essentially three different types of income you need to be aware of: interest income, dividend income, and capital gains/losses. The investment income I will be discussing in the following sections is limited to Canadian-sourced income from investment sources that are generally available to individual investors. Foreign-sourced investment income is subject to a variety of tax treaties, and generally a foreign tax credit regime to recognize the impact of foreign taxes withheld—this is beyond the scope of what is discussed here. Certain types of investments, such as those designed to function as tax shelters, labour-sponsored venture capital corporations, and various private equity investments, among others, may have more intricate income-tax-related implications that should be addressed by tax professionals.

Again, the tax implications discussed below are only applicable to investments held in a taxable investment account. Registered accounts (RRSPs, RRIFs, RPPs, TFSA, etc.) may generate these forms of income, but the Income Tax Act treats these accounts differently than they do a non-registered investment account.

Interest Income

Income from interest is taxed at the same rate as employment or net-business-sourced income. It is added to your taxable income on a dollar for dollar basis and it is taxed at your marginal tax rate. There are zippo taxation favours provided for interest-sourced income.

One of the complicating features of interest income is that it is taxable regardless of whether it is received or not. If you hold investments that have maturity dates that span more than a single year, the government still wants its piece of the income on an annual basis. Each year you must accrue the interest earned up to the anniversary date of the investment and report it for tax purposes.

This accrual requirement applies to most investments that generate interest income for an investor, regardless of how and when the interest is paid. Interest must be accrued on mortgage investments, Canada Savings Bonds, loans to your kids, grandkids, soon to be ex-friends (friendships often don't survive a loan), strip bonds, etc. For some of these types of investments, you will get a T-slip from the issuing institution that can be used to compute your tax obligation. If you do not receive a T-slip, it falls on you to calculate and report the accrued interest income.

Dividend Income

Dividend income results from the distribution of after-tax profits to shareholders by corporations. The income tax system at the investor level has been designed to recognize that dividends have already been taxed and thus there is a form of tax relief applied to recognize the prior tax payment. The complication that arises is that corporate tax rates are not the same as individual tax rates, so there is some dipsy doodle required to integrate the two tax systems that may seem odd, but it has been designed with the intention of being fair.

The amount of the dividend that is included in the income of the investor is not what the investor actually receives, but rather an amount approximating the level of pre-tax income that the corporation would have had to earn to allow it to pay the dividend. In essence, an adjustment is made in an attempt to place the investor in the revenue position of the corporation, and then tax the individual as if they had earned the income directly. In order to do this, the actual dividend received is *grossed up* to imitate the income the corporation would have had to earn and this is the amount included in the investor's income, for tax purposes. The next adjustment required is to recognize the amount of tax already paid by the corporation and eliminate that from the tax obligation of the investor. In order to achieve this effect, the recipient of the dividend is given a credit that approximates the tax that the corporation has already paid.

As if that wasn't enough to comprehend, the corporate tax system is not exactly the same for all sizes of corporation. Some Canadian public corporations and Canadian-controlled private corporations (CCPC) pay tax at a high rate of 38% (dividends distributed by these corporations are referred to as eligible dividends); other CCPCs pay tax at a small business rate, which is lower (dividends distributed by these CCPCs are referred to as ineligible dividends). The dividend gross up and tax credit system is designed to account for this difference in corporate tax rates. By the way, that was an oversimplification of how dividends are categorized for tax purposes, but is sufficient for our purposes.

Eligible dividends, which are the type most often received from Canadian corporations, are taxed as follows:

- The dividend amount actually received is grossed up by 38% and is included in the investor's taxable income.
- A tax credit is applied after the tax payable has been calculated. The federal tax credit is 15% of the grossed up dividend (or 20.7% of the actual dividend received). This is deducted directly from the federal tax payable. A credit is also calculated at the provincial level and deducted from the provincial tax payable.

Ineligible dividends are also subject to the gross up and tax credit process, but the rates applied are different and they are changing over the next few years, so to avoid further complexity, I will leave the discussion at that. The tax slips provided to you through your taxable investment accounts will have all of the information pre-calculated for you in the appropriate boxes.

The important point to take away from this is that dividends are taxed at a lower rate for investors and there is some logic to why this is the case.

At the risk of really testing your patience ... there are two other categories of dividends that an investor might receive depending on the nature of their investments:

- Capital dividends – these are received tax free. Basically, they are viewed as a return of capital to a shareholder. In the normal course of investing, this type of dividend is uncommon.
- Foreign dividends – dividends received from foreign corporations are not subject to the gross up and dividend tax credit mechanism.

Capital Gains and Losses

The KPMG tax-planning book referenced earlier devotes an entire chapter to capital gains and losses, so be aware that there is much more to this subject than I will cover here.

There are a small number of capital gain categories that lead to no tax whatsoever:

- Principal Residence Exemption – any gain realized upon selling your home is completely exempt from tax. Each family is limited to one principal residence at a time (since 1982). So if your family has a house and a cottage that are both ordinarily inhabited, the gain on one of the properties can be sheltered from tax for any given year or series of years while the property was held, but not the other property for those same years.
- Qualified Small Business Shares – up to $848,252 (2018, indexed to inflation) of gains on these shares can be tax exempt.
- There are capital gains exemptions available for qualified farming and fishing property.

While most of us will take advantage of the principal residence exemption at one or many points in time throughout our lives, it is only a select few who will qualify to use the small business exemption or the exemptions for farming and fishing enterprises. A tax pro should be consulted if either of the last two categories applies to you or if you have more than one property that would qualify as a principle residence and you will be selling one of them.

Capital gains or losses arise when you sell virtually any property. Most often for the average among us, a capital gain (or loss) arises when we sell shares of a public corporation. If you sell any personal items, works of art, cars, a personal business, a second residence, raw land, bars of gold, pretty much anything, at a profit, then you have realized a capital gain that could be subject to tax.

Notice that in order to have a capital gain that could be subject to tax, the item of interest must be sold (or deemed to have been sold). If you have an item that has appreciated in value, but you have not sold it, there is no immediate tax implication.

Taxation of Capital Gains

The formula associated with the taxation of ordinary capital gains is relatively straightforward:

Capital Gain = Sale Price (less cost to sell) - Asset Cost (adjusted)

Once you have calculated your capital gain, then you need to determine how much of that gain is actually subject to tax. This piece of the equation has changed a number of times over the years, and I expect will change at various times in the future as governments try to manage their deficits (or dare I say, surpluses). Currently 50% of a non-exempt capital gain is taxable; this portion is referred to on your income tax return as a taxable capital gain.

Taxable Capital Gain = Capital Gain / 2

As an example, say you bought 10,000 Royal Bank shares in 1996 at $15 per share and the commission cost was $.05 per share (or $500) and the shares were held in a non-registered account. Your adjusted cost base for the shares would be $150,500. After your purchase of the stock, you remain quite happy with the prospects of the company so you continue to hold the shares until the beginning of 2017, when you need cash to pay for your daughters' weddings (apparently you skipped the chapter on weddings). All the while, from 1996 through to 2017, the Royal Bank has been issuing dividends to you that you have included each year in your taxable income.

Let's say you sold all 10,000 shares in 2017 at $99 per share and the transaction cost was $10. Your capital gain on the transaction becomes:

Capital Gain = ($990,000 - $10) - $150,500 or $839,490

Of this capital gain, you would have to include 50% in your income in 2017, which equates to $419,745. The actual amount of income tax this would attract will depend on the province within which you reside, and the level of other taxable income you have to report in the year.

There are a couple of things to note from this example (which uses realistic numbers, by the way). First, only half of the gain is included in taxable income. In effect, the tax rates on the capital gain as a whole are exactly half the tax rate applied to interest income. Second, even though the capital gain was built over the period extending from 1996 through 2017, none of the capital gain was taxed until the shares were sold in 2017.

Without a doubt, a better plan could have been devised to realize the gain over time and therefore experience a reduced total tax burden … but when you have an extravagant wedding or two to pay for, what is a parent to do?

Capital Losses

Sometimes—pretty often, actually—the purchase of a capital property does not work out as planned. In these cases, rather than a capital gain, you may find you have a capital loss. If you work through the capital gain calculation above, and the number that comes out the back end is negative, you have a capital loss. Half of your capital loss is called an allowable capital loss. An allowable capital loss can be used to offset taxable capital gains. If the loss cannot be used in the year incurred because there are insufficient taxable capital gains to offset, then the loss can be carried back and applied to any of the previous three years' taxable capital gains or the loss can be carried forward and be applied against future taxable capital gains.

Capital Gains and Losses – Other Considerations

There are a bunch of special situations when it comes to capital gains, far too many to deal with them in any comprehensive manner here. The following will give you a flavour of the types of issues that can come up and perhaps some awareness of when you are doing something a little unusual that may require more research to understand how the *Income Tax Act* may apply.

- The *Income Tax Act* does not define capital property precisely; thus, there can be some confusion about what exactly constitutes a capital gain versus income from a business. The courts have been forced to adjudicate over this distinction many times, resulting in some guidelines, but there is still uncertainty as to where precisely the dividing line resides. Generally, if you do something a bunch of times, it supports the assumption that there is the intent to run a business; business income is taxed very differently than a capital gain. Again, a qualified tax pro should be engaged if you require clarity in this area.

- If you want greater assurance that your stock market trades will be treated as being on account of capital, there is an election available that most people can make (form T123). The form describes who can and can't make the election.
- There are special rules you need to be aware of related to the disposition of personal-use property. Most personal-use property will not be sold for more than it cost; thus, it will not result in a capital gain. In the event that you do sell personal-use property for a gain, though, there could be a tax implication. Losses from the sale of most personal assets are not deductible. The cost of personal-use property is deemed to be at least $1,000, so any sale of personal-use property that generates proceeds of $1,000 or less will not involve the realization of a taxable capital gain.

Listed personal property (LPP), which is a subset of personal-use property, is more "investment-like" and is treated slightly differently for tax purposes. LPP includes artwork, jewellery, rare folios, rare manuscripts, rare books, stamps, and coins, according to the Government of Canada website. When it comes to LPP, losses can be used to offset gains. There are carry-back and carry-forward provisions if an LPP loss cannot be used in the current year. The $1,000 cut-off discussed above still applies.

The bottom line is, if you are selling any of your personal-use items for more than $1,000, you need to take a look to see if there is a profit involved and, if so, then you need to look into the tax consequences because you likely have a capital gain that is taxable.

- Superficial Loss Rules. The superficial loss rules disallow the use of a capital loss if you purchase an identical property within 30 days of the transaction that crystalizes a loss. These rules extend to any such

transaction by your spouse or (if you are a big shot) a corporation controlled by you or your spouse.
- Alternative Minimum Tax. I won't get into the details of minimum tax, but you should be aware that if you are participating in tax preferences in a significant way, then you may trigger minimum tax. Minimum tax can sneak up on you if you participate extensively in tax shelters or you sell the shares of a qualified small business, for example.

I can feel your agony in reading this section, so I think it is prudent to stop there. Rest assured there are many more special situations when it comes to capital property and related tax implications, but the above should cover the majority of situations you might find yourself in.

Bringing it all Together

The tax rates experienced by different sources of income are most easily demonstrated in a table. The combined federal and provincial personal income tax rates for the different sources of investment income applicable to the Province of Manitoba (2019) are presented below. Each province has unique rates due to differences in provincial tax regimes.

If you want to look at the table applicable to your province I would invite you to visit the Ernst & Young website as they have built tax rate and credit tables for all of the provinces and territories and make them available, without charge, to the general public.

Table 8: *Combined federal and provincial personal income tax rates, Manitoba 2019.*[a]

TAXABLE INCOME	BASIC TAX	RATE ON EXCESS	MARGINAL RATE ON		
$	$	Taxable Income[b]	Eligible Dividends[c]	Other Dividends[c]	Capital Gains[d]
0 - 9,626	-	0.00%	0.00%	0.00%	0.00%
9,627 - 12,069	-	10.80%	3.86%	11.52%	5.40%
12,070 - 32,670	264	25.80%	3.86%	18.38%	12.90%
32,671 - 47,630	5,579	27.75%	6.56%	20.63%	13.88%
47,631 - 70,610	9,730	33.25%	14.12%	26.95%	16.63%
70,611 - 95,259	17,371	37.90%	20.53%	32.30%	18.95%
95,260 - 147,667	26,713	43.40%	28.12%	38.62%	21.70%
147,668 - 210,371	49,458	46.40%	32.26%	42.07%	23.20%
210,371 and up	78,553	50.40%	37.78%	46.67%	25.20%

[a] The information embedded in the table is current to June 15, 2019. The table does not apply where alternative minimum tax is in effect.
[b] No tax credits other than basic personal tax credits are reflected in the table.
[c] The rates apply to the actual amount of dividends received from taxable Canadian corporations.
[d] The rates apply to the actual amount of the capital gain. A capital gains exemption is available for certain sources of capital gain; no impact is assumed in the table.

You can see from the table that the type of income you want to generate depends on your tax bracket. In the lower tax brackets, eligible dividends are taxed at the most favourable rate. When it comes to the higher tax brackets, capital gains take over as the most tax-efficient form of income to earn. The same general pattern is consistently observable across the provinces, though the level of income at which the transition takes place is province specific.

LARRY WILSON

Investment Income and Taxes – Other Bits and Pieces

It is not possible to cover all elements of investment income from a tax perspective in the space available. However, there are several aspects that I have come to realize are important to understand, from an investor's perspective. This is not by any means a comprehensive listing of tax issues and applications, but they represent some of the issues I have confronted multiple times over the years:

- Taxes are complicated and continually changing. Don't simply rely on past understanding; do some work annually to refresh your knowledge and gain insight to any new or changed provisions applicable to your situation.
- Don't take overly aggressive positions when it comes to taxation issues without getting qualified advice.
- Mutual funds and taxes. Without getting too deep into it, most mutual funds are structured as flow-through entities for tax purposes. As such, any investment income that is generated within the mutual fund retains its character for tax purposes when distributed. Your account administrator will provide you with a tax slip that segregates the income by type so that it is reported on your tax return, and therefore taxed, in the manner discussed above.
- When it comes to your investments, keep your own record of the adjusted cost base (or verify that your investment firm does it correctly). There are several types of distributions that result in a change to an investment's cost base; be aware of them as they apply to your investment portfolio.
- Pay particular attention to the composition of year-end distributions to ensure that you are treating your adjusted cost base accurately. I have found, with many of the ETFs I hold, there are significant year-end distributions that result in a taxable event, but are not paid out in cash; rather, the value is assimilated back into the shares, with no change to the share price. When this type of distribution occurs, it has been my experience that the company marketing the fund will have an explanation of how to modify the adjusted cost base on their website or in the materials mailed to you accompanying your tax slips.

- When purchasing a mutual fund or ETF in a taxable account, take care not to do so near the end of the calendar year because you may get a taxable distribution that is disproportionate to your responsibility. There are certain types of taxable distributions that are only done at year end, so it may make sense to delay your purchase until the beginning of the next year. Often, the company offering the fund will provide an estimate of taxable distributions a month or so before the end of the year.
- Actively managed mutual funds and ETFs (those that trade holdings regularly over the course of the year) can create significant tax obligations in taxable accounts. As a general rule, you should attempt to keep any funds that are more actively managed in your tax-sheltered accounts (which has the effect of deferring your tax obligation), and those that are less actively managed (e.g., index-based investments) in your taxable accounts.
- If you don't know what you are doing, and are not going to put in the effort to understand what you are doing, get help! The *Income Tax Act* is a daunting publication and is not many people's cup of tea.
- When I say "get help," I mean you need a tax-planning strategy—not simply someone to mechanistically prepare your annual tax return. Don't get me wrong; compiling your tax return accurately is certainly important. However, effective tax planning needs to be done well in advance of tax-return preparation. It is about properly structuring your holdings between accounts, positioning yourself to benefit from any relevant tax credits or incentives, and setting up a record-keeping process that is complete and accurate.
- Keep your investment transaction records current (if you rely on an investment firm for this service, make sure you check what they provide to ensure it is accurate). When you enter into a taxable transaction, make sure to document the transaction details so that you have an accurate record of the tax implications.
- While dividends are sometimes the most tax-friendly income to realize, there are exceptions. One of the most common areas of exception is when you are receiving Old Age Security. The problem with the gross up calculation is that the gross up increases reported net income, and it is

the level of net income that determines if the OAS clawback applies. This is something that well-to-do seniors should keep in mind.
- Minimize your taxes, but never evade your tax obligations. Nothing good comes from tax evasion. If you have done something in the past that you are now questioning, consider making a voluntary disclosure, for more information see the Government of Canada website.
- Don't participate in the underground economy. If someone offers you a deal to do-it-for-cash, it is highly likely that they have no intention to pay their share of tax related to the job. The CRA has an Informant Leads Program where you can report cases of suspected tax evasion. The Government of Canada website has more information.
- While your ability to manage the timing of investment-based income is limited, you do have control over when you realize capital gains and losses. Use this control to your advantage.

I know I have now overstayed my welcome. Over and out.

PART VII – CALAMITY EVASION

I love almost everything related to financial and estate planning. Call me weird, but I enjoy putting together our family's monthly and periodic financial statements. I look forward to the annual process of assessing our financial progress and updating our financial and estate plans. I don't mind doing our income taxes and like to engage in income-tax planning. Assessment of, and perhaps investing in, various investment opportunities is great fun. I read a dozen or two finance-related books every year to stay up to date on the latest developments, trends, and thoughts within the profession. I take courses on all aspects of personal finance to maintain my credentials, but also because I really enjoy the subject matter.

My enthusiasm for almost all things financial planning does not extend to insurance. Insurance for me is the raw broccoli of the financial planning world … it's is generally repugnant, but in the correct doses, it's very good for you.

No matter how much effort, skill, and planning you put into all other aspects of your financial life, if you do not hold your nose and arrange for sufficient and appropriate insurance coverage, bad fortune can come your way without warning and annihilate your finances. You should never leave yourself and your family at risk of ruin; insurance is your protection against the unthinkable.

I prefer to self-insure for risks that can lead to small and sometimes moderate damage. Self-insure means that I do not share the risk with an insurance company through a traditional insurance product. Rather than pay the premium that the insurance company would demand, I accept the risk and implement behavioural changes to reduce the chance of loss or simply accept the risk and any costs that result. Life is never risk free; the smaller stuff is what an emergency fund and living within your means are for.

Insurance and insurance products, in my opinion, have been made to be unnecessarily complicated. I am not an expert on insurance. I believe that insurance is one area where you should seriously consider getting credible and trustworthy expert assistance to supplement your own understanding. While you should seek expert assistance, this does not mean that you should abdicate full responsibility for the analysis and decisions that accompany this element of your plan. I am a firm believer in doing the work necessary to understand the basics so that you have a foundation from which to evaluate and question the options that an expert will present to you.

In my opinion, finding and utilizing the services of a broker who represents many different insurance companies is just common sense. A broker is in a good position to help you find both the coverage you need and the cheapest way to access that coverage.

When deciding on a broker, it is important that you understand any and all conflicts of interest; in particular pay attention to the structure and flow of their remuneration. Good and trustworthy brokers should be both up front and happy to have a compensation discussion with you. Insurance products tend to have hefty front-loaded commissions. You will want to ensure that the primary focus of the broker you select is on finding the product and coverage that is right for you, not the commission that works best for them.

Personal Reflection – Travel Health Insurance

The weather in Phoenix during mid-December 2015 was, as usual, pristine. Clear skies both day and night, the temperatures were in the mid-twenties during the heat of the day and cooled off enough at night to require a light sweater. The lower temperature at night was nice because it made getting into the hot tub a perfect way to end the day, or to loosen up after a run around the neighbourhood. Life was good. Beyond good, actually. It was a privileged existence.

On December 11, 2015 in the evening, I went for a nice run through the residential area around Buckeye. I put in four miles, a common-length run for me when not in training for a half marathon. I had a good sweat going and called it a night. For years I have been running to keep my cardio system in shape and my weight within/near my target range. The next day, the last full day of our vacation, my wife, our close friend Carol, and I climbed a mountain to view some ancient cave dwellings. This is not really my thing, but it is always interesting to see how people lived centuries before and how far we have come since that time. It was a nice light to moderately vigorous hike up that mountain. Later that evening, we had my friend (Jim and I have been friends since grade seven) and his house guest over for the evening ... appetizers and the hot tub were on the agenda. The following day, December 13, was cleaning day before departing to the airport and ultimately back to the frigid December temperatures of Winnipeg ... at least that was the plan.

At 4:30 a.m., I didn't feel quite right. I had been healthy my whole life so I didn't think too much of it. But I did have an odd sensation in my arms, so I thought a precautionary thing to do would be to get up and have a baby Aspirin. I left the light on in the bathroom because I wasn't sure what I was feeling. I got back into bed and my wife asked me why I left the light on, and that was when I informed her that I thought I might be having a heart attack.

It turned out I was. It wasn't just a little heart attack either, it was a 100% blockage of the left anterior descending (LAD) coronary artery.

I remember telling Kim three things while they were carting me off in the stretcher:

1. Tell the children that I love them and am proud of them.
2. Get in touch with Daryl Diamond (the author of *Your Retirement Income Blueprint*[1]) to help manage the family finances.
3. Take the commuted value of my pension.

I am very organized when it comes to managing our finances. When my time comes, I can be comforted knowing:

- we have an adequate investment portfolio,
- our kids' educations will be paid for,
- we have no debt,
- a will is in place that properly takes care of my family,
- if my wife and I were to die at the same time, then trusts will be in place to take care of the kids,

- we have adequate insurance, and
- all of the information is well documented in a secured location that my wife, kids, and trustees are aware of.

Oddly, my wife is not so interested in family financial matters, despite my repeated attempts to interest her; thus, the financial focus on what could have been my last words to her. (I should probably think that through better for next time.)

The staff at the hospital figured out what was wrong in relatively short order and took care of the blockage. A stent, followed by a couple of days in the hospital, and I was sent home.

This situation was completely unexpected. I was not overweight. I was an avid runner, not a fast runner, but quite consistent in getting my training in. I had completed eight half marathons (never exceeding two hours in duration) and lots of ten km races, along with the necessary hundreds/thousands of training miles. Never had my annual check-ups raised a concern that required any attention related to my heart function, and yet here it had happened.

The care I got in Phoenix was top notch and the bill reflected that care. I was fortunate that I had travel health insurance that covered the financial fallout. In all, my treatment cost about $120,000 CDN. As an example of how costly out-of-country care can be; one of the meds I had to procure myself after discharge cost $338 for a 10-day supply in Phoenix, the very same medication in Canada cost me about $25. All of the meds I paid for in Phoenix were much cheaper in Canada. I also discovered that my insurance company was well-equipped to negotiate the charges billed. As I understand it, they never paid the face value of any bill; they knew how to deal with the hospital and negotiated a more reasonable fee for the care provided. I'm not sure if this is the usual practice, but had I been personally responsible, I doubt I would have been negotiating anything (might have even given them a tip) and the final cost paid would have been higher.

Most people don't have an extra hundred grand or two just sitting around to cover a cost such as this. It goes without saying that the cost of this episode easily could have escalated had I had an extended stay in the hospital.

It is this kind of surprise that insurance is perfectly designed to help manage—a low-likelihood event with a potentially high financial consequence. Insurance is the one cash outlay you hope to never gain a benefit from, other than the peace of mind having an appropriately designed insurance strategy provides. It is also the one product that can keep your financial life on track if the unthinkable occurs.

Types of Insurance

The insurance products that make sense to consider purchasing, and the quantum of each, are dependent on the risk profile facing a family. If a risk is evident that could be financially disruptive, then action needs to be taken to either manage the risk or the impact in the event that the risk is realized. Insurance is often the most cost-effective way to manage the financial implications of a risk.

What follows is what I would describe as a *lite* discussion of insurance, meant to whet your appetite as opposed to answer your every question. What I hope to accomplish is simply to have you self-reflect on your situation and determine precisely where the greatest exposures lie for you and your family. A fulsome identification and consideration of the risks that confront a family is the starting point for developing a quality risk-management program.

For some types of risks, you may have the option of simply avoiding the activity that gives rise to a risk. As an example, if you choose to not skydive, then you will have avoided all risks associated with skydiving. If you choose not to drink and drive, well, you get the picture. In other cases, you may simply accept the financial fallout if the risk materializes (self-insure). For example, you may decide to accept the risk that a new big screen TV will die a sudden and premature death, rather than purchase the product insurance that the retailer will inevitably offer you at the time of purchase. In this instance, the cost of the insurance may outweigh the probable cost you will have to accept as a result of forgoing the insurance, and there is no scenario where the financial impact will be devastating. This is exactly the kind of risk that you have built an emergency fund (or financial capacity) to deal with.

There are, however, many other risks that demand you take on the burden associated with the insurance premiums.

Takeaways Part VII

- ✓ Everyone and every family has a portfolio of risks that they must live with and manage; it is just part of the deal in being alive. Some risks are likely to trigger an impact at some point and others are unlikely to do so. We have considerable control over the likelihood of some risks being realized; for others we have limited control. Some risks present a relatively minor financial inconvenience if realized, while others have the potential to devastate the family finances. Proactive risk management is essential to reduce the chance of experiencing a devastating financial outcome.
- ✓ Each family/individual should identify, assess, and analyze each substantial risk they face. For those risks that present a relatively minor financial impact, the risk can be accepted with perhaps some simple behavioural modifications to reduce the likelihood of occurrence. For those risks with the potential to have a meaningful impact, a formal plan of action should be defined and taken. The action can be one of reducing or eliminating the risk through behaviour modification or taking any number of protective measures depending on the specific characteristics of the risk. For many risks, the most cost-effective way to manage the financial implication is through transferring it to someone else—insurance.
- ✓ While the risks faced by an individual or family can be unique to their circumstances, and the financial impact can vary considerably from one instance to the next, the most common areas where insurance should be considered as an option include:

    - Life insurance (temporary or permanent, depending on the nature of the risk)
    - Long-term disability insurance (a person's ability to earn income is often their most valuable asset)
    - Critical illness insurance (can be valuable in many situations, especially where long-term disability insurance is not an option)
    - Automobile, personal property, extended health, travel health, and long-term care are among the insurance products that are also important to consider within your personal risk profile

- ✓ Insurance can be costly. It is important to ensure that you use insurance only for those risks that can be financially significant.
- ✓ Anything that can devastate your finances deserves your attention and in all likelihood should be transferred, at least to some extent, to someone else. You should consider using the services of an independent insurance broker to help you assess your options and keep your costs down. Some of the actions you can take to reduce your premiums include:

  - arrange for a higher, but affordable, deductible,
  - avoid policy riders that you do not need,
  - extend elimination/waiting periods where you have other means available for support in the interim, and
  - pay the premium annually, rather than over time, where there is a cost to the extended payment stream.

CHAPTER 30 – LIFE INSURANCE

My wife and I have insurance on our lives sufficient to cover the level of additional financial burden that our untimely death would have on the family. We have had life insurance in place since shortly after we began our lives together. The face value of life insurance has been adjusted over time to reflect our changing financial exposure.

Early on in our commingling of affairs, the level of life insurance we required was minimal; if something happened to one of us, the other would be able to grieve and then recover financially without much of a hiccup. Little insurance was required at this stage; thus, little insurance was purchased. When we moved into a house and took on greater financial commitments, we felt more life insurance was appropriate and adjusted accordingly.

Then along came the children, our two beautiful bouncing bundles of obligation. This represented a significant change in the profile of our financial responsibilities, one that would endure for an extended period of time. As each of our children entered the picture, we took a hard look at each of the spousal roles and the impact losing either one of us would have on the financial foundation of the family. We then calculated the lump sum of cash that would be required to fund the financial implications should one or both of us no longer be in the picture and purchased enough additional life insurance to ensure that the remaining family could carry on with a comparable lifestyle for the period of time we felt that help was appropriate.

We are now at the point where our two bouncing bundles of obligation aren't so much bouncing as they are sleeping in late, making a mess of their rooms, and questioning the logic of each request we utter (similar to what we did to our parents) as they inch toward taking on independent households. Our kids, of whom we are ever so proud, are reaching a point where we can see their financial dependence subsiding and, therefore, we will soon(ish) be at a point where life insurance needs will diminish substantially. At the same time, over the next few years our term life policies will become very expensive, and with the financial impact of either of our deaths becoming more benign, there will soon be a point at which our circumstances will no longer require life insurance. We will have, hopefully, paid premiums for 40+ years with no need to collect.

In our portfolio of insurance, we do not and never have had any life insurance on our kids. In accounting terminology, our kids—no matter how cute, cuddly and lovable they are to us—can be described as a financial liability: they cost us money. To my way of thinking, you should never insure an expense; you just insure assets. While the death of either of our kids would create unthinkable heartache, the financial consequences would be limited in the short term and positive in the longer term—insurance would not help in any conceivable way should one of the kids die. I know there is an argument to make, however shaky the logic, for insuring a child to ensure they remain insurable in the future. I am unconvinced that this would be money well spent in the vast majority of circumstances. We also don't insure the life of our dog or bunny.

Most families require life insurance to maintain their standard of living in the event that either spouse dies so that their contribution to the family (financial contribution if working or services provided if a stay-at-home parent) can be replaced. The piece of this equation that regularly gets overlooked is the value that a stay-at-home parent provides. In the event of their untimely death, there is a very real financial cost to the family in terms of caring for the children and replacing all of the other valuable work and tasks that they cover off without receiving monetary compensation. Money is not lost, in this case, but money will have to be used to replace the services that were lost and must be accounted for in the amount of life insurance procured.

Before we get into the question of how much insurance is required, let's first take a high-level look at the options available. In broad terms, there are two different types of life insurance: term life insurance and permanent life insurance.

Within the permanent family of life insurance there are two main varieties, whole life and universal life.

a) Term Life Insurance

> One of the beautiful things about term life insurance is that it is simple to understand. I love simple; simple is my specialty. In fact some people refer to me as simple. (I think that is a compliment.)
>
> Term insurance provides a fixed death benefit for a specific period of time at a guaranteed cost. A cash benefit is paid in the event of an insured's death, on a tax-free basis in most cases, to the policy's designated beneficiaries (or the estate). Term insurance is temporary in that once the period of time designated in the policy has expired, you no longer pay a premium and you no longer have any coverage. The term (period of time) covered by the policy can be selected in accordance with your needs—5 years, 10 years, 20 years or longer.
>
> When a person is young, the cost of term insurance is very reasonable (assuming they have a normal risk profile). As a person ages, the likelihood of death increases and the premium, reflecting this increased risk, also increases. Once they get substantially older, the premium becomes very high, and ultimately, term insurance becomes cost prohibitive or it is simply unavailable.
>
> Most term policies are renewable at the expiry of the term, but the premium will be higher than that paid over the course of the previous term, and may be substantially higher than you could get with a fresh application if you are able to demonstrate continuing good health. So one way in which you can keep your term life insurance costs much lower, assuming you are able to qualify based on superior health, is to not simply renew your current policy upon expiry, but rather to reapply. Keep in mind though you should always keep your current policy in place until such time as you have a new application approved. If you allow your policy to lapse and it turns out you are not considered to be insurable with a new application, then you would be out of luck.
>
> Term insurance is great where the risk you need to insure does not continue indefinitely and particularly where the extent of risk you are required to cover reduces as you age. In our case, the need to carry life insurance peaked

and stayed high early in the formation of our family but has trended lower as the financial risk associated with either/both of our deaths has become reduced and our asset base has advanced.

b) Whole Life Insurance

Unlike term insurance, whole life insurance provides lifetime coverage with the added benefit of accumulating cash value over time. Permanent insurance premiums are usually guaranteed when you first buy the policy, some permanent insurance plans enable you to pay for a limited number of years and then never again. Premiums for whole life policies are substantially higher than for equivalent death benefit term policies in the early years but the premiums will remain constant over time as opposed to the rather sharp increase that will occur for term policies as the insured approaches life expectancy. There will come a time when a permanent policy premium will start to look relatively cheap when compared to an equivalent term insurance premium, but the point at which the two premiums intersect takes many years to arrive.

Permanent insurance is perfect for those financial needs that will always be there. Things like funeral costs, estate goals, ongoing support obligations, terminal tax obligations, etc. If you really want to keep a cottage in the family, and there is a huge embedded tax liability due upon transfer as a result of the capital appreciation of the property, it may prove impossible for the heirs to keep the property without some funding from the estate. Permanent insurance could be one possible solution. In a case where you have ongoing financial responsibility for the maintenance of children or a spouse, you may find that permanent insurance is a viable/preferable option.

In situations where you have permanent obligations and you are young, one alternative to permanent insurance that you might want to consider is to purchase term insurance and invest the difference in premiums between the permanent insurance and term insurance. That way, you are building up some additional assets, outside of the insurance policy, that can be used to help manage your portfolio of risks. This would be a strategy you should discuss with your financial planner to maximize the probability that the solution is viable in your particular circumstances.

c) Universal Life Insurance

Universal life insurance is a more flexible and, therefore, more complex type of permanent life insurance that combines insurance protection and a hands-on investment or savings component.

As with all types of life insurance, the policyholder chooses a guaranteed death benefit value that meets their needs. The insurance company determines the insurance cost, fees, and taxes based on the death benefit chosen and the policyholder's personal characteristics. The policyholder then makes deposits to the account in an amount greater than the insurance costs, fees, and taxes, and invests the difference in accordance with the options provided by the insurance company. As you can see, in the case of this form of life insurance policy, the policyholder has a much more involved and ongoing role to play.

The policyholder has flexibility to invest in a broad array of investments, as well as to adjust the amount of the payment within certain limits. In this way, the insurance policy can be used as a method of achieving tax-deferred growth, with the level of risk designed into the investment portfolio being defined by the policyholder.

Lots of very smart people use this type of insurance to build tax-advantaged investment portfolios. When you meet with an insurance professional, no doubt, they will regale you with all the information you could ever want related to this insurance option. My preference for keeping things simple has led me away from this approach, but it seems to be a preferred approach used by many.

Each of the above policy types has a myriad of characteristics that need to be understood in order to be sure you are selecting the policy that is right for you. Working with a financial advisor and/or an independent insurance broker can help ensure that you get the coverage you need, combined with a premium that you can afford.

There were two main reasons my family decided to go with term insurance. First, it did not cost very much to get the appropriate amount of insurance at the time when we needed the most coverage, and needed the coverage most (i.e., when we had a young family and were in the less advanced stages of accumulating net worth). Second, I could easily foresee a time when life insurance coverage would not be required because we would be in a position to self-insure. That time would also coincide with when the premiums for the term policy would start to get more substantial.

An insurance program needs to be affordable. In my view, while it is important that you do not lose sight of any permanent need for life insurance, it is most important that you get the right amount of insurance. Generally, the greatest need for insurance is when you are young, which coincidently is also when you are least likely to have extra free cash flow to fund insurance expenses. In my family's case, freeing up cash flow in our younger years, by utilizing term insurance, also allowed us to more readily pursue other priorities, such as investing for our future.

Life Insurance – Random Observations

- Underwriting is the process whereby the insurance company determines if you are eligible for insurance. The process can take place upon application or, believe it or not, at the time of a claim. Make sure that your policy is underwritten at the application stage. It can be a hassle and may result in some delays, but the last thing you want to happen is to find out that you were not eligible for the insurance when the time comes to make a claim and therefore the insurance you thought was in place is not.
- Always remember, this is not a one-and-done. Get the right amount of insurance for your situation, and review and adjust over time, as your needs change.
- An insurance broker who is equipped to compare quotes from a wide array of companies is a valuable partner to engage. There can be a significant difference in the cost of coverage from one insurance company to the next.
- If you are relying on group insurance coverage to manage your insurance requirements, you must be aware of the risks that accompany this strategy. First, in order to remain covered, you need to remain a member of the "group." That may mean you need to remain employed with a particular company, or you need to remain qualified as a member of the

group that has negotiated the coverage. Second, the terms of the coverage can change over time and you will have no control over the changes. There is greater certainty with a personal/individual insurance policy, though personal insurance is usually considerably more expensive.
- As with all contracts, ensure that you read and understand the policy. The last thing you want to do is expose yourself to a risk that is not covered. When completing the application process, make sure you are entirely truthful in the representations you make. A misrepresentation may negate coverage.

How Much Life Insurance?

Now that we have completed the introduction to the various forms of life insurance, we can tackle the question of how much life insurance should be contracted. The amount you require depends on the risks you need to cover, the assets you have accumulated, and what you want to achieve through the life insurance you purchase.

Typically, when an insured dies there are two cash dilemmas, one-time cash requirements and ongoing cash flow requirements.

The one-time cash requirements include things like funeral expenses and tax consequences that must be paid. If one is married, there are often a number of funding obligations that are not necessarily needed immediately at the time of the first spouse to die, but might be a preference that you want to design into the life insurance equation. For instance, you may want to have cash immediately available to pay off the mortgage, eliminate various sources of consumer debt, fund education, allow the surviving spouse time away from work while they grieve and figure out their new roles, etc. People may also look to insurance to build an estate.

Ongoing cash flow requirements refer to the recurring cash commitments that need to be met in order to maintain the desired lifestyle. For a married couple, how this balance is determined depends on which life is being insured; thus it is important to look at the situation of each partner's death independently to identify:

- income streams that need to be replaced,
- costs that will be added to acquire services that will have been lost, and
- costs that will be avoided because there is one less mouth to feed and one less set of personal expenses that need to be covered.

What the one-time and ongoing cash flow requirements look like are dependent on the situation of the insured, be they married or single, the nature of ongoing support obligations, legacy objectives, etc. This analysis needs to be personalized.

Once you have determined the one-time cash requirements and the ongoing cash flow requirements, the two numbers are translated into a single figure. From that single figure, you will then deduct the wealth that you have currently available to help meet those requirements and the difference will represent the face value of the policy (or policies) you should acquire. Note, there may be certain elements of your current wealth that you do not want to take into account in this calculation, such as your current retirement savings and balances of the like that have a designated purpose and represent an ongoing requirement. Thus, you would only subtract the wealth you have available to apply against the cash requirements the insurance is designed to manage.

At this point, you need to consider the nature of the obligations the insurance will be covering in terms of their degree of permanence. If some of the face value is viewed as being a permanent insurance requirement, then you can look for a whole life or universal life policy to cover that piece of the life insurance puzzle. It is likely that much, if not all, of the requirement you have defined will dissipate as time passes and financial circumstances change. If that is the case in your situation, that portion of your requirement would be a candidate for temporary, or term insurance.

The tricky part of defining the face value of insurance required is that part of the requirement is ongoing and needs to be converted to a single sum. The math can get a little confusing, and I would recommend you have your financial advisor or insurance broker help you with this piece. But if you want a very rough estimate of the level of insurance that is appropriate you can do the following:

1. Add up all of the one-time cash requirements.
2. Decide on how many years you need the ongoing cash flow to be covered and multiply the annual dollar requirement by the number of years you desire coverage.
3. Add the result of the above two pieces together, deduct the current resources you have available to apply to those obligations, and that would represent an approximation of the face value of life insurance that you should purchase.

This approach is only appropriate if you assume that the inflation rate of your planned expenses is approximately the same as the net investment return you will realize on the lump sum of cash that you will invest and draw from on an ongoing basis. You should also recognize that, in using this method, you have planned to use up all of the insurance money at a certain point in time. Again, this approach would provide a rough approximation of your requirement (a little bit on the low side because the net investment return—the return after tax—likely will be lower than inflation), but it should get you into the ballpark of the coverage you require.

An easier way to add some rigour to the calculation would be to go to the internet, search *life insurance calculators*, then enter your information into a couple of different calculators to see what they say. Be aware that the calculators are making some assumptions that may or may not be appropriate, so you should review the methodology they are using. This is also a useful way to check the number you calculated using the above process.

My preference, being old school, is to be more exact and build a spreadsheet that takes into account the expected return on the invested balance, the expected tax rate to be attracted by the investment income, an inflation factor appropriate to the expense profile, and allow for the retention of an appropriate balance at the end of the whole thing to add a cushion in the event of something going awry along the way.

Your independent insurance broker and/or financial advisor can help you work through the specifics to arrive at the level of life insurance appropriate to your situation.

CHAPTER 31 – LONG-TERM DISABILITY INSURANCE

Long-term disability (LTD) insurance provides the insured with income in the event that a disability interrupts their ability to work. (Note, you must have income to replace when applying for this type of insurance.) Given that the ability to produce an uninterrupted flow of earnings is the foundation of most financial plans, this form of insurance is a key element of financial calamity evasion.

Long-term disabilities are particularly insidious from a financial planning perspective because they sap you of your ability to earn a living and yet you continue to incur the expenses of being alive as well as any additional expenses associated with the disability (specialized equipment, alterations to make your home accessible, the cost of an attendant …). According to *A Guide to Disability Insurance*,[1] 1 in 3 people, on average, will be disabled for 90 days or more at least once before they reach age 65. Once a disability lasts for 90 days or longer, it can stretch out to cover a substantial chunk of your working years; therefore, it presents a risk profile that you need to treat with respect.

LTD coverage may well be your most expensive insurance policy. That stands to reason because you are insuring what is potentially a very substantial and long-lasting cash flow requirement, and the odds of becoming disabled over a working career are not as long as many other risks that are generally shared through the use of insurance. Those are two characteristics—a potentially sizable cash flow requirement and a reasonable probability of meeting the criteria for qualification—when combined, that make actuaries sharpen their pencils.

Long-term disability insurance is available in a variety of forms, including:

- group plans,
- individual plans, and
- government plans.

Many workers are covered by a group plan through their employer or through any one of a number of organizations they may belong to, from professional associations to business groups. It may be that this coverage is all that is required to adequately address the financial risks inherent in one's circumstances. However, if this is the coverage you are relying on, it is essential that you understand the details of the plan vis-à-vis your risk exposure. Make sure you read through the coverage details outlined in your policy documentation or discuss the provisions with your human resources department. In many cases, unfortunately, you may find this coverage to be inadequate.

One of the key aspects to keep in mind is that group coverage is only effective while you remain a part of the "group." If it is employer coverage, it is only good while you remain with that employer. If it is coverage provided through a professional association, then it likely remains effective only if you are a member in good standing.

Group coverage is designed with the characteristics of a specific *group* in mind. If your situation is not closely aligned with the average requirements of a group member, then it is not unlikely that there will be gaps in the policy that make it less than ideal for your situation. Also, coverage details are subject to change over time; it is important that you remain aware of any changes to the coverage that could impact its appropriateness in your circumstances.

If you need additional coverage, or if you envision a need for transferable coverage, then you may be best served by arranging for an individual policy. An individual policy will almost assuredly cost you more, but it also can be designed to address your risk profile closely.

A variety of government programs also have LTD elements. These programs include the various provincial Workers' Compensation Programs, CPP/QPP, veterans benefits, and employment insurance. It is beyond the scope of this book to get into the provisions of these programs, but it would be worth your time to do some basic research to ensure that any reliance you are placing on them is warranted. Your insurance professional is a good source of information related to the coverages and limitations that are associated with the various government programs.

When it comes to LTD insurance, there are a number of critical questions that need to be fully considered:

- What is the definition of disability used in the policy and is it right for you?

  Do you need *own occupation, regular occupation,* or is *any occupation* coverage sufficient? Own occupation is the most substantial form of protection and carries the highest price tag. If you have specialized skills, this may be the most appropriate protection for you. It is important that you gain an appreciation for the technicalities of each option and how each applies in any policy you are considering.

- How much income do you need to replace?

  You can't make the insurance decision in isolation from your financial circumstances. LTD insurance policies are designed to provide a percentage of your pre-disability income, often in the area of 60–85 percent. You need to ensure that the cash flow provided by your insurance, together with any other means you have, is sufficient to cover your expected monthly living expenses. Be sure to understand the elements of your remuneration that are and are not included in the definition of income.

- Are the benefits flowing from the plan taxable or tax free?

  Generally, if you pay the full cost of the insurance premiums, the benefits received will be tax free. However, if someone else pays the premiums, the disability benefits will likely be taxable. Make sure you understand how taxation works, in the case of your policy.

- Are the benefits adjusted for changes in the cost of living?

  Regular increases in the Consumer Price Index will have a material impact on the purchasing power of benefits if they are not adjusted.

- How long is the waiting period (referred to as the elimination period)?

  You will need to have sufficient financial capital (or short-term insurance in the form of sick leave or another source) to cover your cost of living for the waiting period associated with your plan.

- Can you afford a longer elimination period?

  If you extend the waiting period, the cost of the policy can be substantially reduced. You should consider this aspect of your LTD policy when you are defining your emergency fund strategy.

- How does LTD coverage integrate with other insurance/income programs?

  The benefits from the various sources of insurance you have in place (group, individual, and government) are likely to be coordinated in some manner, rather than cumulative. There could also be specified dollar limits. You can only fill a gap if you know it exists.

- Is the plan insured or is it an administrative services plan?

  This is particularly important for group plans offered by employers. Certain large employers will offer an LTD plan to employees, but will retain responsibility for paying the benefits. In this situation, the continuing viability of the plan is dependent on the continuing viability of the company. Companies will often hire an insurance company to administer the plan, but the insurance company does not guarantee the benefits associated with an administrative services plan.

It is vital to consider how the disability of a breadwinner could impact the financial situation of their family and take necessary precautions. This type of insurance is expensive. That is because the chance of disability is relatively high and is of substantial financial impact, if realized. Don't assume that the coverage you are provided through work will be sufficient without taking a critical look.

Okay, I can still feel that you are not sold on the importance of this. I just did a Google search and was told that the average starting salary for a college grad in 2018 was expected to be $50,004. Assuming that starting salary and an annual average increase over a 40 year career of 4% annually, the future value of that stream of payments equates to … wait for it … $4.75 million. If you had a 4.75-million-dollar house, would you insure it? If you had a $4.75-million yacht, would you insure it?

CHAPTER 32 – CRITICAL ILLNESS INSURANCE

Critical illness insurance offers a one-time, lump-sum payment in the event you are diagnosed with a listed illness. The purpose of critical illness insurance is to provide a specified volume of additional unrestricted financial resources at a time when you may be off work, undergoing treatment, and otherwise focusing on recovery.

The lump-sum payment is highly desirable in the circumstances that generally accompany a diagnosed critical illness. The payment can be spent in any way the policy owner chooses, providing vast flexibility that can help in garnering whatever type of support is deemed necessary. For example, the insurance can be used to provide additional home care support, help look after kids, pay travel costs to see specialists, or just as a supplement to family income, allowing a spouse more freedom to attend to family needs.

Critical illness coverage is sometimes used in place of long-term disability insurance, which may or may not be appropriate; your circumstances will dictate which is better suited to your needs. The coverage provided by long-term disability insurance tends to have considerably more breadth because critical illness insurance benefits are limited by the conditions in the policy, including the list of applicable illnesses. One factor that may lead you to critical illness insurance is being in a situation where long-term disability insurance is not available. This would be the case for a stay-at-home parent, because long-term disability insurance is only available to applicants with income.

There are several key factors you need to be aware of when considering critical illness insurance, including, but not limited to:

- The definition of what constitutes a critical illness for the purposes of the policy. The conditions covered by critical illness policies are not standard, they can and do vary. The list of illnesses covered can include cancer, stroke, heart attack, dementia, multiple sclerosis, coma, paralysis, organ transplant, and many more.
- Make sure you understand any exclusions that apply to a policy you are considering. Additionally, make sure you understand how any pre-existing conditions would be treated, should they be relevant to your situation.
- Understand the conditions that must be met before the benefit is due and payable, including diagnosis requirements and waiting period requirements that must be survived before the benefit is payable.
- Consider the nature of riders offered and if, in fact, they add incremental value before including them in your policy.

An experienced insurance broker is well placed to provide valuable insight when considering this type of insurance and the relative cost effectiveness of the alternative forms of insurance that should be evaluated given your particular set of circumstances.

I know of a number of people who have opted for critical illness insurance instead of LTD insurance. Often, the stated reason for taking this path was the relative size of the premium. While I am all for reducing costs, it is important to recognize that the coverages are very different. Cost is just one piece to the decision and should not be the sole criteria used.

CHAPTER 33 – LONG-TERM CARE INSURANCE

At some point in your life, you may need to enter a long-term care facility or receive special medical care in your home. Long-term care insurance was designed to help finance the costs associated with this need. Long-term care insurance kicks in when an insured is unable to care for themselves because of a chronic illness, disability, cognitive impairment, or other condition that causes them to be unable to sufficiently perform a specified number of the activities of daily living (defined to include bathing, dressing, toileting, transferring, continence, and eating). The specific details are described in the policy documentation and will vary from policy to policy.

Government healthcare programs do not, contrary to popular belief, universally cover the full cost of specialized care facilities. I live in Manitoba and my mother lived in an assisted living facility that she paid, out of pocket, just north of $3,200 per month to live in. My mother-in-law was in a personal care home, for which she had to pay approximately $85 per day. Neither of our fathers lived long enough to require this level of care. Manitoba government-run personal care homes charge residents a fee, which is based on their income. The fee reaches its maximum at a relatively low level of income. Costs and options vary by province, so be sure to explore the nature of the government programs and associated costs relevant to your circumstances as you are considering this type of insurance.

While this insurance is most often thought of as coverage for the elderly, there are many situations where around-the-clock care can be required for people of all ages.

There are generally two types of payment strategies: one is a reimbursement-style plan the other is an income-style plan. The reimbursement-style plan will specify the expenses that are eligible for coverage. The income-style plan will provide a predetermined periodic payment once qualification has been established. Clearly the income-style plan provides more flexibility with respect to the use of the insurance proceeds, and is more administratively streamlined.

As with all types of insurance, there are a number of characteristics that will determine the premium that will be charged. The most significant include:

- The age of the applicant,
- The state of the applicant's health at the time of application,
- The type and amount of coverage selected, and
- The length of the waiting period chosen.

The alternative to purchasing long-term care insurance is to simply plan to accumulate sufficient investment balances or income sources to cover the risk. This is the route my parents went (though it wasn't a conscious choice, in their case) and my wife and I have decided to do the same.

We know first-hand how expensive this stage of life can be. Our financial projections for retirement have taken these expenditures into account, based on inflation adjusted values of current costs (as experienced by our parents). In our later years, I expect assisted living to be our largest ongoing expense by a substantial margin ... assuming we both get there.

CHAPTER 34 – OTHER INSURANCE

The balance of my family's insurance portfolio at present includes:

- automobile insurance
- personal property insurance (home)
- extended healthcare insurance
- travel health insurance

Of these policies, three have the potential of saving us from potentially debilitating financial hurt, and one is simply there because it was a necessary precursor to obtaining our travel health insurance policy (that being extended healthcare insurance).

Automobile Insurance

Automobile insurance in Manitoba is required by law and it is provided through a provincial crown corporation, so there is little I can offer in the way of sage advice in this set of circumstances. My rule of thumb with all types of insurance is to focus on those pieces of exposure that can become game changers and do what you can to reduce the overall premium cost. With respect to auto insurance, this means focusing on a couple of things:

- Liability coverage. This piece of the premium cost is generally relatively low (at least for the extended portion of coverage) and it is the one form of outcome that really scares me from a financial perspective. Liability judgements against at-fault motorists have the potential to be game changers. My bias is to go for the maximum liability coverage offered and then consider if that is overkill or if the potential risk could reasonably reach that level.
- The deductible. I go for the highest deductible offered to gain the lowest premium. I do this because I can easily afford to pay the higher deductible if the need arises and it has the potential to save me quite a lot of money over the long term.
- Extra coverages. In Manitoba, there are a number of extra coverages available, including:

    - Loss of use
    - Excess value coverage – for vehicles worth more than $50K
    - New vehicle protection – to cover depreciation in the event a new vehicle gets written off, etc.

My general approach to each of these is to consider the likelihood of the event occurring and my ability to cover the additional cost out of my emergency savings, if it does. Sometimes the added coverage will make sense; other times, not so much. I have found my insurance broker to be a good sounding board for these discussions.

Oh, and the best way to keep auto insurance affordable … don't get in any accidents that are your fault and minimize the number of traffic violations that are attributed to you. If you do get in an accident, take pictures, try to get contact information from a witness, and make sure the other driver sees you do this. Their story tends to remain more closely linked to the truth that way. I have experienced a couple of situations where the story has evolved from the time of the accident to the time of insurance resolution. The more you can do at the time of an accident to discourage such evolution, the more likely you are to have the final result closely approximate the truth.

Personal Property Insurance

The personal property insurance policy is a tedious read. (I think they do this on purpose so you won't read it.) I take a long list of questions to my broker every year to get an understanding of everything that has changed from the previous policy; there are always changes in the coverage. I find my insurance broker to be an invaluable asset in determining insurance coverages, and specific riders, that make sense for me to purchase. Again, my general rule of thumb is to do what I can to get the policy premium as low as possible while insuring against outcomes that would be financially meaningful.

Just as with auto insurance above, I like to increase my deductible to reduce the premium, and I like to max out liability coverage. I'm not insuring against the little stuff. I don't like dealing with insurance companies, so I wouldn't be filing a claim for the little things anyway. While it is unlikely that a liability claim will occur, it is the one outcome that scares me the most from a financial impact perspective. Liability coverage is relatively inexpensive and protects my family from risks that have the potential to be game changers.

Travel Health Insurance

We travel a lot, and as depicted in my personal reflection in the introductory piece to this section of the book, the costs associated with a health event out-of-country can be gargantuan. There can even be a substantial personal cost associated with medical treatment in Canada if you are outside of your province of residence when a health situation arises. We always make sure to have sufficient travel health insurance coverage because you just don't know when you will need it.

Extended Healthcare Insurance

Our costs for dental, chiropractic, various paramedical services, and pharmaceuticals have been quite consistent over the last few years. The annual cost of our policy is roughly what we are spending on the services covered, but there are a lot of other things that could arise that are covered by the policy. This is the one policy that we have where the potential for a financial disaster is not so apparent, at least not to me. I would have considered self-insuring this risk, but in order to get the travel health coverage we have in place this coverage was a prerequisite.

PART VIII – ESTATE PLANNING

Assuming you expect to leave behind people and/or causes you care about, giving a little thought to their continuing needs and ability to cope in your absence or incapacity is a responsibility that should override any discomfort you experience thinking about your own death or disability. It is up to you to be sure that your estate is ready for ongoing management when you are no longer able, as well as for orderly distribution upon passing.

An estate plan does a number of very important things for you, including:

- setting out how your assets are to be handled upon death,
- identifying who is to manage your assets, and the powers they have to act in your stead, should you become unable to,
- providing for your loved ones,
- assigning roles and responsibilities that would otherwise have to be doled out by the courts,
- managing your tax obligations efficiently, and
- on and on the list goes …

Put simply, you provide guidance to your loved ones that allows them to act efficiently and effectively, knowing that they are carrying out your wishes. It reduces the burden of decision-making at a time when they need to process what has happened and/or grieve. It gives your survivors a last chance to honour you by knowing they are doing what you wanted rather than feeling guilty for being mad at you due to your lack of foresight and leaving them with a pile of stuff to deal with and no direction.

When people are grieving, do you really want to put them through a longer and more arduous process than absolutely necessary? Do you want your flaky sister acting as your executor, making all kinds of complex decisions on your behalf? Do you want your 18-year-old alcoholic son to have unencumbered access to your hard-earned money the moment it passes to his possession? Do you want the assets you worked so hard to earn to ultimately go to your kids when your significant other passes, or are you equally comfortable with them going to the gong-show your spouse marries after you die? The only way to be confident that the ultimate flow and/or use of your assets corresponds with your wishes is to put some thought into what you want and to build the proper legal framework to guide the actions taken by your appointed representative(s).

There is a lot of ground to cover in this topic area and much of it becomes somewhat technical and dependent on a broad array of factors specific to an individual's situation. In the arena of estate planning, there is a complex mixture of both provincial and federal law that comes into play. The *Income Tax Act*, which is federal law, can have a substantial say in how much of your estate ultimately passes to beneficiaries versus government coffers. Provincial family law has considerable influence over what you can and can't do with certain types of property and there are significant differences between the rules practiced under each province's authority.

All of the legal technicalities that permeate both federal and provincial law make estate planning another area of your financial plan where it is essential to involve qualified and experienced professional assistance. But, having said that, it is also important for you to understand the basics of estate management and distribution to ensure that your plans are properly designed to achieve what you want in a tax-efficient manner. When you are properly informed, you are more able to express to your lawyer what you want to see in your power of attorney (POA) document. With a general understanding of the critical factors, you are able to be an active participant in the will drafting process.

There are a plethora of decisions to be made when planning your estate and we will delve into many of them in a certain amount of detail, but the scope of the book does not permit a comprehensive discussion. An excellent book that dives deeply into the provincial variations and considers several of the topics thoroughly that I can only touch on is written by Christine Van Cauwenberghe, entitled *Wealth Planning Strategies for Canadians*.[1] Her book is an excellent read that I would highly recommend as you study this subject further.

Within Part VIII, we will explore the following subject areas:

a) the will
b) power of attorney
c) trusts
d) probate
e) personal representatives
f) taxation at death

Takeaways from Part VIII

- ✓ Drafting and maintaining an up-to-date will is essential, and the first step in a well-constructed estate plan.
- ✓ An effective estate plan appoints people of your choosing to administer your affairs in the manner you decide. If you don't have a legal will and power of attorney, you have no control and therefore no assurance your wishes will be enacted.
- ✓ A general power of attorney and a will are the perfect financial pairing; they are the wine and cheese of the estate-planning world. One allows your directions to be implemented while you are alive and the other once you have departed. A well-designed will and POA form the cornerstone of an efficient and effective estate plan.
- ✓ Trusts are often thought to be the domain of the rich and famous ... and they are very useful to the rich and famous. However, they can also be extremely useful to many in the middle class. They offer significant control options that are not available with a direct transfer of ownership. Knowing that the benefit of hard-earned assets will flow to whom you want when you want offers immense peace of mind.
- ✓ Probate fees ... YUK ... everyone hates probate fees. There are several very effective techniques available to reduce or even eliminate probate fees. While it makes sense to reduce probate fees, this is only the case where other more significant costs and disadvantages are not realized.

Short-sighted planning in this area can lead to significant unintended impacts.

- ✓ Selecting a primary, and at least one backup, personal representative for all of the potential roles that are required to implement your estate plan is a task that should be thought through with care. Once you have decided who you would like to perform any particular estate role, have a discussion with the candidate to ensure that they are willing to act and understand exactly what you would like them to do and how you would like them to do it. Then do everything you can to make their job easier by being ultra-organized.
- ✓ Income taxes are a huge expense for Canadians and if not properly planned for, they can be even more extreme in the year of death. Upon death, there are a number of taxation realities that crystalize; they need to be fully understood and managed. If you have substantial assets that:

  - are held in unregistered investment accounts and have accumulated sizable unrealized capital gains,
  - are held in registered accounts such as a RRIF or RRSP,
  - are collectibles that have appreciated in value,
  - involve a second property at the lake, in the country, out of the country, etc., which has appreciated in value, and,
  - have otherwise accumulated an as-yet-unpaid tax consequence,

  you need to apply (or purchase) advanced tax knowledge to properly manage the potential income tax exposure.

CHAPTER 35 – THE WILL

A will is a legal document that dictates how your estate will be dealt with upon your death, or more to the point, how loved ones and any causes dear to you will receive benefit from your estate. Depending on your situation at death, it may be that of all the documents you draft and sign over the course of your life, the thousands and thousands of them, your will is the most important. Yet, according to surveys, it appears that well over half of Canadian adults do not have a valid and up-to-date will.

That is brutal. No will means no direction, which leads to uncertainty, perhaps a nice healthy family fight with a lifetime of hard feelings and a confused legacy for the deceased.

Here are ten good reasons to have a valid and current will; perhaps one or two will convince you to boast membership among the prepared minority:

1. You will decide how your estate will be distributed.

   In the absence of a valid will, the provincial government has devised rules (laws of intestacy) that will define how your estate will be doled out. What is the likelihood the rules will match what you would have wanted? Zero?

2. You will decide who will manage your estate.

   Being an executor/executrix is a very demanding role that requires someone to act in an honest, trustworthy, organized, and competent manner. Who knows the skills possessed by potential suitors to this role better than you? A judge you have never met?

3. You can nominate a guardian for your minor children.

   You know your children, you know the potential guardians, you likely even know how your children and the potential guardians get along. Is a judge who doesn't know any of this in an advantageous position to make this decision, or are you?

4. You will decide how to provide for your heirs and any special needs they may have.

   If one of your beneficiaries has a gambling, drug, or out-of-control spending habit, for example, you can build-in safeguards that protect against a bequest being frittered away. If you want your daughter to have access to funds for some uses but not others, you can organize your will to accommodate that. If you want your spouse to enjoy your assets while they are alive, but want also to ensure that your children are the ultimate recipients of your residual wealth, you can design that into the terms of your will. No will = no control.

5. You will decide how to split up responsibilities in your will.

   Assigning roles in your will provides an opportunity to discuss your wishes with the representatives selected and to ensure that they are willing and able to take on the role. By assigning roles to responsible and skilled people, you gain a layer of assurance that just is not there if you leave the decision to chance.

6. The estate settlement process will be streamlined.

   If you can keep the estate out of court proceedings by reflecting your wishes in a manner that fully respects the legal options available to you, not only will the process of settling your estate go more smoothly and quicker, but it will also be substantially less costly. Would you rather your kids have the advantage provided by a few more bucks or would you prefer that a lawyer you have never met drive a nicer car?

7. Tax efficiency can be maximized.

   If you don't write a will, you may lose out on tax-planning opportunities that could enhance the flow to your beneficiaries, as opposed to the government.

8. Once you have satisfied your legal obligations, you can disinherit certain individuals who would otherwise stand to inherit or, alternatively, you can leave a bequest to people and organizations that would otherwise receive nothing.

   It is virtually certain that the formulaic approach applied by the intestacy law of your province will not replicate your wishes. Certainly, if you want to leave anything outside of family lines it will not happen if you don't write a will, name the organization as a direct beneficiary of an asset, or otherwise make formal and legal provisions for the asset's transfer. Even if you are only leaving assets to family, chances are high that intestacy rules will divide your assets differently than you would have wanted.

9. You can change your mind at any time by rewriting your will.

   So long as you are the age of majority and are of sound mind, you can rewrite your will as often as you please.

10. A will allows your survivors to honour your wishes and reduces the chance of family discord.

The guesswork is eliminated where decisions are pre-made and documented. Not everyone may agree with all provisions of your will, some may even challenge your will, but your chance of leaving a family in harmony are maximized if you do them the courtesy of leaving your directions in a legal and binding will.

Oh, may I also point out that there has never been a documented case in the history of civilization where a person has had their death hastened simply because they wrote a will. I feel very confident in saying that you will die when you die, regardless of if you have a will or not, or have thought about death or not. Two certainties in this topic area are: you will die, and if you don't have a valid will when you do, you have screwed up badly.

There are essentially three different forms a will can take:

a) Holographic Will

This is a will that is entirely in the handwriting of the testator (the person who is the subject of the will). This form of will is generally less precise and less thorough, which can lead to ambiguity and ultimately, challenge. Unless you find yourself on your deathbed with no other option, don't rely on a holographic will; properly distributing your estate is simply too important to those you leave behind.

If you want to see the ultimate holographic will do a Google search for "tractor fender will." Apparently the fender is on display at the University of Saskatchewan. Being a Blue Bomber fan I generally don't suggest stopping in Saskatchewan, but it might be worth a look if you are driving past. It offers a strong reminder that you should write your will before you find yourself under a farm implement.

b) Formal Will

Generally, this is a will prepared by a lawyer on behalf of the testator. It is signed by the testator and witnessed in accordance with applicable provincial requirements (usually two witnesses, who do not stand to benefit from the estate distribution). It is also possible to use either a preprinted form or a templated will kit. If "the kit" is properly designed in accordance with the laws applicable to your province of residence and the will is properly signed and witnessed, this approach may work as intended.

My advice would be to not take the chance with any form of off-the-shelf templated will. The cost of legal involvement in writing a will is not onerous in most cases and through the involvement of a qualified and experienced lawyer, you can be sure that it has been done properly and will effectively function to enforce your wishes.

c) Notarial Will

This is a will written by a notary, signed by the testator, and witnessed in accordance with provincial requirements. This form of will is only used in Quebec.

It cannot be overemphasized that a will is not a one-and-done task. As life moves along and your situation changes, the provisions of your will should be reviewed and updated as necessary. Got married? Update the will. Got divorced? Update the will. Got remarried, had a munchkin? Update the will. Your executor, or one of the trustees you appointed in your will has died? Your opinion of the assigned guardian changes? Update the will. Moved to a different province? Review the will to determine if it is still valid.

Even the simple passage of time is likely to alter your estate in a fashion that new planning techniques become applicable. As time goes on, laws change and potential beneficiaries may also change, which require an update of the will. Perhaps you will become more philanthropic later in life, which makes you rethink distribution strategies. A will is reflective of your point-in-time wishes; it is not a living document. The will reflects your wishes when it is signed and incorporates relevant legal provisions at the time of writing. It needs to be made current when either of these two elements change in a material fashion.

The Main Clauses Contained within a Basic Will

Every will is likely to have unique elements in order to recognize the circumstances of the testator. However, there will be a number of common elements.

Identification of the testator (the person to whom the will belongs). In my will, this is one sentence that identifies me by my full legal name and where I live.

Revocation of former wills and codicils. The purpose of this clause is to eliminate authority from prior dated estate instructions. A codicil is a supplementary document that is designed to change, add, or delete wording in an otherwise valid will. Codicils are often used for minor changes rather than rewriting an entire will.

Appointment of an Executor and Trustee. This is the clause where you specify who you assign the role of carrying out the wishes documented throughout your will. It is not a decision to be taken lightly; the time commitment is substantial and the skills required can be extensive and diverse, depending on the complexity of your estate and the expressed wishes. You should name an alternate executor or two in the event that your first choice is unable to act.

Authorization to pay outstanding debts. Just because you are dead doesn't mean your estate can avoid your financial responsibilities. This clause gives your executor authority to pay funeral expenses, debts, fees, administrative expenses, etc. before any bequests are satisfied. This clause goes on for half a page in my will, with all sorts of legal gobbledygook. The reason you are hiring an experienced and qualified lawyer is to get the gobbledygook right. It is your job, with the assistance of your lawyer, to get the strategy right.

Payment of taxes. This provision is designed to provide the executor with both the authority and freedom to deal with taxation issues in the manner that ensures your obligations are met in the most efficient and effective way.

Disposition of property. This is where the rubber hits the road and is the primary purpose of the will. In this section of the will, you express your wishes related to specific assets you want dealt with in-kind, gifts of specific monetary amounts to various people or organizations, and ultimately you provide for the distribution of the *residue* of your estate. The residue is what is left after all debts and expenses of the estate have been settled and the gifts of specific property and cash legacies have been made. The residue is often the largest part of the estate, and if it is not specifically dealt with in the will, it would fall under the rules of intestacy. Just as it is important to provide for alternate executors and trustees, it is important to provide for alternate beneficiaries. This is where you need to consider not only your own mortality, but also that of your beneficiaries. What if your spouse or one of your children predeceases you? What if your whole family dies in a common disaster? What if your favourite charity ceases to exist? It is important to think through alternate flows of assets given changed circumstances.

Experienced estate lawyers have seen a wide variety of outcomes in their practices; they can certainly help with this thought process (and they can assist in more than just the gobbledygook). The more thought you put into the various angles that should be considered, the more likely your will is to adequately deal with any plausible outcome.

When making specific bequests, be careful to ensure that you are not short-changing the residual beneficiaries. If you are donating a large lump sum and circumstances change from the time of writing the will to your eventual passing, you may end up unintentionally penalizing the residual beneficiaries by substantially decreasing the balance of the estate flowing into the residual.

It is within this section of the will that any trust provisions are included. It is through the judicious use of trusts that I can be sure that my estate is enjoyed by those who are most important to me, regardless of how life unfolds in the future for my survivors. The trusts also outline a number of distribution strategies that control the use of funds and timing of fund distribution, with appropriate discretion provided to the trustee. The legal gobbledygook ensures that the trusts are properly formulated.

Appointment of a Guardian for Minor Children. Until your kids get to the age of majority in your province, there is need to provide for their ongoing care and support. As with all other major roles allocated within your will, it is essential that you not only decide who has the skills and wherewithal to effectively serve in the role assigned, but you must also ensure that they are both willing and expect to be able to undertake the role. Again, you should identify a first choice and a backup.

In addition to dealing directly with the responsibility you have for minor children, your instructions should also explicitly deal with your responsibility to look after any pets that might outlive you.

Powers of the Trustee. Trustees are limited to the powers granted in the applicable provincial *Trustee Act,* unless you specify to the contrary. In many cases, the powers specified in the applicable *Trustee Act* may be sufficient, but there can be exceptions. You should discuss the powers to be given your representatives with your lawyer to ensure that they are provided the freedom to act in a manner that makes sense in your situation.

Compensation issues. Wills often are silent on the compensation issue. Many representatives feel uneasy accepting payment; you can relieve them of that by clearly expressing your wishes. The roles doled out can be a lot of work; compensation is a good way to demonstrate your appreciation.

Funeral instruction, organ donation, and other time-sensitive direction. For issues such as these you can certainly include them in your will, if you like. The problem with having them there is that it may well be too late to have them honoured if the will is not consulted before the critical time has been reached. Direction related to time-sensitive matters should either be pre-discussed or left where it can be readily located.

Attestation Clause. This is a clause that states that the will was properly signed and witnessed in accordance with the requirements of your province.

Common Disaster Clause. You should discuss the merits of this clause with your lawyer. Its purpose is to direct that certain actions be taken regarding the estate of the deceased, in the event that their spouse or common-law partner dies at the same time as the deceased or in very close proximity thereto. In the absence of this clause, there is potential for an unfair distribution of a deceased's estate, as well as potential for the need to probate the same assets twice in very close proximity to one another.

In addition to the above-noted clauses there are boatloads of other aspects that may be dealt with in your will as a result of peculiarities of your situation or the law in your province of residence. It is this reason that going the route of involving a lawyer who understands the law in your province, and the details of your specific situation, is so important. If you want your will to function in accordance with your wishes, educate yourself on the basics and hire a qualified professional to assist you in drafting a product that is suitable to your circumstances.

When I was looking for a lawyer to facilitate the writing of our wills, the first couple I interviewed did not have the background in trusts that was required to support our wishes. In each case both, they and I were quick to recognize the gap in their experience base as compared to our needs and they recommended I look elsewhere for service. I quickly moved on to interview further lawyers until I found someone who was well versed in all elements that we wanted our wills to cover.

You need to be an active participant in this exercise if you want to get the end result you desire for those people and organizations that are important in your life. You don't need to be intimidated going through this process—lawyers rely on clients to make a living and are likely to need your business more than you need any particular one of them. You are the boss. You decide who you want to work with.

CHAPTER 36 – POWER OF ATTORNEY

A will takes effect when the testator (the person subject of the will) has passed away. Up until that time, any representatives named in the will have no legal standing to act on behalf of the individual. That said, there are often times when a person requires help making and implementing decisions and undertaking financial or property transactions. It could be that they have lost competency, are out of the country, have physical limitations, or one of any number of other circumstances that make acting on their own behalf inconvenient, difficult or impossible. This is where a power of attorney (POA) comes into play.

A properly drafted, authorized, and witnessed POA document provides authority for someone, of your choosing, to act in your stead. The person selected, in this context, is referred to as an *attorney*. Your attorney does not need to be a lawyer, as the label might imply; in fact, there are few restrictions on who can be named, but they must be a capable adult. The POA essentially comes in two varieties:

1. General POA. This document gives the authority to the named person, or people, to make binding financial decisions and transactions on your behalf.
2. POA for healthcare (which goes by a number of different names, depending on the jurisdiction). This document authorizes someone or some

predefined group to make healthcare decisions on your behalf when you are unable to.

To envision how important it is to have someone with the authority to act on your behalf, just take a moment to think about how things would work if you were unable to act on your own. I'll wait … looked like a bit of a mess didn't it?

Since you don't know what the future holds, it is just common sense for all adults to have both a will and power of attorney in place. And talk about convenient. For a relatively modest cost (my mother had both a will, complete with embedded trusts, and a general power of attorney drafted at a cost of about $500), you can have your lawyer do both of these documents at the same time. That would be a big "to do" off the list. Hey, if you write them on the list individually, you get to cross two things off at the same time. Talk about productivity!

The will and the general POA are the perfect tag team. The POA is effective up until you die, and at that point in time the will takes over. If you decide to name the same authority to take on both the executor and attorney roles, the transition will be seamless.

Some people believe that they really don't need to do anything; after all, if something bad happens someone will step up and take care of things. To this I just say, who is this someone? If you can identify them now, why not just confirm their capability and willingness, then get the paperwork done?

If you have not appointed a POA, in order for someone to act on your behalf, they will likely have to make a court application. This can be time consuming and costly (often thousands of dollars, I am told). In the end, the court may provide these powers to someone whom you would not have chosen to take on the role to begin with. Even if the process goes perfectly and you end up with the right person in charge, why take on the additional cost and add to the already burdensome workload of that individual?

When you take the time to have a POA written, you have the ability to personalize the powers that are granted. You can restrict their powers, or more likely, broaden the powers to include actions that the legislation would not otherwise allow. We live in a world where a trip to Starbucks results in orders like "grande, quad, non-fat, one-pump, no whip mocha" and yet we are happy to accept whatever the provincial government has set for limitations on what our POA can and can't do? I stay clear of Starbucks because they speak a language I don't understand, but I do have a general POA that provides the powers I want my attorney to have when acting on my behalf.

Drafting your General Power of Attorney

Standardized Forms. There are lots of kits and standardized forms available that allow you to design a POA at minimal cost. Similar to the discussion related to such options with your will, employing an experienced lawyer to prepare the document and confirm your intent is much more likely to result in a product that effectively considers any unique elements of your situation.

Your Attorney. Make sure you consider the qualities you want in an attorney and name one only after figuring out who best matches your criteria. Do not take this decision lightly; the person you appoint will be given the power to do almost anything you could do yourself (except write or change your will, give away your assets, or draft a new POA for you … there may be a couple of other limitations, but you get the idea). I will focus on this more fully in a later chapter, but suffice it to say that you will want your attorney, and alternates, to be trustworthy, responsible, knowledgeable about your assets, and able to fill in from a management perspective, should that be required. You will also want them to be a resident of Canada and preferably in your home jurisdiction.

Enduring POA. If the general POA document does not include appropriate wording, it will not maintain its authority once mental capacity is lost. This is exactly the time when you most need someone to act on your behalf, so this is not a misstep you want to make in the drafting process. A qualified and experienced lawyer will be well aware of the need to include this provision and the nature of the wording required in your jurisdiction.

Springing POA. Unless your document states otherwise, your attorney will have the power to begin dealing with your assets from the date on which the document is signed. If you choose, you can sign a springing POA, which will not take effect until some point in the future after specified events have taken place. This condition complicates matters. If you are considering including a provision of this nature, make sure you discuss the potential impact with your lawyer. Your attorney's job is difficult enough without having to jump through a bunch of hoops to demonstrate that the conditions of such a provision have been met.

Other Considerations

- Powers of Investment. If your jurisdiction has significant limitations on the investing options available to an attorney, you may wish to broaden their freedom to act in this regard.
- Compensating the Attorney. There are jurisdictional differences when it comes to compensating an attorney. You should consider if you want to include a clause to specifically outline your views and wishes related to compensation. In my opinion, this is something that should be addressed in the document.
- Designating a Monitor. This is a provision whereby the attorney is required to provide periodic accounting to someone you designate and/or obtain consent from prior to major transactions. If you feel you need or want a second look prior to certain actions, or a global review of accounts at certain points in time, this may be a provision that appeals to you. While this does create more work for your attorney, they may in fact welcome this requirement because it gives them a forum to demonstrate that your wishes are being respected in a diligent fashion.

Power of Attorney for Healthcare

The rules regarding this form of POA are jurisdictional, so it is important that it be drafted by someone familiar with the language required in your province. The difference between a POA for healthcare and a living will is that a living will sets out your wishes regarding medical care and a POA for healthcare appoints your attorney to make a subset of medical decisions on your behalf.

When setting up a POA for healthcare there are a number of elements to keep in mind:

- The POA for healthcare will only be activated upon mental incapacity.
- The scope of decisions that can be made on your behalf are generally limited to those involving medical treatment to prolong life and extend medical treatment.
- You can have multiple original copies of this form of POA. Given the need for immediate access if it is to be of any use, you should ensure that your attorney has a valid copy, and/or keep direction on you (or at least readily available) at all times.
- The wording in these documents can be tricky if it is to precisely communicate the nature of the decisions that you are allocating to your attorney and the conditions upon which they are to be making the decisions. Your lawyer can help make sure that this is done appropriately.

When my father was in the process of dying, I received a call while I was in my car driving to work. By the time I picked up my mother and got to the hospital, the critical point of medical treatment decision-making had passed and the doctor had already made the decision. This resulted in a breathing tube being inserted to assist my dad. The breathing tube kept him "alive" for a few additional hours, but there was never any hope of meaningful recovery. My mother, wife, and I sat there and watched him as his organs shut down one after another and the blood circulation became so constricted that his extremities started to turn blue and became very cold. We watched him struggle for breath and try to speak; he couldn't talk with the breathing tube in his throat. When we finally had the breathing tube removed, it was very difficult for my dad to communicate, though he did seem relieved to have the tube out.

I wish I could have been there to prevent the breathing tube from having been used, and had a meaningful conversation with him as my final memory. It is nice to think that a POA for healthcare will give you some control, but that will not always be the case. Rest in peace, Dad. I miss and love you.

CHAPTER 37 – TRUSTS

I get it. Trusts sound like they are limited to the purview of the rich and famous and you aren't Bill Gates, Mark Zuckerberg, or Jeff Benzos. The fact is that utilizing trusts in your financial plan may be an astute idea for any number of reasons. For instance, at dinner parties you can causally work into the conversation how the latest revisions made to your will included a series of testamentary trust provisions to control the second generation transfer of assets in a manner that protects against the flow of wealth outside of your bloodlines (make sure to wear a turtleneck sweater and use an English accent) … talk about a hot shot! Assuming that didn't do it for you, read on at least for a little bit to see if I can't find something that would make this a strong concept you would be willing to investigate a little further.

Trusts are significantly underutilized, in my opinion. At their core, a trust is simply a way to hold and manage assets in a manner that provides the person transferring the assets more control and greater certainty around the ultimate disposition and/or beneficial use of those assets. (There can also be a series of side benefits, including tax benefits.)

Both my wife and I have included within our wills instructions to establish a trust, or series of trusts, depending on what happens. In the absence of the trust structure, our will would have simply provided for our assets to transfer to each other, assuming the other is alive, and to our kids upon the death of the last survivor between us. This strategy gives the surviving spouse unencumbered access to the estate to do with as they please while they are alive and later, that same unencumbered access would transfer to the kids (assuming they are the age of majority) upon the passing of the last survivor. This all sounds pretty reasonable, until you start to look at a number of different scenarios.

In the case of my wife and I, suppose for a moment that I die first (which is almost guaranteed) and my wife finds another partner. Assume she rewrites her will to follow the same pattern, with the assets transferring first in favour of her new partner, who incidentally has a couple of kids of his own from a prior marriage. My wife takes a trip to her favourite country, Nepal, and experiences an avalanche when trekking to the basecamp of Everest. She died doing what she loved, which is the perfect scenario for her (at least, that is what she tells me). Now all of her assets, and mine, transfer to her new husband. (Hmmmm.) He immediately goes out and has his will rewritten to have his estate transfer, in whole, to his biological kids. My kids at this point, both of whom are living independently, are disinherited from all of the assets my wife and I managed to accumulate over our lifetimes. Crappy, crappy, crap, crap! The judicious use of the trust structure in our wills could have avoided this outcome, while at the same time providing for the needs and wants of the surviving spouse.

You might want to consider the potential benefits of using a trust where you:

- Want to leave financial assets to your adult kids, but you recognize that they are not mature enough to manage a windfall of the value you will be leaving. You decide instead to leave your assets to them in a trust that manages their access to the money over a scaled time frame as they gain the experience, knowledge, and maturity needed to manage their finances. This approach may result in their ending up with a nicely balanced investment portfolio, a fully paid for education, and/or seed money to establish a highly successful business. (You set the terms of the trust and guide the trustee in what you consider to be an acceptable use of the assets placed in the trust.) In the absence of a trust, the kids might have decided to use the funds to pay for lavish vacations, fast cars, and dependent friends, with the end result being a prematurely empty bank/investment account.

- Want to ensure, to the extent that you are able, that your children maintain control over your assets in the event that they experience a relationship failure. A huge percentage of marriages and cohabitation arrangements break down, and if your kids have used your estate to invest in family property, it is highly likely that some of that estate value will flow to their ex-partner (who is no doubt a butt-headed dingbat that you never liked to begin with) unless appropriate structures have been enacted in advance. A trust, designed with appropriate legal advice, would be one way you could consider to help manage the risk of this fate occurring.

- Want your spouse to have full access to your estate (income and/or capital), but you want your children to have the remainder of your assets once your spouse passes on. In this case, you will want to look into the applicability of a spousal trust, which subsequently flows into a trust to benefit your kids upon the demise of your spouse.
- Recognize that a beneficiary will require some assistance with the management of the assets because they are not financially astute. A trust, with appropriately designed terms, can help mitigate the concern.
- Have a disabled child and you want to ensure that their needs are met in a tax-effective manner without inhibiting their access to other forms of social assistance. In this case, you will want to research the Henson trust format as well as look into the benefits and requirements of a qualified disability trust.
- Want to retain access to income from your assets, but in the future you want to leave the remaining capital to a charity, and the tax deduction would be of use to you now. If this is your situation, you will want to look into the applicability of a charitable remainder trust.
- Have a business or other assets (a cottage, perhaps) that you feel will grow in value substantially in the future and you want to freeze the current value and plan for the future tax consequences of additional growth.
- Want to limit the size of your estate to better manage probate fees you may choose to set up an inter vivos trust, an alter ego, or joint partner trust. These types of trusts can also be used in large part as a substitute for a will and/or POA.

- Want to maintain privacy around your assets. You may choose to use a trust structure, in whole or in part, to avoid public access to the information flowing through your will.
- Are in a position that creditors potentially have a claim against your personal assets. There may be an opportunity to effectively use the trust structure to manage that exposure.

As you can see from the above list, which is by no means comprehensive, trusts are very versatile and can be a great way to accomplish many different goals and manage a wide variety of risks and concerns. It is worth your time to gain a general understanding of their use and to ensure that your legal and taxation representatives have a very strong working knowledge of trusts and how they may apply in your circumstances.

The Structure of a Trust (Boring Alert)

There are three parties to a trust: the settlor, the trustee(s), and one or more beneficiaries.

The *settlor* is the person who establishes the trust and contributes the property to the trust. If the trust is set up in a will, the settlor is also the testator or testatrix.

The *trustee* is the person named to manage the property of the trust. The trustee plays a fiduciary role; they are the legal owner of the property, but it is their responsibility to manage the property for the sole benefit of the beneficiary or beneficiaries. The terms of the trust dictate how the assets of the trust are to be managed and are specified in the governing document that caused the trust to be formed (which would be one or a combination of: a trust deed, the governing legislation, or a clause in a will).

The third and final party to the trust is the *beneficiary,* referring to the person, group, or cause to whom the benefit derived from the trust flows. While the trustee has legal title to the trust assets, the beneficiaries are the beneficial owners of the trust assets.

There are two beneficiary distinctions that can be made within a trust. For certain types of formal trusts, the distinction between the two is very important to specify and for the trustee to respect.

- Income beneficiary. This is a beneficiary who receives, or has the right to receive, the income generated by the trust assets.
- Capital beneficiary. This is a beneficiary that receives, or has the right to receive, the assets held in the trust.

The settlor of the trust should use the services of an experienced lawyer, and perhaps a taxation professional, when establishing a trust to ensure it is done correctly.

Types of Trusts (Boring Alert Continues)

Trusts, in general, offer tremendous flexibility in allowing a settlor to structure their affairs in a manner specifically designed to achieve certain goals. The settlor has the option of providing very specific powers to a trustee, to give them substantial discretion, or to enable actions somewhere between these two extremes. While each province has passed legislation providing basic powers to a trustee, the governing document used to create the trust can be used to customize the powers granted.

While there are a number of specific purpose trusts that must contain certain provisions in order maintain their standing as such, there are two broad types of trust to be aware of: inter vivos trusts and testamentary trusts. An *inter vivos trust* is a trust that is created while the settlor is alive. A *testamentary trust* is one that is created upon death, via the terms of a person's will. Delving into the details of specific types of trusts is beyond the scope of this book, but I did want to highlight one particular type of trust that has broad relevance, that being the *spousal trust*.

A spousal trust can be used to ensure that your estate benefits your spouse initially and upon the passing of your spouse, places the assets with residual beneficiaries either for their outright use, or in another trust to further manage asset usage. A spousal trust must be designed carefully to meet the requirements of the *Income Tax Act*. When the qualifications are satisfied, assets can then flow into the spousal trust at their adjusted cost base, thereby delaying the recognition of unrealized capital gains until a final disposition of the assets takes place (either when the trust disposes of the asset or the spouse dies). The deferral of capital gains realization, as we have seen previously, is very beneficial and allows a more controlled realization of tax consequences over time.

A qualifying spousal trust for tax purposes is one where:

- The spouse (common-law spouses also qualify) receives and reports all income realized by the assets held in the trust,
- No one other than the spouse has the right to encroach on the capital of the trust assets for the life of the trust, and
- In the case of a testamentary trust, the trust assets vest with the spouse within three years of the settlor's death.

When the beneficiary of a spousal trust dies, there is a deemed disposition of all assets at current fair market value. A spousal trust is an excellent vehicle to help manage tax exposure while at the same time protecting the ultimate distribution of assets in a blended family scenario.

Certainly, if you have any children with disabilities, you will also want to become well versed in Henson trusts and qualified disability trusts, both of which have benefits designed specifically to deal with the challenges this situation presents. Likewise, if you are 65 or older, joint partner trusts and/or alter ego trusts may be of interest to you. If you are working with a qualified professional and any of these trusts appear to meet your needs, they should bring them to your attention, but don't hesitate to ask for their thoughts.

Taxation of Trusts

For purposes of taxation, a trust is considered to be a separate taxable entity, and has its own tax form (T3 Trust Income Tax and Information Return). It must be completed and filed within 90 days of its fiscal year end.

In general, a trust is taxed in a manner similar to that of an individual, without the benefit of graduated tax rates in most cases (exceptions noted below) and without access to personal credits. What follows are a few taxation highlights; a tax pro should be engaged to ensure that all taxation implications are properly accounted for. Some of the differentiating elements of the taxation of trusts include:

- Most trusts are designed as flow-through entities. This means that any income earned in the trust (assuming it is so structured) can either be taxed within the trust or flow through to a beneficiary and taxed in the hands of the beneficiary.
- Income that flows through the trust to an ultimate beneficiary is deductible to the trust and is instead taxed in the hands of the beneficiary. Certain forms of income retain their character when flowed through to a beneficiary (dividends and capital gains).
- When capital property is transferred into a trust, in many, if not most cases, the transfer is treated as a deemed disposition for tax purposes and the settlor must report the capital gain. There are exceptions for certain types of trusts that will instead receive the capital assets and their associated taxation characteristics (spousal, alter ego, and joint partner trusts).
- In most cases, trusts are taxed with the highest marginal tax rate applied to all earned and retained income. However, there are a couple of exceptions to this general rule:
    - With a graduated rate estate (GRE), the tax rates applied are incremental for the trust in the same fashion they are for individuals. There is a short window where an estate can be taxed in this manner (maximum of 36 months).
    - Graduated rates also apply for a qualified disability trust.
- Capital assets can only accrue unrealized gains for a limited period of time (21 years) before there is a deemed disposition for tax purposes. Some types of trusts are not subject to this rule (spousal, alter ego, and joint partner trusts). Before the end of the 21st year of an impacted trust, a taxation specialist should be consulted in order to consider how best to manage/avoid the pending deemed disposition.
- If property is distributed from a trust to a capital beneficiary, the cost base, for tax purposes, generally flows with the property. There are exceptions to this treatment for certain types of trusts.

As you can readily see from the very brief discussion above, the taxation of trusts has some unique characteristics that add a level of complexity. The services of an experienced tax specialist should be utilized by a trustee to ensure that all of the tax implications are properly accounted for.

Trusts – A Final Thought

There are very real benefits that can be gained by using trusts to manage access to assets, as well as defining interim and final distribution strategies. Additionally, via the trust structure, the settlor has the opportunity to appoint trustees to help the beneficiaries realize the value of trust assets in a prudent fashion. It is well worth your time to explore trust applicability and alternatives in the context of your personal situation with a qualified advisor.

CHAPTER 38 – PROBATE

Probate is the process of confirming that the deceased's will is valid and the executor (or executrix) has the necessary authority to implement the will's instructions. Probating a will involves presenting the last will and testament of the deceased to the provincial court, together with a complete and valued inventory of estate assets, and a series of affidavits and other required documents (including a cheque for the associated probate fees). The court approves the will evidenced by issuing *letters probate* (the name of the approval can vary by jurisdiction). The probate process protects third parties holding estate assets; most financial institutions will not accept direction from an executor until such time as the will has been probated—this is the reason many wills have to go through probate.

The date upon which letters probate is issued also marks the beginning of the elimination period for certain challenges. If the will is delayed for submission to probate, or never probated, then the executor is at risk of liability for a much longer period of time. Thus, while probate has the reputation of being a simple tax grab, it does have some very real implications for the settlement of an estate.

The specifics of the probate process are provincially regulated. Generally, there is very helpful information available through the applicable provincial court website.

Probate Fees

Probate planning has a number of different objectives but is largely about trying to minimize or eliminate probate fees. The quantum of probate fees charged is set on a jurisdiction by jurisdiction basis; often, the fee varies with the size of the estate. The fees charged are subject to change at the whim of the province/territory and there is considerable variability in the probate fee formula applied from coast to coast. Using a probate fee calculator,[1] I ran the numbers for all of the provinces/territories and determined that the probate fees for a $500,000 estate varied from a low of $140 to a high of $7,782.65. For a $1,000,000 estate the range became $140 up to $16,257.65. Quite a difference!

At the time of writing, Alberta had very low probate fees, ranging from a minimum of $35 to a maximum of $525 for estates over $250,000. In Ontario, the fees were titled "estate administration taxes" and amount to $5 per thousand dollars for the first $50,000 of the estate and then become $15 per thousand (or 1.5%) of the gross estate for the remainder. In Manitoba, the fees were roughly half the total in Ontario, with the first $10,000 of the estate attracting $70 in probate fees, followed by $7 per $1,000 (or portion thereof) for the estate value in excess of $10,000.

As you can see from the limited snapshot presented, the fee formula and overall fee level varies markedly from a low- to a high-cost jurisdiction. But even in the most expensive of provinces, the estate was looking at fees of 1.695% on the portion of the estate over $100,000 (Nova Scotia). While this can accumulate to a relatively large payment in the case of substantial estates, as a percentage of the overall estate, the fee is generally not that significant.

When a person engages in probate planning, there are impacts that need to be considered to determine if their efforts to avoid probate fees make sense in the circumstances. In many cases, while probate planning will reduce the gross amount of the fee, there are other costs and limitations that may outweigh the probate fee impact.

Probate Planning

The more common reasons for probate planning include:

- Probate fee avoidance or reduction. The probate fee on a large estate can be a substantial number in some provinces and it makes sense to prudently minimize it if the impact of doing so is not excessive. In several jurisdictions, and in the case of modest estates in virtually all jurisdictions, probate fees are slight and efforts to avoid the fee may end up being more harmful than the value realized by the avoided fees.
- Maintaining privacy. Probated wills and asset listings often become public record. There may be valid reasons for keeping certain information out of the public domain.
- To expedite estate settlement. Avoiding probate altogether gets the assets into the hands of the ultimate beneficiary without significant delay. Probating a will, on the other hand, takes some time.
- To reduce professional fees. Typically, legal fees are based on the size of the estate (the size of the estate is measured by the value of the assets passing under the authority of the will). Trustee fees can also be based on a formula that takes into account the value of the estate.

Probate Planning Techniques

Probate fees are paid on estate assets, and estate assets are those assets that flow through a will to beneficiaries. Probate planning involves dealing with assets in a manner that has them flow to beneficiaries outside of the authority of a will. There are a number of options that can be utilized to achieve this:

1. Adding a Joint Owner with Right of Survivorship to an Asset

    If you add a joint owner with right of survivorship to an asset (assuming it is done properly), when one of the owners dies, the asset passes directly to the surviving owner. As such, for the person who has died, assets owned in this manner do not form part of their estate and no probate fees are applied to the market value of the asset.

2. Giving Property Away

   If an asset is not owned at the time of death, then it will not form a part of the estate and will not attract probate fees.

3. Designating a Direct Beneficiary

   Many different types of registered assets allow the naming of beneficiaries. Where this is the case—as it is with insurance policies, annuities, RRSPs, RRIFs, TFSAs, Segregated Funds, and other registered assets—a beneficiary can be named and the assets will pass directly without becoming encumbered in the probate process.

4. Using an Inter Vivos Trust

   As soon as assets are transferred into an inter vivos trust, legal ownership transfers to the trustee, beneficial ownership to the beneficiaries and, in many cases, the asset will be deemed to have been sold at fair market value. There are situations where the assets can be rolled into a trust at their adjusted cost base. Don't attempt to do any of this without seeking qualified legal assistance and gaining a full understanding of the implications.

5. Insurance Trusts

   If properly set up, an insurance trust may allow the will to govern insurance proceeds distribution, and avoid probate. Again, though, legal advice should be sought in contemplation of taking this action.

From a probate perspective, it is important to ensure that your will is drafted with a common disaster clause. You will recall, this is a clause that states that if you and your spouse die simultaneously or within a short period of time of one another (typically 30 days), your estate will automatically devolve to your contingent beneficiaries. If this clause is not in your will, then your assets may end up flowing through probate on two occasions and result in paying probate fees twice. Not to mention that it would be the second will that would govern the final destination of the assets, which could alter the planned distribution profile significantly and in an unintended way.

Disadvantages of Probate Avoidance

The list of disadvantages associated with avoiding the probate process is fairly extensive, and includes, among others, the following:

- All of the potential benefits associated with testamentary trusts are lost because in order for assets to flow into a testamentary trust they must first form a part of the estate.
- As we have seen, one of the methods of probate planning is to transfer an asset into joint ownership with the right of survivorship. The use of the joint ownership strategy has several perils and costs that need to be considered, including: loss of sole and absolute control over the asset; potential exposure of the asset to creditor and family property claims; as well as the potential realization of capital gains taxes on the gifted portion well before otherwise necessary. It will also create a situation where the asset is ultimately transferred to the joint owner, all else remaining equal, but the tax liability associated with the deceased's ownership interest will be a burden that is taken on by the estate and not by the person who receives the ownership interest in the asset.
- The outright gift of assets will result in loss of control of the asset as well as the immediate realization of any capital gains if the transfer is not to a spouse. The gifted property will also become exposed to the creditors of the new owner, and could introduce the risk of claims under family property legislation.
- Distribution of some assets through the estate and other assets outside of the estate can result in unfair treatment of beneficiaries due to where the tax liability resides. Generally, the estate will end up with the tax burden associated with the deceased's income in the year of death, so those

who receive their inheritance other than through the estate may well have the tax implications associated with their benefit being paid by the estate, reducing the benefit to be received by the residual beneficiaries. It is vitally important to think through and map out the potential tax consequences to understand where the eventual burden will reside (see example, below).
- In addition to an early recognition of capital gains taxes, you could also cause other taxes to be triggered, depending on the property, such as land transfer taxes.

Rather than focusing on probate planning, it often makes more sense to focus on tax planning. Probate fees may *feel* like a big expense, but income taxes *are* a big expense. Also, depending on your situation, the benefit received due to the control features available through the use of testamentary trusts could heavily outweigh the added cost of the probate process.

Case Study: A Poor Probate Planning Outcome

Maybe the best way to take a look at probate planning, and how it can possibly go awry, is through an example. *This example has been simplified, and some shortcuts taken, in order to emphasize certain key points.*

Rick and Marie, residents of Manitoba, lived together in a committed relationship for 35 years. Rick loved car racing, the Winnipeg Blue Bombers, his cottage, and above all else, butter/garlic soaked shrimp. One day, after attending the Grey Cup festivities in the Maritimes, Rick was finishing off a final plate of shrimp at the all-you-can-eat seafood buffet, and was fully satisfied with his meal, when his chair collapsed and he banged his head on the floor, ultimately succumbing to his injuries. Rick died a happy man, with his stomach full of shrimp and having seen the Bombers win their sixth consecutive Grey Cup. Rick left all of his worldly belongings to his lovely and devoted significant other, Marie.

Marie was left behind with their four kids; Xzapion, Jasmin'd, RB, and Pong. Her intention was to have her estate equally distributed to each of the four kids. When Marie died years later, she had the following assets:

Table 9: Estate case study assets list.

ASSET	VALUE	ADJUSTED COST BASE	UNREALIZED GAIN
House	$500,000	$250,000	$250,000
Cottage	$500,000	$50,000	$450,000
RRIF	$500,000	N/A	N/A
Unregistered Investments	$500,000	$100,000	$400,000

Scenario #1 – Marie does no probate planning, all assets flow through the estate and are subject to probate.

In this case, the estate would be valued at $2,000,000 and be responsible for paying probate fees amounting to $14,000 (Manitoba). This may seem like a big number, but keep in mind it represents only 0.7 of one percent of the estate value.

On top of the probate fee, Marie's executor would also ensure that the taxes owing on the capital gain on her house, the capital gain on her investment portfolio, and the tax owing on her RRIF are paid upon filing her final tax return. There would be no tax as a result of the gain on the cottage because it would be declared as her principal residence and exempt from tax. The cottage was ordinarily inhabited by Marie, so it qualifies as a principal residence even though she spent less time there than at the house. The cottage had a greater unrealized capital gain when compared to the house, so it was wise for her executor to declare it as her principal residence to maximize the exemption available.

Marie's final tax return will report taxable income as follows:

Table 10: Case study taxable income, scenario #1.

ASSET	CAPITAL GAIN	TAXABLE INCOME
House	$250,000	$125,000
Cottage	Exempt	$0

ASSET	CAPITAL GAIN	TAXABLE INCOME
RRIF	N/A	$500,000
Unregistered Investments	$400,000	$200,000

Using a tax calculator I found on the internet to approximate the income tax impact, the following is what would be left of Marie's estate:

Estate Assets	$ 2,000,000
Income Taxes	$ 389,320
Probate Fees	$ 14,000
Net Estate	$ 1,596,680
Each Beneficiary	$ 399,170

Thus, with all of the assets flowing through the estate, Marie has achieved the result she was looking for … to have each child receive the exact same value from her estate. (Note: With some well-advised tax planning over the years leading up to her death, Marie could have experienced a better tax outcome.)

Scenario #2 – Marie does some probate planning because she wants to reduce the probate fee that her estate will otherwise be required to pay.

Marie notices that each of her four assets are of equivalent fair market value ($500,000). She figures if she just allocates one of the assets to each of her kids, she will have treated them equally. She takes the following actions:

1. She reregisters the house such that it is jointly owned (with right of survivorship) in the names of herself and Xzapion. When she dies, the house will go to Xzapion outside of the will; this will save some probate fees ($3,500).
2. She reregisters the cottage such that it is jointly owned (with right of survivorship) in the names of herself and Jasmin'd. When she dies, the

cottage will flow directly to Jasmin'd outside of the will; this, too, will save probate fees ($3,500).
3. She designates RB as the direct beneficiary of the RRIF. When she dies, the RRIF will pass directly to RB outside of the will; this, again, will save some probate fees ($3,500).
4. She leaves the investment portfolio to Pong through her will. She could have changed this asset to joint ownership with right of survivorship also, but it has been a long day and her investment advisor was away on holiday.

She feels great relief at having completed all of this heavy lifting. As a treat to herself from her big day of having arranged to save probate fees she goes to the all-you-can-eat seafood buffet … yada yada … and she dies.

Now, what happens to the assets? Are the kids treated equally?

Not even close.

Everything flows as intended outside of the will. The house, the cottage, and the RRIF assets all flow directly to the intended beneficiary without any probate fees. Each of the three kids assumes an asset apparently worth approximately $500,000. The estate, however, is left to pay the remaining probate fees of $3,500 ($500,000 * .007), and the income taxes of about $390,000. Pong just got royally screwed because of the probate planning. The asset left to him was valued equally with the assets left to the other kids, but the tax impact of the other transfers remained with the estate and the only asset left in the estate to pay the tax impact was the investment portfolio.

Pong had a meeting with his siblings to explain what happened and to ask them to share the tax responsibility. His brothers, instead, shared a laugh leaving Pong to hold the tax bag. He now hates his brothers.

Not only that, but fast-forward a couple of years …

- RB develops an addiction to the white powder and very quickly spends the RRIF balance on his habit,
- Jasmin'd has gambling losses that force him to turn over the deed to the house to settle his obligation, and

- Xzapion forgets to renew the insurance on the cottage and accidentally burns it to the ground, forcing him to sell the land because he can't afford to rebuild.

All of this could have been avoided if the judicious use of testamentary trusts had been implemented with a reliable and knowledgeable trustee helping the kids to make reasonable choices within parameters that Marie had a hand in formulating.

Don't get me wrong. Reducing costs is a premise that I wholeheartedly endorse. Especially when it comes to investing, the judicious minimization of cost can make a huge difference in the level of wealth that one is able to accumulate over the course of their lifetime. Reducing probate fees is an admirable goal—so long as it does not create other, bigger, problems. If done correctly, probate fee management is a great idea. If you want to focus on avoiding probate costs, make sure you do so under the guidance of someone who understands your estate plan to ensure the result is well aligned with your intention.

In the course of this example, you may have noted an inordinately high risk of death by attending all-you-can-eat seafood establishments. I know of no such correlation, rather I was hungry as I wrote this piece. I have a weak spot for crab linguini. Perhaps I will go get some; that should give me plenty of energy for tonight's run. It will have to be a long run if I am to get anywhere near calorie break-even.

CHAPTER 39 – PERSONAL REPRESENTATIVES

When writing your will, power of attorney, and trust documents, you are faced with a multitude of significant decisions, not the least of which is the appointment of your personal representative. To be clear, I am using the term personal representative in this context to address all of the different roles where you are appointing someone to act on your behalf. This term will be used to capture the roles of executor/executrix, administrator, trustee, attorney, etc.

Characteristics to look for in a Personal Representative

The first thing you need to get clear in your mind is that you are not bestowing a great honour on someone by asking them to fulfil one of these very important roles. What you are in fact doing is giving them a very important set of responsibilities that includes a list (often a very long list) of tasks that range from complex to mundane and you are asking them to devote their scarce time and energy to complete them all to a very high standard. In some cases, you are even asking your representative to take on potential liability. In effect, what is being asked is akin to helping with a household move that will take many consecutive weekends as opposed to giving them an honorary doctorate or a freshly baked apple pie.

I hope everyone that has named me as their personal representative lives a very long and healthy life, because I love them dearly, and I don't really look forward to acting in the roles they have asked me to perform. They don't much like receiving gifts from me any more either—vitamins, gym memberships, healthy eating books ...

It is important that you thoroughly consider the decision, recognize what you are asking of the chosen representative, and that you get on with it. It is an easy thing to let slide; you don't want to defer the decision so long that it turns out you never get it done. Your loved ones deserve the respect implied in you having made considered, thoughtful, and deliberate decisions related to this element of your legacy. When a personal representative is called on to act, it will almost assuredly be an emotional time for your family; it is up to you to help them through it with the least amount of stress and anxiety possible.

The qualities and skills you should look for in your chosen primary and backup representatives include the following:

1. Trustworthy, responsible, honest, and objective. Most people, I think, will act in a trustworthy and honest manner when the circumstances are right. But you really need to think about your representative, and their situation, in the context of the role you are asking them to perform. Make sure they do not have competing interests that would put pressure on them to act in a manner contrary to your intent. Because their situation may change with the passage of time, you may want to consider building in some other controls, such as a monitor or secondary approval process to add rigour that better ensures appropriate actions are continually taken.
2. Knowledgeable and skilled in the subject matter of the role. If you are assigning a role to someone, you need them to possess the ability to get the job done in an efficient and effective manner.
3. Organized and diligent. The role you have assigned to a representative is likely to be a substantial burden that is now, often suddenly, added to their pile of life's responsibilities. Some of the people in my life are

like my wife's mother, who was a brilliant at keeping track of every date, event, bill, etc. that needed attention. When she was in her prime, you could add a dozen things to her list at any moment and they would seamlessly fit into the schedule. She was as organized as they come, and she could be relied on to complete her commitments to the best of her ability. That is what you need for this role.

4. Professionally discrete. It is inevitable that your representative will be called into action when something rather dramatic has happened in your life. It is precisely this time when there will be more interest expressed in your situation and that will bring with it an elevated opportunity for both enquiries and an audience.
5. Available and willing. In order to be an effective representative, the person needs to possess all of the above attributes, but they also need to have the time to be able to do the job and be willing to take it on.
6. Location and residence. Generally, it is helpful to have a personal representative that lives in close proximity. For some roles, a non-resident would be required to post bond, which could be an expensive undertaking. Also, when it comes to estates and testamentary trusts, the residence of these taxable entities could be impacted by the residence of the personal representative. This can be a huge consideration if you are contemplating naming a personal representative that resides in a different jurisdiction.

Making Your Personal Representatives Task Easier

Given the complexity of the role you are asking your representative to perform, there are a number of activities you should undertake to help assure a smooth transition. The list of tasks depends on the role you have assigned to them, but generally includes the following:

- Have an open and honest conversation with each personal representative about your wishes related to the role and confirm that they are willing to act. Some of the most important elements of your wishes can and should be explicitly reinforced in the governing document (will, trust, or POA), but many of the details of your wishes are best discussed for greater clarity. File a copy of the key points from your conversation with your important documents. Any written instructions outside of the governing documents themselves will not have the full backing of the law, but they certainly can reinforce the representative's actions in the case of any dispute.

- Compile and maintain a detailed inventory of relevant investment assets, valuable personal-use assets, listed personal property, and important documents (will, POA, etc.) in a state that is easy to retrieve and understand. Recent account statements should be maintained in an organized filing system. Ensure that cost details are included in the information to facilitate accurate tax return preparation. I keep an indexed binder that contains the vast majority of the information that my representative will need to know. I update it as information changes and do a global review of content annually to ensure that it is complete.
- Compile and maintain a list of all credit cards, passwords, and contact information for advisors (lawyer, financial advisor, accountant, business partners, etc.).
- Keep a listing of information that is needed to facilitate the efficient running of your household. This would include dates for key payments, a listing of those household costs that are paid automatically by credit card or directly from the bank, and any other type of information that would help your POA take over the household financial operations.
- Keep documents in a fire- and water-proof safe that is properly secured, or a safety deposit box, the location of which is known to your personal representative and to which their access has been pre-arranged.
- If it is important to you, maintain a list of people you would like to have informed regarding any major changes to your situation, complete with contact information.
- If you really want to be helpful, give some thought to what you would want to have included in your obituary, and document the details. If you have specific wishes related to the funeral proceedings, make sure they are known and pre-arranged to the extent possible.
- Ensure funds are available and accessible to allow for the payment of debts, expenses, and obligations that must be settled on your behalf. If

anything is prepaid, make certain that the details are well known to the personal representative so that payment is not inadvertently duplicated.
- You know the family dynamics that will be at play better than anyone else. Make sure these are fully considered when you are designing the roles for your personal representatives. Pre-manage any issues you can foresee by having the necessary conversations ahead of time. Times of stress bring out the idiot in some people.
- Periodically revisit the situation with your personal representative to confirm that they remain willing to act, know where information is kept, and understand the job you have asked them to do.

The role of personal representative—be it executor, executrix, trustee, power of attorney, etc.—is one that is complex, challenging, and time consuming. Don't take for granted that this will magically be looked after in the absence of you doing the necessary planning and preparation.

CHAPTER 40 – TAXATION AT DEATH

In Canada, we do not have estate or inheritance taxes. Imagine that, an opportunity to tax us has been missed (so far). Given how our system of taxation is designed, though, it can certainly feel like we have estate taxes. In fact, it is not unlikely that the final tax return will place the deceased in a tax bracket that is at least as high as that experienced at any time over the course of their entire life. Understanding how taxation works at death, and having a plan to manage the tax burden, is a very important element of an estate plan.

Income taxes are complicated at the best of times, but in the year of death they become more so. Unless the executor/executrix is a tax expert, they should likely seek input from one who is well acquainted with year of death rules and alternatives. If appropriate actions are not taken by the executor to cost effectively manage income taxes, if sued by the beneficiaries, they could experience personal liability. With all of the time and effort an executor puts into settling an estate, likely they are not looking for a *thank you very much* in the form of a lawsuit.

The CRA has prepared a very informative document T4011(E) *Preparing Returns for Deceased Persons.*[1] It would be useful to read through this before meeting with a tax pro so that you can be prepared to have a meaningful conversation and pre-gather much of the information they would be looking for to offer advice applicable to your specific situation.

This chapter is designed to introduce some of the main year-of-death taxation issues, not to make you an expert on the subject.

Filing Requirements

There are two time periods that the executor needs to be cognizant of in order to fulfill their duties as they relate to the Canada Revenue Agency. The first is the time period beginning January 1 and extending to the date of death in the calendar year of the death. The second is the time period after the date of death, running up to the point in time when the estate has been fully distributed.

With respect to the first time period, the executor must file the deceased person's final tax return (as well as any prior tax returns that have not already been filed). The final tax return is completed using the same T1 tax form that would have been filed by the taxpayer had they remained alive (with just a couple of disclosure differences to clearly designate the return as a final return). In recognition of the challenges that an executor faces, the CRA has made certain allowances in the filing deadline, as shown in the following table.

Table 11: CRA allowances in filing deadline for a deceased's tax return.

DATE WHEN DEATH OCCURRED	DUE DATE FOR FINAL RETURN	DUE DATE FOR AMOUNT OWING
Jan 1 – Oct 31	April 30 of the following year	April 30 of the following year
Nov 1 – Dec 31	Six months after death	Six months after death

The CRA has also recognized that it is not unusual for the return applicable to the year prior to death to not have been filed if death occurs in the January to April 30 time frame. In this case, the filing deadline for the prior year return has also been extended. If the taxpayer dies after December 31 but before the normal filing due date, the due date for filing and paying any taxes owing is six months after the date of death.

With respect to the post-death period, income earned and retained by the estate will be subject to tax within the estate. For purposes of this taxation period, the estate is treated as a separate person and must file a trust return for each year until such time as its assets have been fully distributed. A unique opportunity made available to an estate trust is that the executor can take advantage of graduated tax rates for up to 36 months. Only one graduated rate estate (GRE) trust is allowed per deceased individual.

Final Tax Return

The final tax return covers the period from January 1 up to and including the date of death. The deceased will have all of their usual sources of taxable income for this period of time that must be reported. The relevant sources of income will depend on their situation immediately before death, be they working or retired, the nature of investments and investment accounts they have, as well as any business income or other income they may have generated. To this point, the final return looks like it would have had the testator not died, except it is for a shorter period of time than the full year.

In addition to the usual sources of taxable income, there are likely to be some sources of income that are taxable as a result of death. It is this extra piece that feels like an estate tax, but in actuality it is simply the recognition of tax obligations that have been deferred.

Some of the more common additional sources of income include:

- Accrued investment income.

  Income earned but not reported prior to death must be accrued up to the date of death and reported.

- Unrealized capital gains.

  One of the most commonly practiced tax-planning strategies prior to death is to defer taxation for as long as possible as allowed within the rules. Tax deferral is a great strategy, but if consistently practiced, this can lead to substantial asset valuation beyond the cost of the asset, and therein a potentially substantial tax obligation in waiting. Upon death, all capital property owned by the deceased (with the exception of that rolled over to their spouse) is deemed to have been disposed of at fair market value immediately before death.

- Registered investments.

  Remember that tax deduction you got every year you made your RRSP contribution? Remember all of that income earned on your RRSP and RRIF investments that you didn't have to pay tax on because it was compounding unobstructed in a tax-free environment? Well, the government remembers it. When you die, unless you have a spouse or one of a very limited list of dependents to whom your RRSP/RRIF balance can be rolled over, it will all end up on your final return and attract income tax at your marginal tax rate.

It is these last two taxable income items that often have a substantial impact on the final tax return.

There are a number of other tax rules that are peculiar to the year of death that need to be considered by the executor/executrix, including but not limited to:

- Charitable donations limits and carry-back provisions unique to the year of death.
- Medical expense pooling rules unique to the year of death.
- There may be an opportunity to file more than one tax return (up to three in fact), depending on the sources of income earned by the deceased. Generally, if the deceased is in a situation where their representative is eligible to file more than one tax return, there is an opportunity to reduce the cumulative tax liability. In the case where the deceased was in receipt of business income, was the beneficiary of a graduated rate estate, or received certain taxable income payments after death, the executor should research the ability to file additional income tax returns.
- Rollover provisions can be particularly impactful and therefore relevant in the year of death. In the event that a rollover provision is available, and availed of, the tax profile of an investment will be retained by the new owner and further deferral of taxable income will result. Eligibility for rollover is significantly restricted by the CRA rules and is often only available to a surviving spouse.
- Potential spousal RRSP contribution.
- Tax-free death benefits received from an employer.

- Capital loss usage and special applications in the year of death as well as potential carry-back of losses realized in the estate.

Planning for the tax implications of the final return should be a major focus for several years in advance of death to ensure that the estate is in a favourable position to allow the executor/executrix to efficiently manage the tax impact.

What My Parents Did to Manage Final Return Tax Cost

The first brilliant piece of the equation to managing their potential tax problem was for the two mothers to live a long life. Following their lead is highly recommended! What that gave them, or their power of attorney, was a much longer time frame in which to manage the tax liability. Time provides the opportunity to smooth out income realization and thereby take advantage of progressive tax rates.

When my father and father-in-law died, their estate assets, including their embedded tax characteristics, were mostly rolled over to my mother and mother-in-law, respectively. Some gains were realized where it made sense, but the majority were deferred.

My mothers both felt quite strongly that their Old Age Security payment was their right, and both despised the idea of the OAS clawback affecting their pension. So that became our yardstick when it came to net income realization: the OAS clawback threshold. Under no circumstances did either mother want to have their net income exceed the threshold; they did not want to have their OAS confiscated. We managed their income to make sure they did not exceed this amount, while at the same time worked to prudently reduce their registered asset balances and the tax obligations that had accumulated in their non-registered investments (at this time both moms were into their 80s, so the window for deferral was closing).

Through this process, we began to take in a planned amount of income they didn't really need. We were purposely, in a methodical and measured way, giving up the right to earning income in a tax-deferred environment. The practice of managing income to the level of the clawback threshold kept them in the tax bracket they would have been in regardless of the actions we were taking, but we moved them deeper into it in the hope of reducing the total amount of taxes paid over the long run.

In addition to the potential tax liability that my parents had embedded in their registered investments, both had some unrealized capital gains associated with stock investments that also required attention. We managed this deferred obligation in a coordinated manner with the registered asset "problem." As we rebalanced their holdings (selling equities and buying fixed income investments) to match their target asset mix (which was becoming more conservative), we took the opportunity to realize some capital gains in a measured way.

All of these actions require that sufficient time be available to make prudent adjustments in a tax-efficient manner. This is why you want to have a reasonably long time frame over which you are managing your tax profile; it is not something that can be effectively dealt with suddenly.

There is one other common area where some seniors find themselves with a lingering tax problem; this is not one that my parents had to deal with, unfortunately—that being a substantial unrealized capital gain on a vacation property.

One of the great tax breaks afforded by the Canada Revenue Agency is the principal residence exemption. This exemption allows a taxpayer (or a married couple) to declare one property as a principal residence for each year the property was owned since 1971. Any capital gain associated with the principal residence is deemed to be zero for the years designated. If just one property is owned, then there is no further thinking to do; it will be the principal residence for tax purposes and no tax will be payable on the capital gain (though there is a reporting requirement when the property is sold). If more than one property was owned, such as a house in the city and a cottage at the lake, then a choice needs to be made as to which one will be designated as the principal residence for the overlapping ownership time period. A tax pro can help make the appropriate plans when it comes to utilizing this exemption.

For those of you who are more entrepreneurial, there could be additional tax complications and opportunities. Taxpayers who own a qualified small business corporation, or a qualified farming or fishing property, may have a very generous lifetime capital gains exemption available for use. There is a substantial amount of planning that needs to be engaged around these business operations to maximize tax benefits associated with their sale or transfer. Again, Ms. Tax Pro is an invaluable partner to engage so that income tax implications are properly planned for and opportunities availed of.

Final Thoughts

There are a lot of additional complexities and options that need to be considered that are particularly relevant to, or unique to, the year of death. As well, the post-death period will create an entirely new tax filing requirement related to income generated within the estate (T3 Trust Income Tax and Information Return). As you read the above chapter, you were likely finding your eyes glazing over with thoughts of having a chili cheese dog for lunch or wondering if half time is over yet. My advice would be if you, like most people, aren't experienced with year-of-death taxation issues and trust tax returns, purchasing expertise is a wise option to explore.

PART IX – PROFESSIONAL ADVICE

I remember it like it was yesterday. Not because it was particularly surprising, dramatic, or enlightening but because the experience was in such contrast to what I think the financial services industry should aspire to provide.

I had just finished acing the Canadian Securities Course and was taking a peek into career prospects for a relatively new Chartered Accountant in the investment industry. There was an opening at one of the major brokerage houses in my hometown so I applied and won an interview. I took a day off work and went downtown to one of the big buildings near the corner of Portage and Main in Winnipeg, took the elevator up into the sky and entered the well-appointed reception area. The place had the feel of unapologetic affluence. The receptionist could have been cast in one of my favourite TV shows, *Suits*, as she was dressed to the nines and extremely professional in both appearance and motion. The traffic through the reception area was primarily male, very well dressed and everyone appeared to mean business … the place was high energy.

I arrived a few minutes early for my appointment and was shown to a secondary waiting area. I plopped down into my seat, feeling very confident in what I had to offer, but was quietly wondering if this was the kind of environment well suited to my personality … more la-di-da than I generally like. It was clear from the surroundings that there were high expectations and the place had the feel of being a somewhat competitive environment, all of which I had no problem with. Hard work was something I was used to, and the subject matter of this industry was something that intrigued me and I was comfortable with.

I sat and observed. Then I sat some more. I grabbed the *Globe and Mail* from the table beside me and flipped through the business section (I didn't want to get caught looking at the sports). I needed to make the proper first impression, after all. By the time I finished the business section, my appointment time had come and gone, the interviewer was half an hour late, and no one had bothered to update me on his whereabouts; my initial impression of embedded professionalism was out the window. I figured there must be a big new issue or something had happened in the high-paced world of finance and it would become apparent to me in due course ... I waited.

As the wait approached an hour, I had lost patience and was preparing to leave when my interviewer appeared. As it turned out, there was no calamity in the overseas markets, no currency market upheaval that drew the important people to attention, no fraud that had broken requiring immediate action on behalf of clients with a vested interest; rather, his mother-in-law needed a ride to the airport. No meaningful apology, no heartfelt "thanks for waiting," no admission of responsibility.

I remained sceptical but was undeterred. We went to his office and got started on the interview. He talked and talked; apparently this was one of his favourite things to do. When he finally got around to including me in the conversation, within seconds, someone burst into his office and proudly proclaimed that he had unloaded so many thousands of bonds the firm was peddling and he required more to sell. The broker (or salesman) had slicked back blond hair, a beautifully tailored suit (no doubt matched to his convertible Corvette) talked a thousand miles a minute and clearly was the most important person in the world, at least to himself. I'm pretty sure that he didn't notice that I was in the room. They did a quick high-five, he was given the authority he had come in for, and off he went to change the/his world some more.

We got back to the interview and just started to have a meaningful conversation about the markets, financial planning, and my particular aspirations and how they might fit in with the firm's needs when in busted Mr. Important again—no knock, no excuse me, no courtesy. His day was going great. He had unloaded the additional allotment and was after more product to peddle.

I watched this and asked myself if this is what I aspired to become. Did I want the obvious riches that were there for the taking? Okay, sure. Did I want to hit the phones and market to my client base with more concern about what it would mean for me than for the financial future of my client? No. I didn't want to be Mr. Important. I wanted to be important, but to clients. If I was going to do this, I wanted to work hard and honestly help my clients achieve their goals. I wanted to make a good living by bringing value to my clients. Being a big ass was not a path I was willing to follow.

In hindsight, that was one of the best ways I could have spent that day because I learned a lot. I am so thankful that I stayed clear of that piece of the financial services industry. Unfortunately, many people have encountered a big ass and may not have recognized it. It is this kind of thing that, in my opinion, has cast a shadow over an industry that I believe has a vital service to provide.

While progress has been made to improve disclosure in many important ways, there are still embedded conflicts of interest that you need to be aware of and protect yourself from. At the same time, it is always a good idea to have some professional assistance to ensure that your actions are well directed to achieving success. Unfortunately, you need to ensure that any advice you purchase is actually advice that is focused on your best interest and that it comes from someone who is well qualified and appropriately experienced to help you navigate to what you define to be a successful conclusion. You don't need Mr. Important to peddle you bonds, or whatever the highest commissions are on that particular day. You need your goals, risk appetite, personal situation, and means to be the focus of all plans designed and implemented on your behalf.

Good advice does precisely that.

Finding Integrated Appropriate Advice

It is entirely possible that there is no profession where the range of expertise, skill, and specialization is more varied and/or fragmented than it is in the financial services industry. This makes your job a little more challenging to ensure that the people and processes you decide on will lead to the result you are looking to achieve.

Probably the most effective way to proceed is to have a qualified advisor quarterback this process on your behalf. Through this approach, you can ensure that all important elements of your financial situation are considered in a fulsome and holistic way. Many advisors have access to teams of specialists that can professionally deal with all aspects relevant to your financial plan. The key is to find someone you can work effectively with that is qualified to develop a comprehensive financial plan for you and sufficiently connected to bring in relevant specialists to add the necessary details to your plan.

Buyer Beware

I just got home from a wealth management presentation delivered by an investment and wealth advisor who worked for a huge Canadian financial institution with a significant international presence. This particular individual had a team working with him that included:

- Two estate-planning specialists,
- Two financial planners who did comprehensive financial planning and were credentialed to offer insurance products, and
- Organizational support that included substantial investment research capability and investment strategies designed to be scaled for individual investors.

While I was reasonably impressed with the apparent skill and qualifications embedded within the team, I learned enough from their presentation and the question period to know that their investment process did not match my philosophy (in that it did not focus on cost minimization and failed, in my opinion, to properly consider tax impacts).

But the meal, oh, so good! They had a four-course menu with a choice from among several tantalizing entrees. I had the chicken; my wife had the salmon. The smallish room was filled to capacity and we all ate as the speaker delivered his goods. While the presentation was professional, it was slanted to portray benefits and returns in such a light as to WOW the prospects in the room and ultimately sign up new clients; an outcome I'm sure they achieved.

The investing approach they used involved a research team that identified individual stocks to build client portfolios. They used three equity lists—a Canadian, US, and international list—to build diversified portfolios for each of their clients. They demonstrated, in a graph, how their Canadian list produced superior results over the past 17 years when compared to investing in the S&P/TSX composite index. The results looked to be quite impressive, and their portfolio appeared to well outperform the benchmark. Lucky clients! What good fortune I had in being invited to this evening!

When I asked a couple of questions, it was clear that the chart only told a part of the story, the part that made them look like geniuses.

The returns they portrayed were based on the direct appreciation of the stocks included on their list, including dividends. These returns were before transaction fees, before the management fees they charged, and without considering any tax implications. I asked about their fees. The presentation leader proudly stated that they charged 2% annually based on the invested asset total, and no one ever complained because of the value they delivered. (I hadn't asked about the value they delivered, I thought that was the point of the graph.) Clearly they felt 2% was reasonable and to question it was a silly waste of time.

I then asked about how many stocks they had on the list at any given point in time and the rate of stock turnover on their list. They had 26 stocks currently on the Canadian list; turnover averaged out to about 30% per year ... so an average holding period of about three years. This rate of turnover will result in significant transaction cost. Keep in mind also that this was just one of three stock lists; if they intended to purchase in the area of 75 stocks, and turn them over in about 3 years, that is a healthy number of transactions. Implicit in this activity too is the cost that the investor needs to pay outside of the portfolio expenses and management fees, namely taxes. With a 30% annual turnover in holdings, there is potential for significant tax implication for non-registered accounts.

Upon reviewing their presentation materials further when I returned home, I noticed that they didn't define which specific index they were using as a benchmark, so I sent an email asking them if it was the price return index or the total return index. There is a significant difference in the two because dividends form a substantial part of the return of a stock portfolio over a period of time. They were accounting for dividends in the returns they were generating using their stock lists ... that was a key plank he was advocating, dividend-paying stocks of major blue chip companies. In fact, over time, the total return index has outperformed the price return index by about 50% on a fairly consistent basis. I never got a response to my email. They were very quick to respond to my emails when I was setting up the invitation details, not so much to answer questions that maybe they didn't like the answer to.

I want to be clear that in this case, they did not lie. There were seven very small lines on the bottom of the graph saying that the historical compound annual return did not reflect applicable taxes, or account and transaction fees, which would lower returns. No kidding! They likely just forgot to fully define the index they were using. I had asked for the presentation materials before the event and was denied. I was told they had to protect their proprietary information. (A pile of hooey. It is more likely they were protecting against probing questions).

A Better Way to Proceed

It is critical that, when you choose to get advice, you get unbiased and skilled advice to help you set up your plan. While there are skilled and experienced professionals with a number of different backgrounds and credentials, as a rule I lean toward an organization that has a strong educational, testing and a continuing education requirement, the FP Canada Standards Council who award the Certified Financial Planner (CFP) Marks. The FP Canada Standards Council has defined, within its Standards of Professional Responsibility, four sets of standards to which CFP professionals must adhere. Over the course of about twenty pages these standards include:

- A Code of Ethics,
- Rules of Conduct,
- Fitness Standards, and
- Financial Planning Practice Standards.

These standards present a rigorous set of responsibilities that must be respected by those who have earned the right to use the CFP Marks. FP Canada (and The FPSC before it) has/have been working hard for years to overcome some of the issues that have plagued the financial services industry and to set up a process whereby a more consistently designed and delivered product can be expected. However, you are still dealing with people, so there will be variability in skill, experience, and attention to detail, but if the qualifications have been earned and maintained, there is a higher likelihood that a quality relationship will be achieved and financial planning needs effectively satisfied.

The financial planning process espoused by FP Canada was described in chapter 4 and it includes a clear ten-step process[1]:

1. Explain the role of the financial planner and the value of the financial planning process
2. Define the terms of the engagement
3. Identify the client's goals, needs, and priorities
4. Gather the client's information
5. Assess the client's current situation
6. Identify and evaluate the appropriate financial planning strategies
7. Develop the financial planning recommendations
8. Compile and present the financial planning recommendations and supporting rationale
9. Discuss implementation action, responsibilities, and time frames
10. Implement the financial planning recommendations

When interviewing professionals for the role of helping you with your personal planning requirements, it is important that you gain an appreciation for the process they follow; a rigorous process following the distinct steps laid out above should permeate the discussion.

An individual CFP is unlikely to have all of the skills you require to develop and implement each and every element of a comprehensive financial plan. However, they likely have established relationships with other credentialed professionals who can address the details in their given area of expertise, such as:

- CPAs to address your tax-planning requirements,
- Lawyers to tackle your estate-planning concerns, and
- Insurance brokers to service your risk-management needs.

Involving an experienced team of professionals in the development of a financial plan is highly likely to improve the odds of achieving your goals and objectives in an efficient and effective manner.

For more information on the CFP credential, I suggest you visit the FP Canada website. The Canadian website has a slick tool to help find a local CFP who has the particular skills you are looking for. Give it a try and set up interviews until you find the right fit.

As far as ensuring you are getting unbiased advice goes, finding an advisor who works under the fiduciary standard would be ideal. At a bare minimum, understand how the advisor is remunerated and ensure that there is nothing in that structure with the potential to compromise their advice to you. This is why I like the idea of paying a fee for service rendered (preferably an hourly or fixed fee that is directly tied to the effort they are devoting to you). If I am paying by the hour or a fixed fee for a specific output, and that is the sole source of the advisor's compensation, then I can be more comfortable that the focus of their advice is me and my goals, and I have a clear understanding of what the advice is costing me.

Regarding Investment Advice

Let's begin this little piece with some wisdom from Warren Buffet. What follows is from page 20, of his February 28, 2014, letter to the shareholders of Berkshire Hathaway Inc.:

> In aggregate, American business has done wonderfully over time and will continue to do so (though, most assuredly, in unpredictable fits and starts). In the 20th Century, the Dow Jones Industrials index advanced from 66 to 11,497, paying a rising stream of dividends to boot. The 21st Century will witness further gains, almost certain to be substantial. The goal of the non-professional should not be to pick winners – neither he nor his "helpers" can do that – but should rather be to own a cross-section of businesses that in aggregate are bound to do well. A low-cost S&P 500 index fund will achieve this goal.[2]

Further on, Mr. Buffet goes on to say …

> My money, I should add, is where my mouth is: What I advise here is essentially identical to certain instructions I've

laid out in my will. One bequest provides that cash will be delivered to a trustee for my wife's benefit. (I have to use cash for individual bequests, because all of my Berkshire shares will be fully distributed to certain philanthropic organizations over the ten years following the closing of my estate.) My advice to the trustee could not be more simple: Put 10% of the cash in short-term government bonds and 90% in a very low-cost S&P 500 index fund. (I suggest Vanguard's.) I believe the trust's long-term results from this policy will be superior to those attained by most investors – whether pension funds, institutions or individuals – who employ high-fee managers.[2]

What? One of, if not the most successful investor in the history of equity markets advocates low-cost index investing for the vast majority of investors. Huh. Kind of makes you think, doesn't it?

For most people, I believe that the best way to maximize their chance to outperform the average actively managed fund portfolio is to do a few basic things:

- Define an appropriate asset allocation for your situation reflective of your risk tolerance,
- For the equity portion invest in globally diversified, low-cost, indexed products,
- For the fixed income portion use a ladder of investment grade bonds, debentures and GICs,
- Minimize costs at all points in the process, and
- Rebalance periodically (annually, if there are no major market moves).

That's it.

It does not involve taking a day trading course and spending eight hours a day in front of your computer. It does not involve hiring the man with the graph and his team of smartsters to buy just the right stocks for you, from just the right markets around the world, at just the right time. Rather, it involves a bit of self-education, planning, picking the right professionals to help you, and implementing and monitoring your plan.

Again, take a look at the advice provided by one of the most successful and wealthy investors of our time, Warren Buffet. Focus on asset allocation, diversification and cost minimization. This is the approach that a good, qualified, financial planner will lead you through when it comes to the investing piece of your financial plan.

Advice that Pays

As I have mentioned on a number of occasions in the book, it is my view that it is important to develop a foundational understanding of your own in most areas of financial planning so that you are not over-dependent on advisors, but it makes no sense to become an expert in all areas. If you are an expert in one area or another, great, do that piece yourself and maybe have another professional critique your plan to ensure you have not missed something.

The key areas where I believe the average person should involve an expert include the following:

1. The development or review of a comprehensive financial plan.

    The individual should have a very active role in this process, but having a qualified and experienced quarterback to bring it all together would be helpful. If you think you know what you are doing, great! Maybe have an experienced and qualified professional review what you have set up and pay them an hourly fee to offer their opinion related to your plan.

2. Taxation expertise.

    Tax is almost assuredly your largest single area of expenditure; make sure you take advantage of all opportunities to minimize the tax hit. This does not mean evading tax or participating in questionable tax reduction schemes or investments. It means engaging someone to help you plan your tax strategy, or at least review what you are doing from a taxation perspective.

When I say this I am not talking about tax preparation. Tax preparation is likely something you can do for yourself with the assistance of good software. The real benefit comes from involving a tax professional well in advance of April 30 and having them take a close look at your income and investment situation to ensure that you have organized your affairs in the most tax-efficient manner. A Chartered Professional Accountant with a taxation specialty is best suited to help with this. Their assistance is also invaluable when you are setting up the provisions of your will, or if you are an executor or trustee looking for some help with the tax complexities embedded in those roles.

3. Legal expertise.

It is vital that your legal documents be drafted to accurately reflect your wishes and respect the laws of your jurisdiction.

4. Insurance expertise.

You must ensure that you are adequately protected from game-changing outcomes.

With all of the experts you include in your planning process, make sure you discuss fees up front to ensure you identify any potential for bias in their work and to eliminate surprises at the back end. Document the details of the fee discussion and hold them to what they said if the bill presented varies from your understanding.

NOTES

Chapter 2
1. Doug Hoyes, *Straight Talk on Your Money: The Biggest Financial Myths and Mistakes ... and How to Avoid Them* (Oakville, ON: Milner & Associates Inc, 2017), 28.
2. Kevin O'Leary, *Cold Hard Truth on Family, Kids & Money* (Toronto, ON: Penguin Random House, Anchor Canada, 2013).

Chapter 4
1. "SMART Criteria," *Wikipedia*, last edited August 28, 2018, https://en.wikipedia.org/wiki/SMART_criteria.
2. FP Canada Standards Council, *Standards of Professional Responsibility*, (Toronto, ON: FP Canada, 2019), 21-22, http://www.fpcanada.ca/docs/default-source/standards/ standards_of_professional_responsibility.pdf.

Chapter 5
1. Yuri Ostrovsky and Marc Frenette, "The Cumulative Earnings of Post-secondary Graduates Over 20 Years: Results by Field of Study," *Economic Insights* (Ottawa, ON: Statistics Canada, October 28, 2014), 1. https://www150.statcan.gc.ca/n1/en/pub/11-626-x/11-626-x2014040-eng.pdf?st=yAQGoF0W.
2. Ostrovsky and Frenette, "Cumulative Earnings," 3.

Chapter 6
1. "Cost of Post-secondary Education," *Government of Canada*, last modified February 16, 2016. https://www.canada.ca/en/services/finance/education-funding.html.

Chapter 7
1. Gail Vaz-Oxlade, *Saving for School* (New York, NY: HarperCollins, 2013), 4.
2. "Registered Education Savings Plans (RESP)," *Government of Canada*, Rev. 17 (March 22, 2017). https://www.canada.ca/content/dam/cra-arc/forms-pubs/pub/rc4092/rc4092-17e.pdf
3. Mike Holman, *The RESP Book: The Simple Guide to Registered Education Savings Plans for Canadians* (Toronto, ON: Money Smarts Publishing, 2011).

Chapter 8
1. Jen O'Brien, "Wedding Trends in Canada 2015," *weddingbells*, accessed April 17, 2019, https://weddingbells.ca/planning/wedding-trends-in-canada-2015/.

Chapter 9
1. "Home Ownership Rate G20," *Trading Economics*, accessed April 17, 2019, https://tradingeconomics.com/country-list/home-ownership-rate?continent=g20
2. Alex Avery, *The Wealthy Renter: How to Choose Housing That Will Make You Rich* (Toronto, ON: Dundurn, 2018).
3. Nathalie Bachand, Derek Dedman, Martin Dupras, Daniel Laverdiere, A. Kim Young, *Projection Assumption Guidelines* (Toronto, ON: FP Canada Standards Council, April 16, 2019). http://www.fpcanada.ca/docs/default-source/standards/2019-projection-assumption-guidelines.pdf.
4. Canada Mortgage and Housing Corporation, *Homebuying Step by Step: Your Guide to Buying a Home in Canada* (Ottawa, ON: Canada Mortgage and Housing Corporation, February 16, 2017). https://www.cmhc-schl.gc.ca/en/data-and-research/publications-and-reports/homebuying-step-by-step-your-guide-to-buying-a-home-in-canada.

Chapter 10
1. "Driving Costs Calculator," *Canadian Automobile Association*, accessed July 2019, https://www.caa.ca/carcosts/.

Chapter 11

1. Mark Brown, "The Real Cost of Raising Kids: The Updated Figures Might Surprise You," *MoneySense*, April 15, 2015, https://www.moneysense.ca/save/financial-planning/the-real-cost-of-raising-a-child/

Chapter 12

1. "Choosing a Pet," *Ontario Veterinary Medical Association*, 2017, https://www.ovma.org/pet-owners/choosing-a-pet/. Also, see annual costs of owning a dog at https://www.ovma.org/assets/1/20/CostofCaringforDog2017.pdf, and annual cost of owning a cat, https://www.ovma.org/assets/1/20/CostofCaringforCat2017.pdf.
2. "Costs of Owning a Pet," *Winnipeg Humane Society*, 2019, https://www.winnipeghumanesociety.ca/adopt/before-you-adopt/costs-of-owning-a-pet/

Part IV – Debt

1. Matthew Fabian, "TransUnion Q2 2018 Industry Insights Report," *TransUnion*, accessed Sept 19, 2018, https://www.transunion.ca/lp/IIR.

Chapter 13

1. Robert R. Brown, *Wealthing Like Rabbits: An Original Introduction to Personal Finance* (Ajax, ON: Redford Enterprises, 2014), 130/131.
2. David Chilton, *The Wealthy Barber Returns: Significantly Older and Marginally Wiser, Dave Chilton Offers His Unique Perspectives on the World of Money* (Kitchener, ON: Financial Awareness Corporation, 2011), 67.

Chapter 15

1. Kevin O'Leary, *Cold Hard Truth on Men, Women & Money* (Toronto, ON: Doubleday Canada, Division of Random House of Canada Limited, 2012), 37.
2. Moshe A. Milevsky, *Your Money Milestones: A Guide to Making the 9 Most Important Financial Decisions of Your Life* (Upper Saddle River, NJ: FT Press, 2010), 67.
3. "Credit Report and Score Basics," *Financial Consumer Agency of Canada*, modified October 30, 2017, https://www.canada.ca/en/financial-consumer-agency/services/credit-reports-score/credit-report-score-basics.html.

Part V – Investing
1. Andrew Hallam, *Millionaire Teacher: The Nine Rules of Wealth You Should Have Learned in School, Second Edition* (New York, NY: Wiley, 2017), 210–213.

Chapter 17
1. "List of Stock Exchanges," *Wikipedia*, edited April 16, 2019, https://en.wikipedia.org/wiki/List_of_stock_exchanges.
2. "Historical Components of the Dow Jones Industrial Average," *Wikipedia*, edited December 23, 2018, https://en.wikipedia.org/wiki/Historical_components_of_the_Dow_Jones_Industrial_Average.
3. David Blitzer, "Inside the S&P 500: Selecting Stocks," *IndexologyBlog*, July 9, 2013. http://www.indexologyblog.com/2013/07/09/inside-the-sp-500-selecting-stocks/.
4. "Factsheet: Vanguard FTSE Global All Cap ex Canada Index ETF," *Vanguard Canada*, July 31, 2018. https://www.vanguardcanada.ca/individual/mvc/loadImage?country=can&docId=3329

Chapter 18
1. W.H. "Hank" Cunnigham, *In Your Best Interest: The Ultimate Guide To The Canadian Bond Market, Third Edition* (Toronto, ON: Dundurn, 2012).
2. Michael Lewis, *The Big Short: Inside the Doomsday Machine* (New York, NY; London, UK: W.W. Norton & Company, 2011)

Chapter 19
1. Paulette Perhach, "A Story of a Fuck Off Fund," *The Billfold*, January 20, 2016. https://www.thebillfold.com/2016/01/a-story-of-a-fuck-off-fund/.

Chapter 20
1. "Long-Term Capital Management," *Wikipedia*, edited March 27, 2019, https://en.wikipedia.org/wiki/Long-Term_Capital_Management.

Chapter 22
1. This was calculated assuming a one-third investment in each of VCE, VXC, and VAB, and the MERs as at the time of writing. The chosen asset allocation

was used as an example only; it would need to be adjusted to replicate an investor's personal asset allocation to be appropriate for use.
2. The 2019 FP Canada Standards Council, Projection Assumption Guidelines include return values of 3.9% for Fixed Income, 6.1% for Canadian Equities, and 6.4% for Foreign Developed Market Equities—assembled into an equal parts portfolio, this equates to a return of 5.47%. With fees of 0.16%, the gain retained over a 25-year holding period on a $100,000 portfolio would be $264,536, with a loss in value due to fees of $14,102. With fees of 2.0%, the gain retained over a 25-year holding period on a $100,000 portfolio would be $134,618, with a loss in value due to fees of $144,020.
3. Larry Bates, *Beat the Bank: The Canadian Guide to Simply Successful Investing* (Toronto, ON: Audey Press, 2018).

Chapter 23

1. The $1.5 million was calculated assuming the TFSA program remains intact according to the current rules. Indexing was calculated using a 2% rate of inflation; contributions were maximized and invested on the first day of the year earning 5%.
2. "Tax-Free Savings Account (TFSA) Guide for Individuals," *Canada Revenue Agency*, accessed April 17, 2019, https://www.canada.ca/content/dam/cra-arc/formspubs/pub/rc4466/rc4466-17e.pdf
3. Gordon Pape, *Tax-Free Savings Accounts: How to Profit from the New TFSA Rules* (Toronto, ON: Portfolio Penguin, 2015).

Chapter 24

1. Stefania Di Verdi, "Catch Up to Unused RRSP Contribution Room," *MoneySense*, April 23, 2013, updated March 21, 2014, https://www.moneysense.ca/columns/catch-up-to-unused-rrsp-contribution-room/.
2. Bruce Sellery, *The Moolala Guide to Rockin' your RRSP* (Vancouver, BC: Figure 1 Publishing Inc., 2013).
3. "Income Tax Folio S3-F10-C1, Qualified Investments – RRSPs, RESPs, RRIFs, RDSPs and TFSAs," *Government of Canada*, edited October 1, 2018, https://www.canada.ca/en/revenue-agency/services/tax/technical-information/income-tax/income-tax-folios-index/series-3-property-investments-savings-plans/series-3-property-investments-savings-plan-folio-10-registered-plans-

individuals/income-tax-folio-s3-f10-c1-qualified-investments-rrsps-resps-rrifs-rdsps-tfsas.html.
4. "RRSPs and Other Registered Plans for Retirement," *Canada Revenue Agency*, https://www.canada.ca/content/dam/cra-arc/formspubs/pub/t4040/t4040-17e.pdf.
5. "Lifelong Learning Plan," *Canada Revenue Agency*, accessed April 17, 2019, https://www.canada.ca/content/dam/cra-arc/formspubs/pub/rc4112/rc4112-17e.pdf.

Chapter 25
1. Moshe A. Milevsky, *Life Annuities: An Optimal Product for Retirement Income*, CFA Institute, May 17, 2013. https://www.cfainstitute.org/en/research/foundation/2013/life-annuities-an-optimal-product-for-retirement-income.
2. Moshe A. Milevsky, *Your Money Milestones: A Guide to Making the 9 Most Important Financial Decisions of Your Life* (Upper Saddle River, NJ: FT Press, 2010).
3. Moshe A. Milevsky, *Are You a Stock or a Bond? Create Your Own Pension Plan for a Secure Financial Future* (Upper Saddle River, NJ: FT Press, 2009).

Chapter 26
1. "Pooled Registered Pension Plan – Information for Individuals," *Government of Canada*, modified November 9, 2016, https://www.canada.ca/en/revenue-agency/services/tax/individuals/topics/pooled-registered-pension-plan-prpp-information-individuals.html.

Chapter 27
1. "Governance," *CPP Investment Board*, 2019, http://www.cppib.com/en/who-we-are/governance-overview/
2. *27th Actuarial Report on the Canada Pension Plan, as at December 31, 2015* (Ottawa, ON: Office of the Superintendent of Financial Institutions Canada / Office of the Chief Actuary, 2016). http://www.osfi-bsif.gc.ca/Eng/Docs/cpp27.pdf.
3. "Canada Pension Plan – How Much Could You Receive," *Government of Canada*, modified May 7, 2019, https://www.canada.ca/en/services/benefits/publicpensions/cpp/cpp-benefit/amount.html.

4. Doug Runchey, "How to Calculate Your CPP Retirement Pension: updated with 2018 rates," *Retire Happy*, accessed April 17, 2019, https://retirehappy.ca/how-to-calculate-your-cpp-retirement-pension/.
5. "Archived - Backgrounder: Canada Pension Plan (CPP) Enhancement," *Government of Canada, Department of Finance*, modified September 19, 2016. https://www.fin.gc.ca/n16/data/16-113_3-eng.asp.
6. "Old Age Security Payment Amounts," *Government of Canada*, modified April 1, 2019, https://www.canada.ca/en/services/benefits/publicpensions/cpp/old-age-security/payments.html#tbl1.
7. Nathalie Bachand, Derek Dedman, Martin Dupras, Daniel Laverdiere, and A. Kim Young, *Projection Assumption Guidelines* (Toronto, ON: FP Canada Standards Council, April 16, 2019), 11. http://www.fpcanada.ca/docs/default-source/standards/2019-projection-assumption-guidelines.pdf.
8. Frederick Vettese, "Why You Should Wait Until You Are 70 to Collect Your CPP Benefits," *Financial Post,* October 17, 2016, https://business.financialpost.com/personal-finance/retirement/why-you-should-wait-until-you-are-70-to-collect-cpp-benefits.
9. Frederick Vettese, *Retirement Income for Life: Getting More Without Saving More* (Oakville, ON: Milner & Associates Inc., 2018).

Chapter 29

1. Milagros Palacios, Charles Lammam, "Canadians Celebrate Tax Freedom Day on June 10, 2018," *Fraser Research Bulletin* (Vancouver, BC: Fraser Institute, June 20, 2018), https://www.fraserinstitute.org/studies/canadians-celebrate-tax-freedom-day-on-june-10-2018.
2. The federal and provincial tax rates presented do not consider alternative minimum tax provisions, which could apply in certain circumstances. Only the basic personal amount has been accounted for in the tables; other federal and provincial tax credits may also apply. The Government of Canada website should be consulted for current tax rate information. https://www.canada.ca/en/revenue-agency/services/tax/individuals/frequently-asked-questions-individuals/canadian-income-tax-rates-individuals-current-previous-years.html.
3. Milagros Palacios, Charles Lammam, "Taxes versus the Necessities of Life: The Canadian Consumer Tax index, 2018 Edition,"

Fraser Research Bulletin (Vancouver, BC: Fraser Institute, August 14, 2018), https://www.fraserinstitute.org/studies/taxes-versus-necessities-of-life-canadian-consumer-tax-index-2018-edition.
4   KPMG, *Tax Planning for You and Your Family 2019* (Toronto, ON: Thomson Reuters, 2018).
5   Evelyn Jacks, *Family Tax Essentials: Know More. Keep More. How to Build a Wealth Purpose with a Tax Strategy* (Winnipeg, MB: Knowledge Bureau Newsbooks, 2016).

Part VII - Calamity Evasion
1   Daryl Diamond, *Your Retirement Income Blueprint: A Six-Step Plan to Design and Build a Secure Retirement*, Second Edition (Oakville, ON: Milner & Associates, 2014).

Chapter 31
1   *A Guide to Disability Insurance* (Toronto, ON; Montreal, QC: Canadian Life and Health Insurance Association Inc., January 14, 2016), 1. http://clhia.uberflip.com/i/199350-a-guide-to-disability-insurance/0.

Part VIII – Estate Planning
1   Christine Van Cauwenberghe, *Wealth Planning Strategies for Canadians 2018* (Toronto, ON: Thomson Reuters, 2017).

Chapter 38
1   "Canadian Probate Fee Calculator," accessed December 18, 2018, https://www.legalwills.ca/canadian-probate-fee-calculator.

Chapter 40
1   "Preparing Returns for Deceased Persons," *Canada Revenue Agency*, modified February 12, 2019, https://www.canada.ca/en/revenue-agency/services/forms-publications/publications/t4011/preparing-returns-deceased-persons-2016.html.

Part IX – Professional Advice

1. FP Canada Standards Council, *Standards of Professional Responsibility*, (Toronto, ON: FP Canada, 2019), 21-22, http://www.fpcanada.ca/docs/default-source/standards/ standards_of_professional_responsibility.pdf.
2. Warren E. Buffet, T*o the Shareholders of Berkshire Hathaway Inc.*, February 28, 2014, 20. http://www.berkshirehathaway.com/letters/2013ltr.pdf.

DEDICATION

To my two beautiful children, Kaylee and Dan, thank you for being great kids and for all the chocolate, Jets gear, and highlighters—you know me well. Also, this book is pre-inheritance required study. A test will be administered upon the reading of my will.

To all those who have played a part in helping Kaylee and Dan become the wonderful young adults they are—Kim, teachers, coaches, family, and friends—I thank you from the bottom of my heart. I see your influence in their thoughtfulness, kindness, and wisdom each and every day.

A special thanks to Kim and Carol for slogging through the earlier, and much longer, version of this book. Your dedicated review removed many of the head-scratchers from the final version.

Kim, I'm sure there were times when other projects should have received a higher priority than writing and rewriting this book. You never made me feel as though I was neglecting my duties or my family. Your continual support was very much noticed and appreciated.

Printed in Canada